THEMES IN AFRICAN LITERATURE IN FRENCH: A COLLECTION OF ESSAYS

THEMES IN AFRICAN LITERATURE IN FRENCH: A COLLECTION OF ESSAYS

Edited by

Sam Ade Ojo and Olusola Oke

Spectrum Books Limited
Ibadan
Abuja• Benin City • Kaduna • Lagos • Owerri

Published by
Spectrum Books Limited
Spectrum House
Ring Road
PMB 5612
Ibadan, Nigeria

in association with
Safari Books (Export) Limited
1st Floor
17 Bond Street
St Helier
Jersey JE2 3NP
Channel Islands
United Kingdom

Europe and USA Distributor
African Books Collective Ltd
The Jam Factory
27 Park End Street
Oxford OX1, 1HU, UK

© Nigeria French Language Village

First published, 2000

ISBN 978-9-7802920-65

Contents

Notes on Contributors

Cyril Mokwunye is an Associate Professor in the University of Benin, Benin City, Nigeria. He studied at the University of Ibadan where he obtained the Master of Arts in French and at the University of Bordeaux, Bordeaux, France where he obtained the Doctorat de 3^e Cycle. He has taught French and Francophone Literature at the University of Benin for over twenty years. His major research interest focuses on Caribbean Literature in French. He has published many articles in learned journals.

Sam Ade Ojo is a Professor of French at the University of Lagos and the current Director of the Nigeria French Language Village, Badagry. He studied at the University of Toulouse where he obtained the Maîtrise ès Lettres and the Doctorat de 3e Cycle. He has taught French and Francophone Literature for over twenty-five years at the University of Lagos and other universities in Nigeria. His areas of specialisation include French as a Second Language, Twentieth Century French Literature and Francophone African Literature. He has published many articles in learned journals both national and international. He is one of the co-ordinating editors of the "African Literature Series".

Joseph Obinaju is an Associate Professor at the University of Uyo, Nigeria. He studied at the University of Nigeria, Nsukka, where he obtained the Master of Arts in French and at the University of Port Harcourt, where he obtained the Ph.D. He has taught French and Francophone Literature in Uyo for more than fifteen years. His research focuses on Francophone African Literature.

Adebo Adejumo is an Associate Professor at the Nigeria French Language Village, Badagry Nigeria. He studied at Syracuse University, USA, where he obtained a Master of Arts and a Ph.D. in French Literature. He has taught extensively in the University of Jos and for nearly a decade at the Nigeria French Language Village. His major areas of research are French Literature, Surrealism and Cultural Studies. He has published several articles

Cletus Ihom currently teaches African Literature in French at the Nigeria French Language Village, Badagry. He has completed a Ph.D programme at the University of Jos, specialising in the African Francophone Novel. He has also published articles in learned journals in this area.

Tar Adejir lectures at Ahmadu Bello University, Zaria, Nigeria.

Raymond Elaho is a Professor at the University of Benin, Benin City, Nigeria. He studied at the University of London where he obtained the Ph.D in French Literature of the Twentieth Century. He specialised on the "nouveau roman". His research focuses on French Literature, particularly the "nouveau roman", on Francophone African Literature and on Francophone culture in Africa. He has taught French and French Literature in Nigerian universities for more than twenty years. He has published *Entretiens avec Le Nouveau Roman* and many articles in learned journals.

Tunde Fatunde lectures at Lagos State University. He studied at the University of Bordeaux, Bordeaux, France where he obtained the Maitrise ès Lettres and the Doctorat de 3e Cycle in French and Comparative Literature. He has taught French and Francophone African Literature for more than two decades at both the University of Benin, Benin City, and Lagos State University, Lagos. His research focuses on Francophone African Literature and "liberation struggles" including feminism.

Aloysius Ohaegbu is a professor of French and African Literature at the University of Nigeria, Nsukka, and currently Head of the Department of Foreign Languages and Literatures. He holds the Licence ès Lettres of the University of Lovanium and the Doctorat de 3e Cycle of the University of Paris-Sorbonne. He has published extensively in his areas of specialisation – African Literature of French expression, Language Education and Culture. He is co-editor of *Nsukka Studies in African Literature* and consultant editor of many reputable journals.

Mattiu Nnoruka is a professor of French at the University of Ilorin, Nigeria. He studied at the University of Besançon where he obtained the Licence ès Lettres de Lettres Modernes, Licenses ès Lettres de Français Applique and Maîtrise ès Lettres de Lettres Modernes. He was at the University of Laval, Quebec, where he obtained the Ph.D in French Literature. His areas of specialisation include Francophone African Literature, French Literature and Civilisation. He has to his credit chapters in books and several articles published in learned journals.

Affin Laditan currently teaches French at the Nigeria French Language Village, Ajara, Badagry. He studied at the University of Ibadan, the University of Geneva and he is about to conclude a Ph.D programme at the Université de Franche-Comté, Besançon in France. His areas of specialisation include the teaching of French as a Second Language; "narratology" and French African Literature. He has published many articles in learned journals.

Yetunde Osunfisan holds M.A. and Ph.D degrees from the University of Lagos, Nigeria. She has been lecturing at the University of Ilorin, for close to 14 years. Her areas of specialisation are Stylistics and Discourse Analysis with particular reference to African Literature of French expression. She is also very much interested in Translation and has done a lot of practical work in this field.

Yemi Mojola lectures at Obafemi Awolowo University, Ile-Ife, Nigeria. She did postgraduate work at the University of Laval, Laval, Canada where she obtained the Maîtrise ès Lettres and the Doctorat ès Lettres in Twentieth Century French Literature. She has taught French Language and French Literature for more than twenty-five years at the Obafemi Awolowo University. Her research focuses on Twentieth Century French Literature and Feminist Literature in Francophone and Anglophone Africa. She has published articles in learned journals and chapters in books.

Gertrude Edem is based in the Department of French, McGill University, Canada.

Tundonu Amosu is an Associate Professor at Lagos State University, Nigeria. He did postgraduate studies at the University of Dakar, Dakar, Senegal, where he obtained the Maîtrise ès Lettres in French and in the University of Bordeaux, Bordeaux, France, where he obtained the Doctorat de 3e Cycle in Francophone and Comparative Literature. He has taught French and Francophone Literature for more than twenty years at both Obafemi Awolowo University and Lagos State University. He has published articles in several journals on Francophone Literature and Translation.

PREFACE

The *African Literature Series* in which this book appears is the collective work of lecturers of French in Nigerian universities. The contributors to this volume in the series have been brought together by the Nigeria French Language Village, Ajara, Badagry to work on a network research project that seeks to project African Literature in French beyond the circle of Francophones into that of Anglophones within and outside Africa. Anglophone Africans in particular and the Anglophone world at large have paid considerable attention to African Literature in French and have written extensively on it sometimes in French, the original language of the literature, but most often in English. They have brought into the discussion of the literature the experience that they have gathered through their study of its Anglophone counterpart.

In the comparative enterprise in which Anglophones study Francophone literature, they have often succeeded in drawing attention away from the pet obsession of the Francophones with textual analysis, "analyse littéraire". They have stretched their vision into thematic issues that can only be ignored at the risk of reducing the literature to its less vital linguistic and formal attributes. Because of its very nature of a client literature, African literature in European languages owe more to European literature in its formal and linguistic aspect. Its language and style are often direct products of African tutelage under foreign teachers in colonial and post-independence African schools and universities, where the study of foreign literatures was often done more for the linguistic advantages than for any other more serious cultural attributes.

The essays that appear below arise out of the collective preoccupation of the teachers and lecturers of French and African literature in French in Nigerian universities with the issues and themes that feature promptly in Francophone African literature. We are conscious of the disparateness that comes along with our kind of book. A collection of essays is necessarily a forum for the display of separateness, sometimes even of irreconcilable views and ideas but it is also and more importantly an avenue for bringing together probing minds whose collective output would by far outspace the efforts of single minds, however excellent.

This is Volume 2 of the African Literature Series; it is directed primarily at the Anglophone readers of African Literature in French, especially those who do not speak French at all. As for the Anglophones, who speak some French, they should find the book very rewarding. Efforts have been made to ensure that both the French originals as well as the translations of the texts that have been studied and analysed have been referred to extensively. Quotations have been made in both the original French versions, very often one after the other. It is also expected that some Francophone readers with adequate knowledge of English will draw immense benefits from the book.

The book is divided into three sections that deal severally with poetry, the novel and drama. In the poetry section, attention is focused on the most vital form of poetry that has been written by Africans in French, that is Negritude poetry. The debt to Léopold Sédar Senghor in this domain is clearly acknowledged in the fact that two of the four chapters in this section are devoted to the renowned poet. David Diop and Tchicaya U Tam'si are each accorded a chapter. Both of them are substantial poets who highlight the poetic legacy that both the Negritude movement and Senghor have helped to nurture in Francophone Africa. The four chapters are written by researchers who have a wide experience in the teaching of Francophone poetry in African universities.

There are nine articles, which touch on the technical and aesthetic aspects of the novel, on various themes, on characters in general and women characters in particular. They are written by lecturers and professors, who have previously examined the various issues mentioned in lectures, conferences and seminars as well as in academic forums where the African novel in French has been discussed. Mongo Beti and Sombene Quesmane are highlighted alongside Alioum Fantouré, Henri Lopes and Sony Labou Tansi. The first two are the masters of the African novel both in French in the colonial and post-independence eras, while Alioum Fantoure and Henri Lopes are notable post-independence Francophone novelists. Ahmadou Kourouma receives attention predictably on account of his "revolutionary" language while female authors are treated in chapter thirteen and around the issue of women and womanism, which is a prominent feature in the Francophone African novel, especially of the post-independence era.

Theatre is treated in two chapters: one of them draws attention to the female characters in Francophone African drama while the other examines radio plays. Radio plays constitute a rather large proportion of the published drama of Francophone Africa.

These essays do not cover all the notable authors nor, indeed, most of them. While acknowledging the inexhaustiveness of the essays, we hope, however, that the significant issues that they raise would sustain the interest of the reader and probably sensitise him to the variety of themes that are visible in Francophone African literature.

Sam Ade Ojo and Olusola Oke
Badagry,
August 1999.

POETRY

.

1

SENGHOR AS PRE-INDEPENDENCE NEGRITUDE POET

Cyril Mokwenye

Pourquoi étudier Senghor? Parce que c'est le premier
poète noir? Parce que c'est le meilleur? Le plus connu?
Parce que c'est un fondateur du mouvement de la
Négritude? Parce qu'il fut Président du Sénégal? Parce que
c'est le premier Noir à être reçu à l'Académie Française?

(Kesteloot, 1997:32).

PREAMBLE

Léopold Sédar Senghor, whose profile Lilyan Kesteloot tries to
capture in our epigraph, deserves to be studied by scholars of
African literature, for all the reasons the critic has suggested here.
Born in 1906 in Joal in Senegal, Senghor is one of the few surviving
key Negritude poets of the pre-independence era[1] and remains to
date one of the most accomplished African poets of the pre and
post-independent periods. Senghor is more than a poet and literary
giant; he is also an astute politician and statesman who led his
country for two decades without blemish.[2] An intellectual of high
repute, 'aggregé', prolific writer and lover of the French language,
he became the first black man to be accepted into the prestigious
Académie Française. Above all, Senghor has remained an African
and a black man, committed to the cultural, political and social
emancipation of his race, a struggle he embraced in the 1930s in
Paris, using Negritude as his greatest weapon.

Senghor fought the battle for the liberation of the African,
essentially through the Negritude movement which he co-founded
with the Martinican, Aimé Césaire, with the aim of resisting the
racial victimisation of the black man in a white dominated world.

3

In the Europe of the 1930s, in which Senghor and Césaire lived, the black man was a victim of racial discrimination and oppression and was regarded as being inferior to his white counterpart. The treatment meted out to the blacks was primarily a result of the erroneous and racially biased treatise of such European ethnologists of the day as Lévy Bruhl, de Gobineau and Spengler, who claimed that black people were barbaric, had under-developed brains, had neither a history nor a past and lived on trees.

With the arrival in Paris of black students from Africa and the West Indies, who were soon in close contact with their white counterparts both within and outside the classrooms, the myth of the so-called white superiority over the blacks on the intellectual plane was soon broken, as black students in every way measured up to their white colleagues. More importantly, in fact, was the appearance eventually, on the social and intellectual scenes, of progressive ethnologists like Levy Strauss, Maurice Delafosse and Leo Frobenus, who painted a better image of the black race, thereby giving impetus to the already growing desire among the young blacks to challenge the Europeans' negative and biased opinion of their race.

Already in the United States of America in the 1920s, the Black Renaissance Movement had begun to react against such theories as propounded by the racist ethnologists. African American writers like Claude Mackay, Jean Toomer, Langston Hughes and Contee Cullen mounted a campaign against racism in all its forms in the United States and other parts of the black world. It was not until the 1930s that the Black students in Paris (comprising Africans and West Indians) came in contact with the Movement through the effort of Andrée Nardel, who, together with Dr Sajous, a Haitian, founded the *Revue du monde noir*. This review thus laid the foundation of a black cultural renaissance in France.

The first response to the enlightenment which *Revue du monde noir* had brought to France came from the West Indian students, mainly from the Martinique, through the publication, in 1932, of their protest journal, *Légitime défense*. In it, they condemned the French government for its repressive policies against the Islands and at the same time denounced their compatriots who, as authors, did no better than ape the French writers both in their style as well as in their thematic preoccupation. Because of its radical language and revolutionary stance, the journal was visited with repressive measures meted out to it by the French government and so could not produce a second number. Following the proscription of *Légitime défense*, the West Indian students, in collaboration with their African counterparts, decided to found another organ through which they could make their voices heard. This led to the birth of *L'Etudiant noir*, in 1934, a journal which had as its founders West Indians like Léonard Sainville, Aimé Césaire, Léon-Gontran Damas and Aristide Maugrée; Africans like Léopold Senghor, Birago Diop and Ousmane Socé. The journal was conceived as a rallying point for all black students in Paris, irrespective of their nationalities. Léon Damas had this to say of the review:

> *L'étudiant noir*, journal corporatif et de combat
> avec pour objectif la fin de la tribalisation, du
> système clanique en vigueur au Quartier Latin.
> On cessait d'être plus qu'un seul et même
> étudiant noir.[3]

If *Légitime défense* had as its prime objective the struggle for political revolution, *L'Etudiant noir* preached more of cultural renaissance, mainly through literary activities. The influence of Senghor as a key leader of the *Etudiant noir* group made it possible for the members to adopt African traditional poetry as a form of literary expression, a situation which afforded the non-African members of the group an opportunity of discovering the African worldview. Aimé Césaire and Léon Damas were thus so exposed to the traditional African poetic tradition that when, for instance, in 1937, the latter published his *Pigments*, it was discovered that the poems contained a good number of African poetic forms.

Negritude was, therefore, born out of the concerted efforts of the authors of *Légitime défense* and the founders of *L'Etudiant noir.* Both journals, while articulating the aspirations of the Blacks in Paris at the time, paved the way for a more ideological philosophical and literary-oriented movement which Negritude became. Because of its omnibus ambition, critics have not been able to pin down Negritude to one single and all-encompassing definition. However, Léopold Sédar Senghor, one of the founding fathers of the movement and its most celebrated proponent, defined Negritude in its broadest sense to be "l'ensemble des valuers culturelles de l'Afrique noire."[4] He goes on to add that Negritude is "le refus de l'Autre, le refus de s'assimiler, de se perdre dans l'Autre... Le refus de l'Autre, c'est l'affirmation de soi."[5] Aimé Césaire, the man who coined the term "Negritude" and used it for the first time in his *Cahier d'un retour au pays natal* in 1939, defines it as "la simple reconnaissance du fait d'être noir, et l'acceptation de ce fait de notre destin de noir, de notre histoire et de notre culture".[6]

From these important definitions coming from the founding fathers of Negritude, it is clear that Negritude's major pre-occupation was the reappraisal of the Black man and his culture especially in his contact with the white man's world. The very first concern of Negritude was therefore with culture. As a cultural manifestation of being black, it aimed at not only projecting Africa's culture and civilisation, but also at resisting the negative image which the Europeans created of blacks and Africans.

Literature was the most efficient medium of manifesting Africa's culture and civilisation, while poetry became the most effective genre for expressing it. Senghor was in turn the most important Negritude poet committed not just to illustrating and defending Africa's cultural values through his poetic creations, but also to the rehabilitation of Africa's damaged image, especially during crucial pre-independence years.

*   *   *

The 1960s saw a large majority of French-speaking African colonies gaining their independence with little or no arms struggle. In the French-speaking countries south of the Sahara, the year 1960 could be regarded as the year of independence as nearly all of them obtained their independence that year.[7] Even though it may not be possible here to quantify precisely the amount of influence literature had in bringing about political freedom in the Francophone world, it is certain that Negritude literature did in fact play a major part. Senghor himself recognised this fact when in 1966, at a Conference in Beyrouth, he stated:

"C'est grâce à ces vertus de la Négritude que la
décolonisation s'est faite sans trop de sang ni
de haine au sud du Sahara qu'une coopération positive
fondée sur le dialogue et la réciprocité des services",
s'y est instauré entre anciens colonisateurs et
anciens colonisés, qu'un esprit nouveau a soufflé à
l'ONU, où le non et le coup de poing sur la table ne
sont plus signes de force".[8]

SENGHOR AND THE DEFENCE OF AFRICAN CULTURE

In our preamble, we were able to observe the fact that Africa, during the colonial era, was portrayed in very bad light especially from the cultural point of view. For the Negritude writers in general and for Senghor in particular therefore, literature was to serve as a weapon for the enlightenment of the white race concerning the blackman's culture and civilisation. More than through any other genre, it was through the poetic genre that Negritude was to seek to accomplish this task.

Senghor's pre-independence poetry dates back to his early literary activities, which cover the period 1930 to 1961. This period saw the publication of four important volumes of his poetry namely *Chants d'ombre* (his first collection of poetry written between 1930 and 1939 but published in 1945), *Hosties noires*, (published in 1948), *Ethiopiques* (published in 1956) and *Nocturnes* (published in 1961). The poet's main preoccupation in these early volumes of his 'oeuvre' was to portray his deep love for Africa's rich cultural heritage, which was despised by the white race. By so doing, he hoped to bring about a change of attitude on the part of the white man, which would lead eventually to the cultural and political emancipation of the black man. Much of Senghor's pre-independence poetry is anchored on his personal experience in France, first as a student and later as a soldier in the French Army. His 'exile' in France enabled him to experience the antithesis between Europe and Africa and consequently affected his life and determined the emotional tone of his poetry. Even though Senghor's pre-independence poems could be said to show a deep concern for his personal situation, Senghor was able to give his poetry a universal touch by his concern also for his people and mankind as a whole.

Some of the dominant poetic moods to be found in Senghor's poems of this era are those of exile, isolation and nostalgia, as displayed mostly in the first two collections: *Chants d'Ombre* and *Hosties noires*. A typical poem that evokes those feelings of nostalgia, exile and isolation is 'Joal'. In this poem, the poet recalls his childhood days in his native village in Senegal and contrasts them with the cold, isolated life he was living in Paris:

> Joal!
> Je me rappelle
> Je me rappelle les signares à l'ombre verte
> des vérandas
> Les signares aux yeux surréels comme un
> éclair de lune la grève.

> (Joal!
> I remember
> I remember the signares in the green shadow
> of the veranda
> Signares with eyes surreal as moonlight on the beach).

This poem reveals to what extent the poet, exiled in far away Europe, misses his ancestral birth place, his family warmth, friends and such cultural activities as singing of songs, wrestling, marriages and so on.

We find the same emotions equally displayed in another poem "In Memoriam". It is in this poem that the poet's sentiment of estrangement and isolation in a foreign land is greatly revealed. The poet's longing for home in the poem is overwhelming:

> C'est Dimanche
> J'ai peur de la foule de mes semblables au
> visage de pierre
> De ma tour de verre qu'habitent les migraires les
> Ancêtres impatients
> Je contemple toits et collines dans ma brume
> Dans la paix - les cheminées sont graves et nues.

> (Sunday
> The crowding stony faces of my fellows make me
> afraid

> Out of my tower of glass haunted by headaches
> and my restless Ancestors
> I watch the roofs and bills wrapped in mist
> Wrapped in peace... the chimneys are
> heavy and stark).

"In Memoriam" describes the French people on a typical Sunday morning and, through this description, it evokes the poet's feeling of loneliness and alienation in the white man's land. The poet further uses the opportunity not only to define his place among his fellow beings, but at the same time to comment on the European way of living which he considers soulless. As an African, used to a world of warmth, he cannot fit in properly into the European way of life. In consolation, the poet casts his mind back to his native Africa:

> Je contemple mes rêves distraits le long des rues
> Couchés au pieds des collines
> Comme les conducteurs de ma race sur les rives
> de la Gambie et du Saloum
> De la Seine maintenant, au pied des collines...
> . . . .
> O morts défendez les toits de Paris dans la brume
> dominicale
> Les toits qui protègent mes morts
> Que de ma tour dangereusement sûre, je descende dans
> la rue
> Avec mes frères aux yeux bleus
> Aux mains dures.
>
> (I watch my dreams listless along the streets, sleeping
> at the foot of the hills
> Like the forerunners of my race on the bank of the
> Gambia and Saloum
> Now of the Seine, at the foot of the hills
> . . . .
> O dead, defend the roofs of Paris in this sabbath mist
> Roofs that guard my dead
> That from the dangerous safety of my tower, I may go
> down into the street
> To my brothers whose eyes are blue, whose hands
> are hard).

The poem "Nuit de Sine" is equally pervaded by the same feelings as one finds in the two poems we have seen above. "Nuit de Sine" is a poem that celebrates 'Africanness' and 'blackness', while at the same time revealing the author's intense love for his motherland. According to Mezu,

" `Nuit de Sine' celebrates the beauty of the tropical night, not just the stars and countryside but the human warmth, the togetherness, the light touch of life, in a quiet village, lost to modern civilisation but happier because of this Eden-like purity".[9]

Femme pose sur mon front tes mains balsamiques,
    tes mains douces plus que fourrure
Là-haut les palmes balancées qui bruissent dans la
    haute brise nocturne
A peine. Pas même la chanson de nourrice.
Qu'il nous berce, le silence rythmé.
Ecoutons son chant, écouter battre sang
    sombre, écoutons
Battre le pouls profond de l'Afrique dans la
    brume des villages perdus.
Voici que décline la lune lasse vers son lit de
    mer étale
Voici que s'assoupissent les éclats de rire, que
    les conteurs eux-mêmes
Dodelinent de la tête comme l'enfant sur le
    dos de mère
Voici que les pieds des danseurs s'alourdissent,
    que s'alourdit la langue des choeurs
        alternés.

(Woman, lay on my forehead your perfumed hands
    softer than fur
Above the swaying palm trees rustle in the high night
    breeze
Hardly at all. No lullaby even
The rhythmic silence cradles us
Listen to its song, listen to our dark blood beat, listen
To the deep pulse of Africa beating in the midst of forgotten
villages
See the tired moon comes down to her bed on the slack sea
The laughter grows weary, the story-tellers even
Are nodding their heads like a child on the back of its mother
The feet of the dancers grow heavy, and heavy the voice of
the answering choirs).

In another typical nostalgia poem titled "Que m' accompagnent kôras et balafong" ("Let Koras and Balafongs accompany me"), the poet not only evokes his childhood, but also his love for his native land. He uses the occasion to celebrate Africa's past (before the incursion of the whites into the African continent) by singing the praise of his dead ancestors and other past heroes:

> Tokô Waly mon oncle, te souviens-tu des nuits d e j a d i s
> quand s'appesantissait ma tête sur ton dos de patience?
> Ou que me tenant par la main, ta main me guidait par
> ténébres et signes?
> Les champs sont fleurs de vers laisants; les étoiles se posent
> sur les herbes sur les arbres.
>
> C'est le silence alentour.
> Seuls bourdonnent les parfums de brousse, ruches
>   d'abeilles rousses qui dominent la vibration grêle des
> grillons
> Et tam-tam voilé, la respiration au loin de la Nuit.
>
> (Tokô Waly, my uncle, do you remember those long ago
> nights when my head grew heavy on your patient back?
> Or how you took my hand in yours and guided me
>   through signs and shadows?
> The fields blossom with glow worms; stars alight in grass
>   and trees.
>
> There is silence all around
> The only stirrings are the perfumes of the bush,
>   hives of russet bees that dominate the crickets
> And muffled tom-tom the distant breathing of the night.

In similar poems of exaltation and celebration of the African heroes, ancestors, nobility, in which Senghor recounts their exploits, it is the same sense of responsibility and duty to his African race that guides the poet. Poems like 'Au Guélowar', 'Totem' 'Prière aux masques', 'Le retour de l'enfant prodigue', are poems, which reveal Senghor's commitment to African dignity and cultural richness. In Senghor's desire to uplift the African and promote his culture, he devotes particular attention to the African woman and glorifies her as a symbol of Africa's beauty and richness. It is for this reason that a poem like 'Femme noire' (Black woman) becomes significant as a pre-independence poem, for through this poem, written in the 1930s, Senghor achieves a remarkable revolutionary feat. This is because before then, it was only the beauty of the white woman, as celebrated by such European artistes as Dante, Bouccacis and Spence that was talked about. That Senghor came out boldly to sing the beauty of the black woman, can be regarded as a major breakthrough in the struggle for the cultural rehabilitation of the black person:

> Femme nue. femme noire
> Vêtue de ta couleur qui est vie. de ta forme qui est
> beauté!
> J'ai grandi à ton ombre: la douceur de tes mains bandait
> mes yeux
> . . . .
> Femme noire, femme obscure
> Fruit mûr à la chair ferme. sombres extases du vin noir.
> bouche qui fais lyrique ma bouche.
>
> (Naked woman. black woman
> Clothed with your colour which is life. with your
> form which is beauty:
>
> In your shadow I have grown up: the gentleness of your
> hands was laid over my eyes?
>
> Naked woman. dark woman
> Firm-fleshed ripe fruit. sombre raptures of black wine mouth
> making lyrical my mouth).

Through the themes of nostalgia and exile, Senghor is at his best, pouring out his personal emotions. He uses the occasion of his exile in the white man's land as an opportunity to closely x-ray Europe not just from the physical point of view, but also from the psychological angle, thus bringing into sharp focus the cultural and climatic differences between Europe and Africa. The poet thus elevates the theme of nostalgia and exile to that of a racial issue, underlying, as it were, the problems confronting the colonised man in the white man's land As an antidote to cultural racism, his poetry prescribes the celebration of Africa's cultural values and achieves this through contrasting European individualism with Africa's brotherliness, Europe's coldness with Africa's warmth and by generally appraising Africa's finest traditions as evidenced in the poems we have discussed above.

As a pre-independence Negritude poet, Senghor's responsibility to his race and people was not only a matter of seeking his people's cultural emancipation through a positive portrayal of the cultural attributes of the black race. Senghor, as a father of Negritude, who knew what the Negritude movement stood for, saw his task also as that of raising a voice against the ills of colonial domination in Africa. With regard to this aspect of his commitment to political emancipation, the poetry of Senghor has suffered considerable criticism among African critics for its middle-of-the-road and rather ambivalent posture towards the colonialists. However, we cannot be too categorical in writing off Senghor's pre-independence poetry on the basis of non-commitment to political struggle, since Negritude poetry was founded on the platform of protest. As Jacques Chevrier reminds us: "La Négritude est d'abord effectivement réaction à la situation coloniale de l'Afrique d'avant 1960".[10]

It must be noted that Senghor's pre-independence poetry bears testimony to the author's commitment to Africa's liberation if we consider the way which some of the poems level accusation against the colonial overlords. Nowhere is this desire better illustrated than in the collection titled: *Hosties Noires*. By giving the collection 'Hosties Noires' as title, Senghor is drawing attention, in a symbolic way, to the fate that befell his fellow Africans who had become victims of Europe's oppression and discrimination. Written mostly during the Second World War (between 1939 and 1945), the poems are concerned with the social and political conditions of the black man in his interaction with the white man. According to Abiola Irele, the poems in *Hosties Noires* are the most committed of all Senghor's work. In his opinion,

> The peoms of *Hosties Noires* can be seen as a comprehensive *critique* of Europe. Because they are in a strict sense war poems, they provide a specific moral viewpoint for Senghor's appraisal of the contradiction of Western civilization. They are a documentary on public events as well as a judgement on human passions behind those events, through which Senghor attacks the European claim to superiority over the rest of the World.[11]

One poem, which illustrates Senghor's commitment to the cause of the African, is 'Prière de paix' (Prayer for Peace) in which he enumerates the grievances of the black man and levels accusation of injustice against Europe and the white race:

> Seigneur Dieu[........ ....]
> Et il est vrai, Seigneur, que pendant quatre
>   siècles de lumières elle a jeté la bave et les
>   abois de ses molosses sur mes terres
> Et les chrétiens, abjurant Ta lumière et la
>   mansuetude de Ton coeur
> Ont éclairé leurs bivouacs avec mes parchemins,
>   torturé mes talbés, déporté mes docteurs et
>   mes maîtres-de-science.
> [. . . . .]
> Et ils m'ont fait une vieillesse solitaire parmi la
>   forêt de mes nuits et la savane de mes jours.
> Seigneur la glace de mes yeux s'embue
> Et voilà que le serpent de la haine lève la tête dans
>   mon coeur, ce serpent que j'avais cru mort...

> (Lord God, ...
> It is true Lord, that for four enlightened centuries
>   she has scattered the baying and slaver of her
>   mastiffs over my lands
> And the Christians, forsaking Thy light and the
>   gentleness of Thy heart
> Have lit their camp fires with my parchment tortured
>   my disciples, deported my doctors and masters
>   of science.
> . . . .
> And have made for me a solitary old age in the forest of
> my nights and the savanah of my days. Lord the glasses of
> my eyes grow dim. And lo, the serpent that I believed was
> dead raises its head in my heart.)

SENGHOR, THE AMBIVALENT POET

Senghor's direct attack here on the white oppressors does not end with his condemnation of the European christians who have not lived up to expectation, but goes on further to attack the French administration in particular for its high-handedness:

Qu'elle aussi a porté la mort et le canon dans mes villages
   bleus, qu'elle a dressé les miens les uns contre les autres
   comme des chiens se disputant un os
Qu'elle a traité les résistants de bandits, et craché sur les
   têtes-aux-vastes-desseins.
Oui, Seigneur, pardonne à la France qui dit bien la voie droite
   et chemine par les sentiers obliques.
Qui m'invite à sa table et me dit d'apporter mon pain, qui
   me donne de la main droite et de la main gauche enlève
   la moitié.

(She too has brought death and guns into my blue village,
   has set my people one against the other, like dogs
   fighting over a bone.
Has treated those who resisted as bandits and spat upon the
   heads that held great schemes.
Yes, Lord, forgive France that shows the right way, and goes
   by devious paths
Who invites me to her table and bids me bring my own
   bread, who gives with the right hand and takes away
   with the left).

In his reaction against the effects of the Second World War on
blacks, Senghor, pays tribute to the contribution of African soldiers
to a war which was not their own. He considers the Senegalese
soldiers who died fighting in foreign lands as victims sacrificed
unjustly and so decides to honour them in "Poème liminaire":

Vous Tirailleurs Sénégalais, mes frères noirs à la main chaude
   sous la glace et la mort
Qui pourra vous chanter si ce n'est votre frère d'armes, votre
   frère de sang?
Je ne laisserai pas la par les le aux ministres, et pas aux
   généraux
Je ne laisserai pas-non! –les louanges de mépris vous enterrer
   furtivement.
Vous n' êtes pas de pauvres aux poches vides sans honneur
Mais je déchirerai les rires *banania* sur tous les murs de
   France.

   (You *tirailleurs* of Senegal, black brothers, warm
      handed under ice and death,
   Who but I should sing of you, your brother
      in arms, in blood?
   I will not leave the speeches to ministers nor to
      generals

I will not leave you to be buried stealthily with a
little contemptuous praise.
You are not poor with nothing in your pockets
without honour
I will tear down the *banania* smiles from
every wall in France).

In a poem like "Neige sur Paris", Senghor does not spare the white race whom he denounces for their many atrocities against the black race:

Les mains blanches qui tirèrent les coups de fusils qui
croulèrent des empires
Les mains qui flagellèrent les esclaves, qui flagellèrent
Les mains blanches poudreuses qui vous giflèrent
les mains peintes poudrées qui m'ont giflé
Les mains sûres qui m'ont livré à la solitude
et à la haine...

(White hands which shot guns that demolished empires
White hands which whipped the slaves, which whipped
White powdery hands which slapped you, powdered
painted hands which slapped me
Confident hands which abandoned me to solitude and
hatred). (My translation).

Through these poems, Senghor can be seen to be protesting and raising a voice against such colonial vices as oppression and domination which characterised the pre-independence era in Africa. As in all his poems, we find here also that his protest poems are marked by his personal experiences and feelings and so lend his poems a particular emotional significance. But, certainly, this personal aspect of his poetic posture plays down his commitment to the collective cause of the Africans as a people, for the poet allows his privileged personal attachment to France and Europe to mellow down his reaction. The consequence is that rather than witness an outright condemnation and total rejection of France and Europe, the way we see it in the poems of David Diop, what Senghor offers us is an act of 'forgiveness' and 'pardon'. It is, therefore, disturbing for the African who expects Senghor to come out boldly to condemn the whites, but who, at the end of the long list of grievances in poems like 'Prière de paix' or 'Neige sur Paris', finds such verses as these:

> Seigneur, pardonne à ceux qui ont fait des Askia des
> maquisards, de mes princes des adjudants
> De mes domestiques des boys et de mes paysans des salariés,
> de mon peuple un peuple de prolétaires.
> Car il faut bien que Tu pardonnes à ceux qui ont donné la
> chasse à mes enfants comme à des éléphants sauvages.
> Et ils les ont dressés à coups de chicotte, et ils ont fait d'eux
> les mains noires de ceux dont les mains
> étaient blanches,
> Car il faut bien que Tu oublies ceux qui ont exporté dix
> millions de mes fils dans les maladreries de leurs navires
> Qui ont supprimé deux cents millions.

> (Lord, forgive those who made resistance fighters of the
> Askias, who turned my princes into sergeants
> Made houseboys of my servants, and labourers of
> my folk, who turned my people into proletariat
> For you must forgive those who hunted my children like
> wild elephants.
> Who trained them with whip and made them the Black
> hands of those whose hands were white.
> You must forgive those who stole ten million of my sons in
> their leprous ships
> And who suppressed two million more).

From Senghor's posture in the above stanza, the poem, which otherwise would have brought considerable credit to his pre-independence poetry, fails to do so because of the poet's lack of courage to drive home his indictment of Europe. He adopts an ambivalent posture which subtracts from his reputation as a pre-independence Negritude poet, whose major preoccupation would have been to fight for the political emancipation of his oppressed brothers, through the adoption of a more positive and radical poetic approach. In this regard, when compared to a pre-independence Negritude poet like David Diop, Senghor's Negritude poetry can be said to be non-committed. Senghor's ambivalence can be explained by the fact that he was too deeply assimilated into the French culture which he greatly admired. While claiming his Africanity, he did not want to lose his Frenchness and so preferred to preach reconciliation and peace in his poetry. This is why, in her assessment of the poem "Prière de paix", Lilyan Kesteloot, some fifty years after, cannot forgive Senghor for his ambivalence and lack of genuine commitment towards the total condemnation of France and Europe over their colonial iniquities. Comparing

Senghor to other Francophone intellectuals of about his generation and after, she asks:

> "Tous nos intellectuels (Pathé Diagne, Aly Dieng, Doud'Sine, Birago, Houtondji, Aguessy, Towa, Melone, Belinga, Mudimbe, Lopes, Obengu, Tati et même Cheik Anta Diop ou Iba Der) n'ont-ils pas fait leurs études en Europe, souvent avec latin? N'ont-ils pas été marqués par le rationalisme cartésien, et parfois beaucoup plus profondément que Senghor? N'écrivent-ils pas la langue française comme Senghor, n'ont-ils pas eu des amis français comme Senghor, des femmes françaises ou étrangères? Mais évidemment ils n'ont pas tous écrit "que Dieu pardonne à la France" ni proné la réconciliation de Demba-Dupont".[12]

AFRICAN ORAL TRADITION AND SENGHOR'S POETRY

In spite of Senghor's serious concern with the cultural aspect of Africa's contribution to world civilisation, his pre-independence poems laid the foundations for the emergence of modern African poetry. Senghor was concerned with the form of the African poem and so paid considerable attention to poetry as a form of art, which to him mattered even more than the thematic aspect. This was why he categorically asserted that:

> Ce qui fait la Négritude d'un poème, c'est moins le thème que le style, la chaleur émotionnelle qui donne la vie aux mots, qui transmue la parole en verbe.[13]

In other words, even though the Negritude poets saw themselves as fighting a committed battle on the cultural, psychological, ideological and political levels, they nevertheless did not lose sight of their primary concern with art. Senghor considered himself first and foremost as a literary artist, a practitioner of the literary art of poetry and so remained essentially a manipulator of language in the creative process; thus fulfilling, in another sense, the purely literary aspect of the Negritude aspiration.

Senghor's pre-independence Negritude poems provide an enormous variety in terms of the poet's style. As a poet, Senghor uses a lot of the French classical poetic forms, which he fully masters and skillfully adapts to his African subject matter. Senghor shows great talent in not just the way he adopts the style of Paul Claudel, but also in the way he uses the elements of traditional African poetry in his works. From the French, Senghor inherited the use of the alexandrine versification but which he adapts to suit his use of the free verse. He does this by combining various verse forms to achieve syllabic groups, which are accentuated by pauses. In doing so, Senghor remains as close as possible to the alexandrine which, to a very large extent, can be said to dominate his poetry. For example, we find in a poem like 'Chaka' the dominance of regular syllabic structures characteristic of French versification:

> Je ne suis pas le poème, je ne suis pas le tam-tam
> Je ne suis pas le rythme. Il me tient immobile
> Il sculpte tout mon coeur une statue de Baoulé

> (I am not the poem, and I am not the drum
> I am not the rhythm. It holds me still, it
> carves all my body like a statute of Boule).

Negritude poetic style is one which can be said to derive, in the main, from African oral tradition, in the sense that virtually all the poetic devices explored by the Negritude poets are adaptations from African oral poetry. In the case of Senghor, even though we have noted that the influence of Paul Claudel is paramount in his poetry, he excels in the use of African cultural references which he adapts in order to lend his poem that peculiar African colour and meaning. There is, thus, in Senghor's pre-independence poems in particular, the frequent introduction of local words and expressions as well as the infusion of African names and words like: 'Ndessé', 'Serère', 'signares', 'Kora', 'dang', 'Kor siga', 'saras', 'Téring-Ndyare', 'dyoung-dyoung', 'taga', 'tama' and so on. The use of local colour references in his poems of course forms an important part of Senghor's attempt at domesticating African poetry and making it more relevant to the cultural realities of his people. Such cultural references equally enable the poet to illustrate the elements which symbolise, in certain ways, Africa's past glories and civilisation.

Apart from the direct use of local cultural references, Senghor uses images and symbols to represent Africa, which is the source of his creative inspiration. Africa, being the centre-piece of Negritude poetry, Negritude poets use various images and symbols to represent her. Senghor, for example, uses 'Night' and 'Blackness' as his most common symbols of Africa. As Irele points out, "Night can be considered the governing symbol of Senghor's poetry".[14] It is not therefore surprising to find 'Night' and 'Blackness' occurring frequently in his poems and in the titles he gives to them: 'Nuit de Sine' (Night of Sine), 'Femme noire' (Black Woman), 'Elégie de minuit' (Elegy of midnight), 'Masque nègre' ('Negro Mask') 'Chants d'ombre' ('A Song of Shadow'), and so on. In a poem like 'Que m'accompagnent kôras et balafong' (Let Kora and Balafongs accompany me), we find the following stanza which reveals the place of 'Night' in Senghor's poems:

> Nuit d'Afrique ma nuit noire, mystique et claire noire
>
> ....
>
> Nuit qui fonds toutes mes contradictions, toutes contradictions dans l' unité première de ta négritude
> Reçois l'enfant toujours enfant, que douze ans d'errance n'ont pas vieilli.
>
> (Night of Africa my dark night, mystical and lightning
>
> ....
>
> Night that dissolves all my contradictions, all contradictions
> Receive your child still a child whom twelve
> years of wondering has not made old).

In addition to the use of the imagery of 'night', Senghor uses some other images in his poems to represent Africa. For example, the 'black woman' is used as the symbol of life, the muse of the poet and mother of the prodigal child ('L'enfant prodigue'). 'Blood' is also used as an image and is linked to the black woman in reference to Africa, a typical example being in the case of the poem "Nuit de Sine" where we read:

Ecoutons son chant, écoutons battre notre sang sombre,
 écoutons
Battre le pouls profond de l'Afrique dans la brume des
 villages perdus.

(Listen to its song, listen to our dark blood beat, listen
To the deep pulse of Africa beating in the midst of
 forgotten villages).

The 'River Congo' is celebrated also in Senghor's pre-independence poetry as a symbol of Africa's vitality, a source of abundance and fecundity, as a mother:

Oho! Congo oho! Pour rythmer ton nom grand sur les eaux
 sur les fleuves sur toute mémoire
Que j'émeuve la voix des kôras Koyaté!...
. . . .
Mère de toutes choses qui ont narines, des crocodiles
 des hippopotames
Lamantins iguanes poissons oiseaux, mère des crues
 nourrice des moissons

(Oho! Congo oho! I move the voices of the *Koras* of
 Koyaté to make your great name their rhythm
Over the waters and rivers, over all I remember...
. . . .
Mother of everything that has nostrils, of crocodiles, of
 hippopotamus
Sea-cows, iguanas fishes, birds, mother of floods and
 fields).

The use of repetition, a device common in traditional African poetry is explored by Senghor in his poetry as a poetic technique, a device he makes the cornerstone of his versification. Thus we find in virtually every poem the repetition of words and phrases which, at times, function as refrains. In a poem like 'Joal', the phrase 'Je me rappelle' ('I Remember') opens all the six stanzas; the same is also true of 'Femme noire' (Black Woman) where the phrase ('Femme nue femme obscure' (Naked Woman, dark woman) opens all the stanzas of the poem, except one. The same applies to such poems like 'Neige sur Paris' (where 'Seigneur' is repeated many times), 'Prière de paix' 'Seigneur' is repeated, at the beginning of every stanza. In 'A l'appel de la race de Saba', 'Mère sois bénie' is repeated at the beginning of every stanza of the poem. By using this device, Senghor is able to achieve the effect of emphasis as they enable him to stress the point he is making in the poem.

Another important role which the use of repetition in Senghor's poems plays is that it affords the poet the possibility of enumerating, drawing parallels as well as juxtaposing related figures which he has taken directly from the African oral tradition, especially as it concerns the African praise poem. In a poem like "Au Gouveneur Eboué", Senghor pays tribute to the first colonial Governor of French West Africa in a typically African praise style through the use of comparison and drawing of parallels:

> Eboué! Et tu es le Lion au cri bref, le Lion
>   qui est debout et qui dit non!
> Le Lion noir aux yeux de voyance, le Lion noir à la crinière
>   d' honneur

> (Eboué! You are the Lion with the sharp cry, the Lion
>   who stands and says no!
> The black Lion with prophetic eyes, the black Lion with
>   the name of honour).

As a master of the African praise poem, Senghor uses another device known as the 'apostrophe' in his poems. The use of the apostrophe, apart from conferring on the poems the status of a direct address, also lends to them an incantatory tone. A number of Senghor's pre-independence poems open with the apostrophe. In 'Lettre à un prisonnier' (Letter to a prisoner), the poem begins thus:

> Ngom! Champion de Tyâné!
> C'est moi qui te salue, moi ton voisin de
>   village et de coeur.
> Je te lance mon salut...................

> (Ngom! Chamption of Tyané
> It is I who greet you, your neighbour in the village,
> your neighbour in heart.
> I fling my greeting to you...

In 'Prière aux masques' (Prayer to Masks), the opening lines are a direct address to the ancestral gods:

> Masques! O Masques!
> Masque noir, masque rouge, vous masques
> blanc et noir
> Masques aux quatre points d'où souffle l'Esprit
> Je vous salue dans le silence!
>
> (Masks! Masks!
> Black mask, red mask, you white and black masks
> Masks of four points from which the spirit blows
> In silence! I salute you).

The same devise is used in the poem titled 'Lettre à un poète' (Letter to a Poet), a poem dedicated to Aimé Céssaire, Senghor's intimate friend. He addresses him thus:

> Au Frère aimé et à l'ami, mon salut abrupt et
> fraternel!
> Les géolands noirs, les piroguiers au long cours
> m'ont fait goûter de tes nouvelles
>
> (To a loved brother and friend, my blunt and
> fraternal greetings!
> The black gulls; the far travelling cause-master
> have brought me some taste of your news).

The poem 'Taga de Mbaye Dyôb' (Taga for Mbaye Dyôb) strikes us as one poem in which the poet perfects his adaptation of the African poetic tradition by the way he presents the poem. Senghor adapts the Senegalese praise chant known as the 'taga' (sung by griots) and accompanied by the drum, sings his own praises to Dyôb, while in the second part of the poem, he adopts and transposes into French a Senegalese song usually sung by village maidens:

> Mbaye Dyôb!. Je veux dire ton nom et ton honneur.
> Dyôb! je veux hisser ton nom au haut mât du retour, sonner
> ton nom comme la cloche qui chante la victoire
> Je veux chanter ton nom Dyôbène! toi qui m'appelais
> ton maître

(Mbaye, Dyôb'. I will speak your name and your honour
Dyôb! I will hoist your name to the high mast of the ship
returning, ring your name like the ball that sounds victory)
I will sing your name Dyôbène, you who used to refer
to me as your master).

In adapting this technique, however, Senghor introduces a new approach to the praise poem, in the sense that, rather than sing the praise of a hero who has performed an exploit, his poem exalts an ordinary soldier who has not recorded any triumphant or heroic achievement, as we see in the following stanza:

Dyôb! qui ne sais remonter ta généologie et
    domestiquer le temps noir, dont les ancêtres
    ne sont pas rythmés par la voix du tama
Toi qui n'as tué un lapin, qui t'es terré sous les
    bombes des grands vautours
Dyôb! qui n'es ni capitaine ni aviateur ni cavalier pétaradant,
pas seulement du train d'équipages
Mais soldat de deuxième classe au Quatrième
Régiment des Tirailleurs Sénégalais
Dyôb! je veux chanter ton honneur blanc.

(Dyôb: - You who cannot trace your ancestory and bring
    order into black history, your forefathers are not sung
    by the voice of the *tama*
You who have never killed a rabbit, who went to ground
    under the bombs of the great vultures
Dyôb! you are not a captain or airman or trooper, not even
    in the baggage train
But a second class private in the fourth
Regiment of the Senegalese Riffles
Dyôb! I will celebrate your white honour).

CONCLUSION

We have attempted in this essay to examine Senghor's early poems within the context of pre-independence Negritude poetry. We have equally tried to show that Negritude was largely manifested in literature through the poetic genre, with Léopold Sédar Senghor as one of its earliest and foremost practitioners. His pre-independence poems stand out distinctly among his poetic oeuvre, as they articulate the poet's earliest commitment to the illustration and defence of Africa's cultural values. These poems also helped to lay the foundation for the birth of modern African poetry through Senghor's adaptation of African traditional oral poetry forms, thus providing a model for a number of younger budding African poets after him. As a poet committed to the cultural rehabilitation of his people and race, Senghor's pre-independence poems do honour to Africa's cause by the way the poet celebrates the African village and society, glorifies the ancient heroes of Africa and exalts the African soldiers who died in the white man's wars in Europe. All these add up to give Senghor a place among African writers who, in their own way, contributed to Africa's eventual independence, even if they were not in the forefront of political radicalism as shown in their works. As Clive Wake puts it, African poetry:

> ... is a poetry that owes its particular atmosphere to a definite situation in history. This factor suggests the themes of colonialism, independence, race, culture and also the idea that poetry should by its commitment contribute to the struggle of freedom. Where there is little talent, much of African poetry is only this, but often there is a broader vision which transcends the immediate political preoccupations of the poet and his contemporaries. At this level, in a poetry that is called by circumstances to speak of the oppressed and liberation of the black man, the poet shows a deeper concern with his personal situation and from there with that of his people and finally, of mankind and so gives his poetry a universal validity which it would not otherwise have".[15]

In this connection, it is apparent that through his pre-independence poems, Senghor's preoccupation was not overtly political, but the poet shows adequate concern for his people and his race by the way he celebrates African values using the benefit of his personal experiences either as a child in his native Joal, as a student in Paris, exiled from Africa, or as a soldier fighting for France. His intimacy, however, with France clearly affected his reaction to European colonial policies against Africa and so places the poems at a disadvantage when considered as politically committed poems. As we have shown in the essay, his posture of forgiveness and pardon for the oppressors of his people and race constitute the crunch of the criticism levelled against his pre-independence poems by younger and radical African writers and critics.

All considered, Senghor's pre-independence poems, more than his later poems, helped to provide a model in terms of style and themes for the younger generation of African poets in search of an 'African' direction in poetic expression. His poems, being the most abundant, (among Negritude poets) in terms of number, thus provided enough variety for the student of modern African poetry to choose from. This is why we agree with Kesteloot when she observes that there is a certain "fascination de cette poésie qui a servi de modèle de jeunes gens s'exerçant à mâtriser leur plume".[16]

Notes

1. His contemporaries were notably Léon-Gontran Damas, Aimé Césaire, Birago Diop, Ousmane Socé and David Diop.

2. Senghor was the president of Senegal from independence in 1960 to 1980 when he handed over to President Abdou Diouf.

3. Cited by Lilyan Kesteloot. *Ecrivains noirs de langue française.* Bruxelles: Institut de Sociologie de l'Université Libre de Bruxelles, 1965, p. 91.

4. *Ibid.* p.11.

5. *Ibid.* p.112.

6. *Ibid.* p.113.

7. Bénin, Togo, Cameroon, Congo Brazzaville, Côte d'Ivoire, Niger, Mali, Burkina-Faso, Senegal, Central African Republic, Democratic Republic of the Congo, Mauritania - all became independent in 1960.

8. Cited by P. Decraene. "Senghor et la négritude" in *Ethiopiques*

No. 59: 1997, p. 86.

9. Okechukwu Mezu. *The Poetry of Léopold Sédar Senghor.* London, Ibadan, Nairobi: Heinemann, 1973, p. 16.

10. Jacques Chevrier. *Littérature nègre.* Paris: Armand Collin, 1974, p. 49.

11. Abiola Irele. *Selected Poems of Léopold Sédar Senghor.* London, New York. Melbourne: Cambridge University Press, 1977, p. 16.

12. Lilyan Kesteloot. "Pourquoi étudier Senghor?" in *Ethiopiques, op.cit.:* p. 32.

13. Cited by J.P. Sartre in *Anthologie de la nouvelle poésie nègre et malgache*, L.S. Senghor (ed.). Paris: Presse Universitaire de France, 1948, p. XXIX.

14. Abiola Irele. *Selected Poems of Léopold Sédar Senghor.* p. 27.

15. Clive Wake. *An Anthology of African and Malagasy Poetry in French.* London: Oxford University Press, 1965, pp. 3-4.

16. Lilyan Kesteloot. "Pourquoi étudiér Senghor?" in *Ethiopiques:* p. 35.

Bibliography

Chevrier, J. *Littérature négre.* Paris: Armand Colin, 1974, 288p.

Guibert, A. *Léopold Sédar Senghor.* Paris: Serghers, 1966, 215p.

Irele, A. *Selected Poems of Léopold Sédar Senghor.* London, New York. Melbourne: CUP, 1977, 134p.

Kesteloot, L. *Ecrivains noirs de langue française.* Bruxelles: Institut de Sociologie de l'Université Libre de Bruxelles, 1965, 340p.

Mezu, O. *The Poetry of L.S. Senghor.* London, Ibadan, Nairobi:

Heinemann, 1973, 101p.

Nwoga, D. *West African Verse*. London: Longman, 1974, 242p.

Reed, J. and C. Wake. *French African Verse*. London, Ibadan, Nairobi: Heinemann, 1972, 213p.

Senghor, L. S. *Anthologie de la nouvelle poésie nègre et malgache*. Paris: PUF, 1948, 227p.

Senghor, L. S. *Poèmes*. Paris: Editions Seuil, 1964, 254p.

Towa, M. *Léopold Sédar Senghor. Négritude ou servitude?* Yaounde: CLE, 1971.

Wake, C. *An Anthology of African and Malagasy Poetry in French*. London: CUP, 1965.

Journal Articles Consulted

Irele, A. "Léopold Sédar Senghor as Poet". *Odu*, No.1, New Series: April 1969.

Irele, A. "Negritude - A Philosophy of African Being". *Nigeria Magazine*, Nos.122-123: 1977, pp.1-13.

Decraene, P. "Senghor et la négritude". *Ethiopiques*, No. 59: 1997, pp. 85-89.

Kesteloot, L. "Pourquoi étudier Senghor?". *Ethiopiques*, No. 59: 1997, pp. 32-35.

2

THE MILITANT POETRY OF DAVID DIOP

Sam Ade Ojo

"Nous savons que certains souhaitent nous voir abandonner la poésie militante (terme qui fait ricaner les "puristes") au profit des exercices de style et des discussions formelles. Leurs espoirs seront déçus car pour nous la poésie ne se ramène pas à "dresser l'animal langage" mais à réfléchir sur le monde et à garder la mémoire de l'Afrique.

Comme l'écharde dans la blessure
Comme un fétiche tutélaire au centre du village.

Ce n'est qu'ainsi que nous pourrons pleinement exercer nos responsabilités et préparer le renouveau de nos civilisations."

David Diop: *"Contribution au débat sur la poésie nationale"*[1]

DAVID DIOP: THE MILITANT POET OF NEGRITUDE

David Mandessi Diop became better known by the reading public from late 1948, when he was featured with fifteen other Negro-African writers including ten West Indians and five other Africans in Senghor's *La Nouvelle Poésie Nègre et Malgache de Langue Française*. Before then, in January 1948, Présence Africaine had published three of Diop's poems ("Le temps de Martyr", "Celui qui a tout perdu" and "Souffre pauvre Nègre"). Though only five poems of his were included in that Senghor's seminal and historic anthology of Negro-African poetry, David Diop's selection was certainly a testimony to the outstanding quality of his poetic fervour and distinction as well as a recognition of the enviable and exemplary position which he occupied among the new and young generation of African writers, particularly those who were acclaimed, at that time, as the spokesmen and intellectual props of Negritude. It must, of course, be noted that Negritude has, by 1948, already established itself as the philosophical rallying-point and the battle-cry adopted by Negro-African writers to assert the cultural distinction, the socio-political identity, the geographical uniqueness, the distinction of pigmentation and the intellectual presence of the black race in a world that was dominated by Eurocentric norms and biases. Negritude was also the demystifying literary movement relied on by Blacks to negate and reject the stultifying and humiliating myths and prejudices used by negrophobic whites to define the black man.

That Diop, in spite of his tender age of 21 years, was identified by Senghor, who did the compilation of the 1948 anthology, as being worthy of being counted among the acknowledged pillars of the Negritude movement, showed that his brand of poetry must have been seen as constituting a useful facet and a complementary counter-point of Negritude poetry. This fact needs to be very well emphasised, given the critical evaluation made of Diop's poetic distinction by Senghor. In spite of the admission by the latter that Diop's poetry is "a violent expression of a strident racial sensibility",[2] Senghor was not quite at ease with the style of Diop. This was how he expressed his reservation about the young man's poetic specificity:

> "Il comprendra que ce qui fait la Négritude d'un
> poète, c'est moins le thème que le style, la chaleur
> émotionnelle qui donne vie aux morts, qui
> transmue la parole en verbe".[3]

Senghor was rather too hasty in his appreciation of Diop, since it must be admitted that five poems ought not to have been used to fully do justice to the quality of a potential creative writer and that the age of a poet ought also to have been taken into consideration in making an acceptable assessment of the poet's work. Moreover, in the specific case of Diop, Senghor, the respected co-founding-father of Negritude, who was later to become the first African member of the prestigious French Academy, ought to have been more responsive to the inherent quality of Diop's poems, just as he should also have known that creative quality and specificity derive from factors that are intrinsically personal and sociological as well as intimately human. It would have been clearer to the poet-president and the first African "agrégé de grammaire" that Négritude could not have had a monolithic and straight-jacketed orientation and that, even as at that time, it already exhibited the potentials of becoming a volcanic literary philosophy that would eventually explode, with many ambivalent consequences and complementary tributaries.

This, indeed, was actually how Negritude developed. And so, we later on had the serene, peaceful, collaborative and conciliatory Negritude à la Senghor; the passeistic, sarcastic and demystifying version of Negritude à la Césaire and the acidic, aggressive, tempestuous, provocative and revolutionary Negritude à la Diop.

It is this caustic Negritude à la Diop that this chapter would attempt to bring to light. It is this assertive and forceful Negritude, the militant and revolutionary Negritude, that is charged with an iconoclastic fervour and that is fed by revolt, anger, disappointment, anguish, reality and naked truth that we would analyse from the only volume of Diop's poems, entitled *Coups de Pilon*.

This thin volume of 30 satirical poems is militant both in its style and theme which both fuse into each other and complement each other. No wonder Diop, in a veiled response to Senghor's reservation about his poetic quality, says that "the style is expected to serve the theme" ("la forme n'est là que pour servir l'idée."). [4] Diop's militant Negritude is borne out of his personality, his life experiences, his literary mission and vision and his personal philosophy; in one word, the reality which he knew, lived and experienced. His caustic and uncompromising Negritude which permeates each of his 30 poems also grows out of the pains which our poet personally suffered as a result of his emotionally imbued assessment of an African continent that has been viciously and sadistically bled to near-extinction, that has been rapaciously battered and dismembered, that has been wickedly sapped of its energy and resources, and of a black race that has been wantonly humiliated, alienated, divided, decivilised and stunted in its growth and of the panhuman subjugation of the so-called inferior races and underdogs to rapacious and egotistical exploitation, oppression and dehumanisation by those who see themselves as politically, economically and technologically superior.

It is a combination of all these factors that makes Diop's Negritude differ from Senghor's but similar to the revolutionary fervour of such West Indian creative firebrands as Aimé Césaire, Paul Niger, Jean Brière, Jacques Roumain, Léon-Gontran Damas, René Depestre, W. E. B. Dubois, Frantz Fanon and to the militancy of Pablo Neruda and Augustino Neto. This is why Diop could not but be an unrelenting polemist, imbued with a revolutionary humour[5] and fired by an obsessive animosity and a vengeful indignation against all exploiters and oppressors, against all predators and hypocrites, against all cheats and deceivers, against all arrogance and superiority deriving from colour as well as special political and economic identities. Diop has been a victim of all these indignities and so he would not want other human beings not to be fully sensitised to the modus vivendi : tricks, dualism, norms and strategies of the operators of sadistic deprivations to justify and defend their wicked acts so that their innocent and unwary victims would not be easily taken in. This should, from the view point of Diop, be the duty of all writers because:

> "La littérature est l'expression d'une réalité en mouvement, elle part de la réalité, la capte, saisit ce qui n'est qu'un bourgeon et aide à le mûrir ... (Il faut donc que) le poète puise le meilleur de lui-même cc qui reflète les valeurs essentielles de son pays et sa poésie sera nationale ... (Il suffit de) dire à partir de la sève dont il a été nourri, tout le reste étant que surajouté à son fond propre."[6]

David Mandessi Diop therefore built his poetry on himself, projected it from himself, around himself, and also from and around his immediate environment. This is why Diop's poetry is so real, so authentic, so fresh and so striking. A little examination of his life would help to drive home this point very well.

LIFE EXPERIENCE IN THE PERSONAL SERVICE OF CREATIVE SENSIBILITY

Much more than his contemporaries, David Diop, the precocious and sensitive artist, the visionary humanist, the satiric genius, "the extremist voice of Negritude," "the Maiakovsky of African revolution" and the principal Negro-African representative of the poetry of protest, 'the revolutionary Ariel' is a pan-Africanist, being born of a Camerounian mother (Maria Engômé Mandessi Bell, whose grandfather's name, David, he was to be the first to bear in the family) and a Senegalese father (Mamadou Yandé Diop). His being an exogamous product therefore precluded him from being bugged down by a narrow nationalism or a simplistic patriotism that would have resulted from the exigencies of the ethnic, chauvinistic and socio-cultural imperatives of belonging to a single country. He therefore, seemed to belong to two nationalities and, in fact, to Africa which he loved with an enduring passion, with unmitigated commitment and a ravishing excitement. His singular decision to join hands with Sekou Touré in building up his newly independent Guinea in 1958, (after the decisive vote of September 28, 1958) with the attendant withdrawal within 48 hours of all the French workforce in Guinea, by offering to contribute to the supply of the much needed professional manpower is a clear testimony to the pan-African zeal of Diop. Let's listen to this committed and pragmatic poet of love and of Africa, as he made known his decision to his brother in-law Alioune Diop to leave for Guinea:

> "Je pars pour la Guinée au début de la semaine prochaine en compagnie de Abdou Moumouni, de Joseph Ki-Zerbo et quatre autres professeurs africains. Comme je l'ai écrit, il est des cas où celui qui se prétend intellectuel ne doit plus se contenter de vœux pieux et de déclaration d'intention mais donner à ses écrits un prolongement concret. Seule, une question de famille m'a fait hésiter quelque temps, mais après mûre réflexion, ce problème ne m'a pas paru être un obstacle à mon départ."[7]

And so to Guinea, and specifically to Kindia's Ecole Normale Supérieure as a teacher he went in October 1958 and it was from there that he was returning, on his way to take up a job in Senegal, when his plane crashed on August 29, 1960 and he died along with his second wife, Yvette (to whom he was married after Virginie Kamara who bore three of his five children).

But, before 1958, Diop was living in France where he was born (in Bordeaux in "the country of pale human beings - O Mbêng'a - Bekala") on July 7, 1927. He lost his father at the tender age of 8, in 1935. It was therefore his mother who had to bear all the moral and financial responsibilities of bringing up Diop first as a young boy, later nicknamed Gorgui, in Dakar (1931-1938). From 1938, he was in France specifically in Nîmes (1938-1943), in Joinville - le Pont near Paris (1943-1945) and Paris (1945-1951) where, in this foreign environment, blacks were generally treated with disdain, hypocrisy and hatred. It was in this hostile French milieu that he actually grew up. Not only was he as well as his fellow blacks subjected to all the ills and pains of racism, he also had to go through another form of racism during the war years and the Occupation : the pangs of Nazism with its repressive and rapacious racism. Diop was therefore a victim of a double racism.

But, with his mother and his three sisters and two brothers by his side in their crowded Parisian residence in 32 rue des Ecoles, Diop enjoyed the warmth and tenderness of a happy home. It was a home that was built on love, care and respect for others and that was enlivened by some measure of the traditional African "joie de vivre". David's mother talked a lot to her young boy about Africa: her past and her present, her virtues and her vicissitudes, her lost glory and her potentials. According to his friend of many years, Bakary Traoré:

> C'est dans le cœur de cette maman qu'il apprit l'Afrique et la misère des déshérités de toute origine. C'est à travers les épreuves et les richesses spirituelles de celle que, pour plus d'un Africain en exil, offrit le reflet de la chaleur maternelle de l'Afrique que l'on expliquera la vision chez le poète de *Coups de pilon*, du monde, des humains, de la joie de vivre, de l'amitié, de l'égalité fraternelle, de la noblesse de l'homme.[8]

The discussions with his mother would have made the young boy to imbibe most painfully the pangs of alienation and of living in an imposed exile.

This exile was definitely more than a geo-political one for David, who had to keep on moving, always moving, from France to Africa, from Africa to France, with the attendant psychological and cultural dislocation on his development. It was indeed an exile from self, from the warmth and beauty of Africa, from the natural exuberance and raw joy of the typical African child, exposed to an unadulterated nature that was not yet soiled by the trappings and artificiality of Western technology. This was why the theme of exile features prominently in David's poetry. And on each occasion that it is treated, it is with sadness and bitterness, with nostalgia and a sense of loss. This is so because his imposed exile which constituted the essence of his migrant life was full of physical and psychological contradictions, conflicts, dichotomies and oppositions for David. He tried, with a lot of bravado and an exemplary *joie de vivre,* to surmount the attendant dualism and the sense of "homelessness" which were deep in him.

Apart from the physical agony, humiliation and alienation to which Diop was subjected as a result of his imposed exile as a young boy growing up in Nîmes, Paris and Monpellier, he also lived most of his life as a semi-invalid. This predicament forced our future poet to abandon, in 1951, his medical studies at the University of Grenoble, for Arts in the University of Montpellier as a result of his long hospitalisation of almost two years at the Saint-Hilaire Senatorium. His health problem was made worse by a leg problem, osteomyelitis, which almost made him a one-legged man. Again, he had a very bad bout of pneumonia which cost him one of his lungs. With all these unfavourable health conditions, David was forced to see life as a bitter battle that had to be courageously fought.Let's listen to Senghor (his uncle and his teacher at the Lycée Marcelin Berthelot at Saint - Maudes Fossés) describe this predicament, in his speech at the cemetery of Bel-Air on September 2, 1960:

> "Mon cher David, ta jeunesse n'a été qu'un long calvaire. Ton
> mérite a été d'avoir toujours surmonté la souffrance, d'avoir
> affronté des études difficiles, d'avoir fait de celles-ci et celle-
> là, un tremplin pour t'élever plus haut"[9]

This heroic approach to life would be strongly reflected in his poetry
in which his dramatis personae are shown first of all as victims of
uncompromising and hostile forces which had to be seriously
challenged, attacked and repelled by them with determination,
courage and resourcefulness.

It was little wonder that our young poet became attracted to the
Communist Party towards 1947 through the series of debates and
conferences held in 184 Boulevard Saint-Germain. Marxist
philosophy must have supplied Diop with a strong intellectual tonic
to pep up his personal conviction about the essence of man and
about the equality of man to man regardless of his colour, creed or
geographical location. More powerfully than the other revolutionary
philosophies that appealed to the young revolutionaries of the time:
freudism, bergsonism and surrealism, which seriously challenged
such conservative ideals as cartesianism, positivism, scientism and
bourgeois humanism, Marxism was particularly ruthless in its
virulent attack of the raison d'être of oppression, of colonisation
and of assimilation. Marxism considers man as "a cosmic
phenomenon" worthy of being accredited with the same qualities
wherever he is ; it denounces whatever principles are used to justify
exploitation, repression and alienation which constitute the tripodal
substratum on which colonisation reposes. Diop found therefore
in Marxism the philosophical springboard to rationalise his
commitment to the liberation of all the oppressed peoples of the
earth and the castaways of every country and to completely reject
any form of institutionalised oppression and repression. This
explains why he found it a lot easier to see the blackman's problem
from a much wider perspective than Senghor saw it. For Diop, the
black man's predicament is just one aspect of a cosmic or panhuman
problem. The black man was therefore presented by our poet as
belonging to the panhuman family of all world underdogs who were
ceaselessly exploited, sadistically depersonalised, viciously
humiliated and heartlessly deculturalised by oppressive regimes,

by dehumanising principles or by domineering constraints. No wonder therefore that the Negritude that is revealed in Diop's poetry has a more panhuman coloration than that of Senghor. It must, of course, be emphasised that this panhuman dimension of Diop's poetry does not in any way remove anything from Diop's Africanness or his love for Africa. Rather it complements it. This point was very poignantly made in Diop's statement (quoted above) in which he also underscored his panhuman and nationalistic mission as a writer:

> Que le poète puise dans le meilleur de lui-même ce qui reflète les valeurs essentielles de son pays et sa poésie sera nationale (...). Mieux, elle sera un message pour tous, un message fraternel qui traversera les frontières.[10]

Indeed, the message of Diop's poetry goes beyond Africa, it is not centred on only the black man. Its dramatis personae, as pointed out above, are all those who are the victims of institutionalised exploitation or any form of oppression or domination. These are found in all parts of the world, from Africa to America, from Europe to Asia, from the West Indies to China.

From the above, it is clear that Diop's poetry, which is "an outcry mixed with violence, a song motivated only by love"[11] would have an orientation that would reflect his background and vision. Having lived in such charged environments and having imbibed such revolutionary ideas as we have just described, his poetry would also be charged and incisive. And so, all his published poems, written between 1942 (when David was in Class Three at the Lycée Marcelin Berthelot) and 1958, reflect our poet: his love, ambitions, inhibitions, fears, biases, convictions, attitudes and world-view. They also give a picture of Africa: pre-colonial Africa, colonial Africa and a hopefully decolonised Africa: three phases of Africa's evolution or history made up of its past, its present (as seen in the 50s) and its future (from the years of independence). The African or the black man comes out in the poems, as a sample of the castaways of the earth. While analysing these themes in Diop's poems, we would also show how his poetic style has very strongly helped to convey the militancy of Diop as a poet.

THE ESSENCE OF DIOP'S MILITANCY

The militancy of Diop, as hinted at above, is both in his style and the themes of his poems. Militancy, basically, connotes attack, opposition, negation, refusal and rejection. It implies taking a violent option to neutralise a situation. The violent option is generally forceful and aggressive: its objective is certainly iconoclastic and radical. It aims at changing a situation or negating a position that is considered unbearable, unacceptable, unfavourable, unsatisfactory, untenable and unrewarding. It implies neutralising a condition that is intolerable and painful, putting an end to a status that is no more tolerated, checkmating a development whose consequences would henceforth not be condoned or positively entertained. It is a mental or physical or psychological approach that attempts to put a stop to a situation or condition that is seen as inimical, unhealthy, inclement, unwholesome and distasteful to one's interest, integrity, personality, success, joy and dignity, in one word to one's present and future.

For Diop, the situation which was seen as inimical to his interest and dignity and to those of the peoples to whom he was committed (Negro-Africans and all the oppressed peoples of the world) was the one created by *slavery* (with its concomitant alienation, uprootment and dehumanisation), by *colonisation* (with all its *modus operandi* including exploitation, assimilation, mystification, racism, brainwashing and alienation) and by *exploitation* (with its psychology and principles of domination, oppression and superiority complex). The status that could no more be tolerated was that of subjugation and exploitation. The situation that had to be negated was that of the oppressed and the alienated. The approach that was adjudged unacceptable henceforth was the brutality of colonialism as well as the dogmatism and hypocrisy of its cultural arrogance. The denigration of human value and dignity that was justified by slavery, imperialism and capitalism could no more be tolerated. Certain Eurocentric connotations, terms and norms used in identifying the black man were no more considered acceptable. Particular approaches of the Negro-African and the oppressed to life generally : passivity, self-pity, conformism, inferiority complex, purposeless actions, lethargy and resignation were henceforth considered inappropriate and basically unhealthy to their survival and overall happiness.

And since militant negation is usually accompanied by assertion, the philosophical and stylistic approach adopted by Diop is to provide a counterpoise for each unacceptable situation or condition. Hence, we have the following oppositions or antithetical positions: colonisation and decolonisation, racism and anti-racist racism, exploitation and equality, self-pity and self assertion, fatalism and activism, inaction and apathy, suffering and joy, misery and happiness, dependence and self-reliance, pessimism and optimism, hypocrisy and reality/honesty, lies and truth, selfishness and unity/ fraternisation, a negative and positive change, defeatism and victory, hopelessness and hope, shame and pride, humiliation/indignity and self-assurance, inferiority and superiority, protest and revolt. And to convey the transformation or passage from the situation of insatisfaction, contempt and wrath to a tolerable situation, and also a salutary condition, which normally involves a fundamental change and which reflects the dialectical structure of Diop's poem. Diop always has recourse to iconoclastic words : adverbs, conjunctions, verbs and nouns.

But, the militant tone of the collection is first of all supplied by its title,[12] *Coups de Pilon.* This very authentic African imagery which the first translators of the work to English distorted by changing it to an Eurocentric imagery (by replacing *pilon* which is pestle by *marteau* which is hammer) has a strong iconoclastic connotation. The idea of blows, on its own, is forceful and aggressive. Allying the blows, however, to those coming from a hammer, as the first English translation of the text tried to convey, reduces the impact of the forcefulness and incisiveness of the blows. Diop is always very careful in his choice of terms because, for him, poetry is action and words are meant to convey ideas aptly. The original French title is therefore charged with a poetic objective, which is to make of Diop's poetry a forceful literary driving force that is aimed at "breaking the eardrums of those who do not want to listen to it and to slam like sounds of shark on the egoism and the conformism of the conservatives. [13] The objective of Diop is therefore to drum his violent message forcefully into the eardrums of the operators of unacceptable conditions and norms. It even aims at breaking their eardrums. Only blows that are strong can do that. Anyone familiar with the driving force that goes into pounding with pestles, as witnessed in African rural settings of yesteryears, would be able to understand the full implications of Diop's imagery. We therefore wish to reject the English translation of the title of the text and stick to its literal translation of "pestle pounding" in order to fully do justice to the implications of the mortal, forceful and energetic pounding that the title of the text should convey.

The blows that are to come from the choice of words and ideas, from the assault on age-long myths, norms and biases about both the whites and the blacks, from the break from a distasteful status quo of the Black man and from the debunking of the hypocrisy and brainwashing engineered by colonialism and assimilation, all representing a whole process of "dememorisation,"[14] are expected to have strong psychological and even physical impacts on all the actors and counter-actors in Diop's poetic landscape, as their hearts, consciences, psychologies and bodies are to be jolted and subjected to rude shocks and reverberating cacophonies. Another aspect of the imagery of mortar/pestle sounds is the notion of united action that this common African culinary activity connotes. Not only does pounding involve energy and determination, it also calls for combined and multiple action so that whatever is being reduced to a paste can be effectively and quickly done. The action that the poetry of Diop calls for would bear very positive fruits, if only there is unity of purpose and action, if there is a merging of forces and intentions and if there is an iron determination on the part of the oppressed and the wretched of the earth to reverse their unbearable conditions and situations.

It is particularly through this approach that the violent blows of anger, of venom, of defiance and of disintegration would terminate the plague of racism, the cancer of colonialism and neo-colonialism, the cankerworm of exploitation, the locust of hypocrisy, the ravaging disease of assimilation and dispossession as well as the shame of humiliation and inferiority complex. It is with these that "the tenacious carapace of our false paradises" (of white civilisation, white Christianity, white hypocrisy, white flattery) would be shattered to pieces with "the hard blows of stones".[15] Mention must also be made of the rhythm that the mortar and pestle give.

The militant action to put an end to the intolerable and unhealthy situations described above would inspire dithyrambic songs, dances and celebrations to which the music of pounding invites. The full impacts of the mortar (mortal) blows and the accompanying celebrations would be made clearer as we examine the presentation of Africa in *Coups de Pilon*.

THE REHABILITATION OF AFRICA IN *COUPS DE PILON*

Africa is the heart-beat of *Coups de Pilon*. It is the central preoccupation of the poet in the work; every movement in the whole collection and all the themes treated are centred on Africa. It is actually the driving force, the motivating spirit and the catalysing power that helped to release the creative resilience and tonic that enabled our poet to translate his ideas into powerful words which charged him with the emotional energy that makes the whole collection to reverberate with effusion, vitality and reality.

Our poet did say in one of his most African and most powerful poems, symbolically entitled "Africa":

Afrique mon Afrique	Africa my Africa
Afrique des fiers guerriers dans	Africa of proud warriors in the
les savanes ancestrales	ancestral savannahs
Afrique que chante ma grande-Mère	Africa of which my grandmother sang
Au bord de son fleuve lointain	On the banks of far-away river
Je ne t'ai jamais connue.	I have never known you.

This last statement was taken by some critics to mean that Diop did not know Africa. In actual fact, because of the long years that our poet spent in Europe (France) and what was expected to be the attendant effects of this on his overall comportment and attitude, a few people around him, who did not fully understand him, would be tempted to accuse Diop of being the prototype of the alienated black man described by Fanon as "peau noire, masques blancs". In fact, one young lady was actually reported to have tagged him in a language that is close to this at a conference organised at that time by African students in Paris on the theme, "Role of the African woman in the modern society". The young lady was said to have violently rebuffed Diop, by shouting him down when he stood up to talk in that conference, in the following words:

"Tu n'es qu'un 'Toubab' ! Tu ne connais pas l'Afrique" [16]

This accusation was certainly misplaced, because Diop knew Africa, lived as an African (whether he was in Africa or out of it), thought like an African and felt for Africa. And as it was said by his brother, Iwiyé Kala-Lobè:

Il vit en osmose avec l'Afrique, "son Afrique"[17]

It may be true that he did not physically know the precolonial Africa that had already been destroyed by the white enslavers, colonisers and missionaries. It would be unrealistic to expect him to have had any direct contact with that Africa, with its martial glories and heroic past, with its unadulterated beauty and paradisiacal peace. But, he had read a lot about that phase of Africa's evolution ; he had heard about it from knowledgeable and well-informed people including his mother and on the few occasions that he visited the continent. He could not but have a feeling of loss and the nostalgia for that Africa that was no more, that had been thrown into the dustbin of history and that was just a pale shadow of its old self. It was therefore useful for him to show his readers, both African and non-Africans, that unique Africa which had now become a victim of years of denigration and assimilation, of bastardisation and self-negation, of exploitation and brain-washing, of prejudices and crimes, and of humiliation and hypocrisy; a continent that was grossly misunderstood, a continent that was presented by the West as being barbaric, uncivilised, empty, crude, darkened by basic human weaknesses and traits. It was needful for Diop to rehabilitate the continent that Europeans had made to look like good only to be exploited and used to service their civilisation and technology, so frail that it needed to be energised by their technology and

Christianity, too undeveloped and shamefully devoid of any history and civilisation to warrant being subjected to white technology and Western norms and seriously in need of being fed with white civilisation to prevent its extinction.

The rehabilitation that was done by Diop involved showing what Africa was not and what it was ; what Africa had lost and what it has become. This rehabilitation, aimed at showing how Africa was before the arrival of the whites in the continent, indeed of pre-colonial Africa, is vigorously pursued in the following poems: "Afrique", "Auprès de toi", "Nègre clochard" "Celui qui a tout perdu" and also in the few poems devoted to the poet's mother and lovers in which Africa came out as mother-Africa : "A ma mère", "Rama Kam", "Hommage : Rama Kam : Beauté Noire", 'A une danseuse Noire', 'Je sais', 'Poem to Remember', 'Détresse', Où étiez-vous, "Ton sourire", *"Demon"*.

It must be pointed out that the rehabilitation done by Diop is not the type of romanticisation of Africa that is aimed at giving a bloated image of a pre-colonial continent that was perfect, idyllic, harmless, blissful and Edenic, as it is seen in the poems of Senghor. We are not presented with a continent which was an epitomé of innocence and peace, as seen in the works of many Négritude poets who use this pervasive nostalgia as an evasion or as a means of rejecting European culture and civilisation. Rather, we are made to see that Africa has a definite and distinct identity that rubs on each African or each black man, that Africa has a socio-cultural reality which is quite different from that which the West tried to present to its own peoples, and that it has a verifiable geo-political distinction from which every African receives his raison d'être.

Africa is therefore accorded an identity in *Coups de Pilon*. This identity comes alive either through its name, Africa, its topography, vegetation and climate, its ancient empires of Ghana and Tombouctou, its cities and its peoples. It is singularly individualised by being identified by a second person singular pronoun 'toi' or 'tu', with the objective of underscoring the very close familiarity of the poet with the continent that had been made so strange, distant and unknown by the West. Our poet presented the continent in the following ways :

"Tu es l'idée de Tout et la voix de l'Ancien ("A une danseuse noire")".

Ô mon Afrique ma mure espérance	Oh my Africa, my mature hope
Brisant la stupeur vénéreuse de mon corps	Breaking the pernicious stupor of my body
Je chante pour ton sourire	I sing for your smile
Je chante pour ta parole ("**Je sais**")	I sing in your defence

Africa was appropriated by Diop, as a jewel, as a treasure jealously valued, as a possession that is

"Mon amante basculée à son de trompe panique" ("**Je sais**")	My lover knocked off at the sound of panic trumpet
"Afrique mon Afrique" ("**Afrique**")	Africa my Africa
"Ma terre d'énigme et mon fruit de raison" ("**A une danseuse Noire**")	My land of enigma and the reward of my mental commitment

Africa is presented therefore as a continent that cannot but be cherished with love, care, tenderness and concern.

This is particularly so because, for the pan-African poet that Diop was, (and also for all genuine Africans), Africa remained the only geophysical reality that accorded him his identity, that gave him the feeling of a home, that allowed him to have an indisputable origin. His imposed exile in France and the resulting dichotomy and dislocation on his personality did not make our poet forget that Africa was his home. This was powerfully expressed in '**Auprès de toi**':

Auprès de toi j'ai retrouvé mon nom	In your presence I have rediscovered my name
Mon nom longtemps caché sous le sel des distances	My name that was long hidden under the salt of distances.
J'ai retrouvé les yeux que ne voilent plus les fièvres	I have rediscovered the eyes which are no more to be clouded by fevers
[......]	In your presence I have rediscovered
Auprès de toi j'ai retrouvé la mémoire de mon sang".	the memory of my blood.

Our poet could not avoid the pull that was relentlessly drawing him to Africa. It was a biological and physical pressure; it was also a socio-cultural and psychological one. It was equally extremely emotional.

It was partly to underscore this point that he equated Africa to a mother, the giver of life. Not only did he see Africa as his "mère-patrie" (motherland), the continent is also shown as the motherland of all blacks:

O mère mienne et qui est celle de tous Du nègre qu'on aveugla et qui revoit les fleurs ("**A ma mère**")	O my mother and mother of all Of the black man who was blinded and sees the flowers again ("**To my mother**")

In personifying Africa as a mother, Diop was definitely attracted to the mother's attributes of maternal tenderness, love, care, concern, commitment and softness for her child; he was also motivated by such other features of the mother as the care-taker and protector of her fragile, innocent and tender child (mère - protectrice), as the feeder of her young baby who depended on her milk (endowed with an energy-giving force) and love to grow (mère-nourrière) and as the energiser of her feeble child (mère-distributrice de l'énergie). Thus, was discredited the role hitherto accorded to France by the early Francophone writers, who, in the same vein as Bakary Diallo in *Force-Bonté* (published in 1926) saw in France the protective, supportive, caring, helpful mother(land), whose invaluable support was needed by the helpless, spineless, hapless and feeble African, who was also presented as a perpetual child who could not grow into maturity without France which had egotistically appropriated the legal and natural right to completely assimilate the virtually lifeless child that was devoid of any distinct identity.

Africa was also presented by our poet as another protective element, a tree:

"l'arbre - gardien", ("**A une danseuse snoire**") "l'arbre robuste et jeune" ("**Afrique**")	the guardian-tree the robust and young tree

The full meaning of this great symbol of a tree would be better appreciated when viewed against its accompanying attributes of root, foliage, shadows and fruits and also projected to the totemic attributes of the tree (= wood) which is used to 'create' or 'represent' gods and goddesses on whom Africans depended for their survival and protection before the arrival of the white missionaries. Indeed, the shape of Africa, with its root stoutly buried in South Africa, its branches solidly extended to East and Central Africa and its foliage spreading out in West and North Africa shows the sturdiness and robustness of Africa. This particular essence of Africa is symbolic of its latent power. Though it was / is battered by incredible (political) hurricanes, it would also remain unbent and unshaken, though it was/is afflicted by (economic and physical) parasites, it would not fail to continue to put forth new shoots – all these, showing the latent and generative force of Africa and its distinctive capacity of being able to preserve most of the vital and natural (God-given) qualities which Western civilisation and technology had lost and which the West, with its parasitic agents, had sought to sap away:

Cet arbre là-bas	That tree over yonder, Splendidly
Splendidement seul au milieu de	alone amidst white and faded flowers,
fleurs blanches et fanées	That is Africa, your Africa which
C'est l'Afrique ton Afrique	is growing again
qui repousse	Which is patiently and obstinately
Qui repose patiemment	growing again
obstinément	And whose fruits acquire little
Et dont les fruits ont peu à peu	by little
L'amère saveur de la liberté.	The bitter taste of liberty.

To do full justice to the correct and realistic presentation of Africa, Diop tried to present to his reading public the three phases of Africa's evolution: pre-colonial Africa, colonial Africa, independent Africa or decolonised Africa. Each phase is presented from the African viewpoint as against the Eurocentric perspective through which Africa had been known to the Western world and which had also been forced down the throats of most Africans for years. The Negrophobic and Eurocentric sensibility that nurtured the Africa of chauvinistic Europeans created an imaginary African continent of European dream. It was a land replete with nothing but negative and obnoxious qualities. It was an Africa of deficiencies, an Africa that was distinguished by a chequered history that could not attract nor induce respect from anybody. Instead, it evoked paternalistic pity, contempt and condemnation from Europeans who convinced themselves of the justice, validity and indispensability of their civilising mission to a crude and barbaric continent which very badly needed to be helped and built up by a superior and better race. The justification of slavery, imperialism, colonisation, Christianity and neo-colonisation and also their enabling props and rationalising philosophies was premised on their beneficial impacts to Africans and the continent.

These points formed the basis of the position taken by our poet on the Eurocentric views on Africa, on the civilising mission of Europeans to Africa and on the philosophical standpoint taken by Europeans to justify their claims of superiority to Africans. Diop's position could not but be iconoclastic, militant and radical. As pointed out earlier, not only are ideas, biases, principles and norms on Blacks revalorised and overturned by Diop to favour the black race and those other underprivileged peoples of the world who share identical predicaments with the Blacks, our poet subjected all the actors involved in the panhuman and cosmic injustices and wrongs which have for long plagued the world underdogs to a thorough bashing in his *Coups de Pilon*.

PRE-COLONIAL AFRICA

The first major Eurocentric prejudice that Diop tried to overturn is the one based on the wrong premise that Africa did not have a past and that even if any past could be carved out for it out of sheer magnanimity by Europeans, it should be a past without any glamour, without any distinction, without any virtues that anybody could be proud of and without any worthy civilisation that could be copied or inspired from. The commonest derogatory stand of such hard chauvinists as Gobineau and his ilk, was that Africa was such a god-damned continent, populated by half human cannibals and brutes who were created specifically to serve the superior races and were expected also to subject themselves to their orders, ways of life and traditions. For them, Africa was condemned to carry the burdens of the civilised world and to remain subordinate to the superior races.

For Diop, Africa had a virtuous and exemplary past that could compare favourably with the past of other so-called civilised countries of the world. That past was characterised by a distinguished history, a distinctly enviable way of life and other outstanding qualities that should inspire the pride of all blacks and that should make the civilisation built on it appreciated and admired. While Europeans tried to attract Africans to their civilisation which was presented as the best, the worthiest and even the only one which could carry the name of civilisation, African civilisation, before being impregnated, impaired and disturbed by Western adventurism and imperialism, was shown by Diop to be distinguished and worthy of being espoused and cherished. Missing it was shown by Diop as missing the milk and essence of life, loosing it was presented as loosing the kernel of joy and human warmth ; merging it with another was shown as subjecting it to a stultifying pollution or adulteration. This was forcefully painted in the poem "Celui qui a tout perdu":

Le soleil riait dans ma case
Et mes femmes étaient belles et souples
Comme des palmiers sous la brise des soirs
Mes enfants glissaient sur le grand fleuve
Aux profondeurs de mort
Et mes pirogues luttaient avec les crocodiles

The sun used to laugh in my hut
And my women were lovely and lithe
Like palm-trees in the breeze.
My children would go gliding over the majestic river
Whose waters were deep as death.
And my canoes would wrestle with the crocodiles

La lune, maternelle, accompagnait nos danses
Le rythme frénétique et lourd du tam-tam
Tam-tam de la Joie Tam-tam de l'Insoucjance
Au milieu des feux de liberté.

The motherly moon would accompany our dances
Frenzied and heavy was the rhythm of tom-tom
Tom-tom of joy, tom-tom of care-free life
Amid the bonfires of freedom.

The blissful communion between nature and Africans reminds one of the symbiotic communion between nature and man of the biblical Eden.

Nature was in touch with man; the two were joined together in harmony and love ; they blended together as friends ; they related to each other as partners with reciprocal interests and concerns. The unity between man and nature generated peace and joy ; it inspired confidence and freedom ; it brought satisfaction to the pre-colonial African, it brought him heavenly motivated power and seemed to assure him of the supervisory control of the natural forces: "the motherly moon would accompany our dances". All these would be brought to an abrupt end by the arrival of the Whites. It was a monumental loss to Africans. It was like the loss of everything to them : loss of life, land and properties, loss of their peace, joy and human warmth, loss of their dignity, personality and pride. It was also the loss of their civilisation. The loss extended to all that distinguished the African, to all that characterised Africa as a geo-political reality and as a budding economic power. It was the beginning of Africa's tragedy and the end of its unity with nature. In fact, it was as if nature was replaced by the Europeans who imposed on Africa their civilisation and technology which took the place of nature which used to exert superintending control over the lives of Africans. The colonised continent was sapped of its original distinction and was restructured to reflect whatever the colonial masters wanted to make of it.

COLONIAL AFRICA

The dichotomic nature of the transition from pre-colonial Africa to colonial Africa was forcefully conveyed by the first line of the second part of "Celui qui a tout perdu":

"Puis un jour, le silence."　　　"Then one day, silence ..."

It was a sudden, abrupt, unexpected and strange intrusion ; it was a destructive, catastrophic and deadly irruption. The other verses of the remaining part of the poem conveyed the damage, violence, commotion and sadism which characterised the arrival of the white intruders who subjected the continent to rapacious tortures and its innocent and defenceless inhabitants to various indignities including rape, deportation, slavery, hard labour and other shameful deprivations.

This presentation of the arrival of Europeans in Africa is radically different from the manner that it used to be presented by the Whites and their apologists. For the latter, the arrival of the Whites in Africa had very positive consequences on the continent because it brought an exemplary civilisation and culture to the uncultured and uncivilised *"Niggers"*. It was presented as bringing relief to the Niggers from their agonising years of suffering, pains and depression. It was painted as salutary, beneficial and helpful to Africans.

But Diop, in the same vein as Césaire, had a different view. The traditional defence of the civilising mission of the West was shown to be a blatant lie, an indefensible affront to the Blacks and a reckless exploitation of a defenceless, innocent and peace-loving people. Rather than being a civilising mission, it was presented as a de-civilising and destructive adventure which brought suffering, unhappiness and dislocation to the black race in its train. Three vectors of this adventure were singled out, so as to show its ugly and negative features. These are slavery, colonialism and Christianity.

Slavery, presented as a dehumanising exploitation of man by man, came out as a monstrous humiliation of the black race. The physical, material, psychological and spiritual dimensions of this ruthless and sadistic commercialisation of the black man are revealed in many of the poems. In fact, slavery, from its initial take-off point in Africa through its route to its field of exploitation and operations are vividly described by Diop. From the time "the steel-eyed conquerors" imposed their uniform of iron and blood "on the black men ("Celui qui a tout perdu") through the "metallic hell of the routes" ("Les Vautours") to the "agonising shouts in the plantations" ("Les Vautours"), the blacks are seen as the victims of very humiliating tortures, perpetrated by whites who came out in the poems as merciless exploiters, sadistic killers, sexual monsters and inhuman savages. Many other poems also describe other aspects of slavery. "L'agonie des chaînes", "Le temps de martyre", "Souffre pauvre Nègre" and "Liberté" are some of these poems through which the traditional notions about the Whites as civilisers were reversed by Diop.

Colonialism came out of most of the poems in *Coups de Pilon* as a very pervading process of decivilisation and destruction, as a ravaging plague, as a mechanism predicated on a certain kind of brutal force and as a tyrannical logic of minority power. Colonialism was thoroughly condemned in all its ramifications; its traditional claims were radically overturned; its operators were bitterly lambasted and its manifestations were roundly condemned.

As already pointed out, colonialism could not be justified according to Diop, on any ground, because it was inhuman and damaging; it was an administrative machinery of impostors and usurpers; it was built on institutionalised violence (physical, psychological and spiritual). The killing, flogging, maiming, imprisonment and insults ("L'agonie des chaînes", "Souffre pauvre nègre", "Pleurs", "Le Temps de martyre", "Ecoutez Camarades", "Afrique"), the rape, sexual orgies and moral perversions ("Le Temps de martyr", "Celui qui a tout perdu"), and the various acts of exploitation, violence, humiliation and wickedness which characterised colonialism could not but portray it as a system specifically invented and effectively exploited by white savages and sadists to dehumanise a weaker race. Specific features of colonialism were presented as asphyxial. Assimilation, for example, was particularly singled out as a hypocritical brainwashing which turned blacks to spineless apes and helpless human sponges, who naively absorbed strange and incongruous manners and ways of life ("Nègre Clochard", "Renégat", "Un blanc m' a dit"). Western civilisation was revealed in its true character of being the way of life of the whites, which makes it to be therefore strange to Africans who have their own distinct and home-grown civilisations. In fact, civilisation was shown by Diop as a way of life of a people; and its identity and specificity were shown to derive from the totality of the life, mentality, culture, literature and history of the people in question. If Western civilisation, as shown and presented to Africans, were to be really appreciated for what it is in reality and practice, it would be seen to be fundamentally materialistic, selfish, hypocritical, exploitative, mercenary, oppressive and heartless.

The purveyors of the above civilisation who were also the white colonialists and the white masters come out therefore in *Coups de Pilon* characterised by the above features. The avidity, hypocrisy, moral cupidity, double-edged philanthropy, sanctimonious arrogance and heartlessness of the whites whose people Diop's poetic landscape clearly portray their civilisation as a civilisation of lies, of sterile intellectualism, of self-centredness and of plundering. This is very powerfully conveyed in the way Diop portrayed the white colonisers in the poems. Apart from acting and behaving as real human beings operating in their various roles as (white) enslavers, masters, soldiers, administrators, traders and missionaries, they are made to behave (and are referred to) as animals, specifically as carnivores: vultures, hyenas, beasts, panthers and jackals, who therefore manifest animalistic instincts, who operate with the ruthless and sadistic jungle law of the survival of the fittest and who are motivated continuously by the primitive animal concern for self. The so-called superior race therefore emerges from Diop's poems as a race of vultures, jackals and hyenas: of voracious, violent and rapacious people who selfishly exploit and mutilate their preys by devouring (i.e. destroying) these with impunity. Very few African poets have done such a radical analysis of whites and of white civilisation and have attacked their self-arrogated myths of superiority and their biases with such a violent anger as Diop did.

Christianity was another European-created system, which came under Diop's militant scrutiny. It is shown as being a brainwashing sustainer of colonisation which it defends, particularly with its morality of meekness and abnegation, with its philosophy of unquestionable obedience to the master and also its other mystifying strategies and manipulations. Diop places Christianity in the same pedestal as other mystifying philosophies through which the white man tried to subjugate the wretched of the earth, to justify their domination of these dispossessed peoples and to build up various myths to actualise their claims to superiority. In many poems ("Les Vautours", "La route véritable", "Les Heures", "Aux mystificateurs", "Le Renégat", "Ecoutez Camarades"), the hypocrisy, falsehood and ambivalence of Christianity as well as other European created myths are painstakingly described. This is very well revealed in the various contrasting imageries in the poems, in the antinomic notions of the Whites, their dualistic attitudes, discrepancies between their intentions and actions, between their feelings and realisations, between their hidden intentions and appearances, between their covert and real identities and also in the differences between their beliefs and actions, all showing the wide gap between what was claimed to be and what was in reality.

Under this asphyxial situation, the black man could not have been seen as the beneficiary of the blessings of colonialism and Western civilisation, an idea that was commonly shared by the apologists of western civilisation. Instead of this, the black man was shown as an undeserving victim of the curses of western civilisation, which was distinguished by tricks, intrigues, tortures, wickedness and dispossession. As we have pointed out, it was the beginning of their loss of all that they hitherto had and also the take-off of their journey on the path of white oppression and exploitation, of inferiority complex and subordination. Africa became like a quenched volcano, exposed to the laughter of others (the Whites) and to their greed. Africans became a confused lot, with little or no hope, but covered with shame, distinguished by a sense of despair and subjected to a European orchestrated and carefully guarded dehumanisation.

The plight of Africans under colonialism, was also presented by Diop as being akin to that of other dispossessed and oppressed peoples of the earth, with whom the black race should share fraternal ties. These 'castaways of the earth', to use Claude Mackay's words, are not subjected to identical geographical and racial parameters. They belong to an economic and panhuman family whose members are victims of institutionalised oppression, exploitation and repression. These peoples are located in the different parts of the world (Vietnam, Suez, Hanoi, Africa and U.S.A) where the technologically weaker races and the economically underprivileged are used as producers of the wealth of others referred to as "brothers" and "comrades" in adversity and misery. 'These wretched of the earth' have common characteristics. They are all exploited because of their social status; they are all dispossessed because of their economic identity; they are all subjected to sadistic victimisation and humiliation because of either the colour of their skin or because of the level of their material success or failure. While these members of international proletariat are generally presented in five poems ('Vagues', 'L'Agonie des chaines', 'Ecoutez Camarades', 'Certitude' and 'Appel') in which various aspects of their misery and depersonalisation are described, Diop was more specific in a particular poem. In that poem, "A un enfant noir" was presented the case of Emmett Till, the fifteen year old Afro-American boy lynched and drowned in Money, Mississippi by the Ku-Klux-Klan for daring to look admiringly at a white girl. The collective justice of lynching, invented by the Americans to do jungle justice against the blacks, shows the duality and savagery of the white capitalist oppressors. In the U.S.A. where technology, with skyscrapers and air-conditioners, has reached its peak, where Bible-waving fundamentalists pretend to exhibit the Christian norms of love and kindness and where every day life is expected to be built on Christian virtues, the black race has been singled out as a valueless race by callous and hypocritical white racists. But then, Diop foresees an end to this indignity and oppression, which could be achieved if the oppressed join hands together to fight for freedom and fairness and to create a new *MAN*.

INDEPENDENT AFRICA

It is from Africa that the oppressed panhuman race can best learn its lessons of creating this new man, by the ability of man to liberate himself from the strangulating hands of white oppressors. From the hopelessness and the hellish atmosphere of yesteryears, Diop created an opening for hope, regeneration and survival for the new man.

The structure of most of the poems demonstrates in a very positive way the inexorable movement towards a triumphant affirmation of liberation and a complete reversal of former myths and stereotypes. By the time our poet was foreseeing this triumphant evolution of Africa towards independence, virtually no African country had become independent! Diop was indeed prophetic in his militancy! The trend suggested in the poems was to be followed by most liberation movements. It is generally a move from despair and resignation to hope and revolt. While most poems open with an indictment against the various manifestations of exploitation, by describing the brutalities and hypocrisy of the white oppressors, they close on a note of optimism leading to a happy future of reconstruction and renaissance, during which the white oppressors would be shown the way out. Each of the poems underscores this optimistic movement from gloom to bliss, from subjugation to freedom, from agonies to a happy future – a future that is translated by images of light, sun, stars and dawn shattering the darkness and piercing through clouds and mists.

Diop returns to the original unity between man and nature of the pre-colonial period. In spite of the technological and economic superiority of the white man, the exploited man, aided by natural forces, would have the last laugh. The oppressed man, in cosmic alliance with the natural elements whose indomitable energies would come to his aid to perfect his strategy for vindication and redress, would have a more durable victory.

But then, this victory could not be achieved and retained passively. It has to spring from an iconoclastic action: combat. The struggle has to be resolute and decisive. "Le Défi à la force" describes this very poignantly:

Toi qui plies toi qui pleures	You who stoop, you who weep
Toi qui meurs un jour comme	You who one day die just-like that
ça sans savoir pourquoi	without knowing why
Toi qui luttes qui veilles	You who struggle, who watch
pour le repos de l'Autre	while the other sleeps,
Toi qui ne regardes plus avec	You with no more laughter in your look
le rire dans les yeux	You, my brother, with this face of fear
Toi mon frère au visage de	and anguish
peur et d'angoisse!	Rise and shout "Non".
Relève-toi et crie Non	

This militant call for positive revolt and action, promising freedom from the shackles of oppression and exploitation whose chain is formed by capitalism, slavery and colonialism, is addressed to all those who are victims of all forms of injustices, resulting from colour, status, religion or place of birth. The role of unity in this strategy for liberation is indispensable. The oppressed peoples have to come together to form a united front, since unity is strength. But it is basically when people have identical interests and are pushed together because of deeply felt needs that they can come together and fight together. ("La Bête affolée", "Vagues", "Ecoutez Camarades", "Aux mystificateurs", "Nègre Clochard", "Certitude"). With all the strategies for liberation very well harnessed, the dispossessed shall possess his possession and be in a position to reconstruct his past and recreate his identity.

This is why the unrepentant 'assimilé', the whitewashed African and the American Uncle Tom are very violently lambasted by our poet. In three poems : "A une danseuse noire", "Nègre Clochard" and "Le Renégat", Diop presents to us the ridicule of this traitor to his people's cause who, with his easy-go-lucky ways, is over-intoxicated by western honours and his lugubrous and incongruous European manners. We are made to see the ugly side of this self-alienated black man who is thoroughly westernised and culturally whitewashed and who could not but look grotesque and odd, wherever he finds himself, in Africa or in Europe. He cannot but be pitied and jeered at as he plays the role of a comic figure in his self-created comedy.

THE NEW AFRICAN

In place of the traditional African created by the Europeans : the epitomé of inferiority, of backwardness and of savagery, who brings out the white man's myth of the lazy, mediocre, good-for-nothing *"nigger"*, Diop created a new African. In the spirit of anti-racist racism, he replaced the black ugly savage of negrophobic European invention by the white man who was made to bear the old anti-Negro myths and biases and who, at the end, cut the image of a contemptible and condemnable figure. Indeed, the table of racism was turned against the whites. To the question: Can the White give the best model of man?, Diop replied in the negative, by presenting the white man in his moral bankruptcy and his wild sadism, as the archetype of hypocrisy and as a vicious agent of dehumanisation and alienation.

On the other hand, the black man comes out in Diop's poetry as a victim of circumstances beyond his control. The reading public cannot but sympathise with him, as a victim of a tragic manoeuvring. Indeed, he comes out as a tragic hero of a classical tragic play who is generally a pun in the hands of an inexorably wicked fatality. In this tragic manoeuvring, the black man is admired, just as in a classical tragedy, for his audacity and efforts, which end generally on a pathetic note. His strength of character also demonstrated his exemplariness. One aspect of the black man's personality that has to be admired, in spite of the enveloping tragic atmosphere in which he has been positioned is his blackness.

The essence of blackness is particularly emphasised in the black woman who features in many of Diop's poems: "A ma mère", "A une danseure noire", "Rama Kam", "Hommage à Rama Kam". In each of these poems, we are made to witness the dethronement of the conventional myths, based on Caucasian norms, used in defining the blacks. Instead of feeding ourselves with the usual tradition of seeing blackness as the pejorative term to denote everything that is negative, ugly or condemnable: mourning, sadness, pessimism, shabbiness, crudeness, misery, vice and frustration, Diop shows that black is beautiful and virtuous. These qualities are to be particularly appreciated in the dark Venus, the black woman who symbolises beauty, warmth, passion and generative force. Every aspect of the black woman, her physique and movements, inspires respect and appreciation. Her pervading, sensuous and captivating beauty, her magnetic attraction and her exotic seduction are completely devoid of the trappings of Western civilisation. She is in complete contrast to the Caucasian woman, whose artificial coarseness receives its strength from her make-up, which cannot inspire authentic passion and love.

Above all, the black Venus symbolises Africa, a land of beauty, of joy, of peace and human warmth. This helps to see the new African as a model of beauty and the generator of peace and warmth, as an agent of positive change, as an harbinger of hope for panhuman understanding.

CONCLUSION

Diop has succeeded more than many other Negro-African poets to use poetry as a powerful instrument of renaissance and rehabilitation, as a means of destroying debilitating and negative myths about the black man and as a goading force to incite man to assert his real identity, to re-create his buried virtues and to win back his lost paradise. With a powerful style, supported by the choice of strong words and sustained by a biting irony and an iconoclastic sarcasm, Diop has most brilliantly succeeded in making his militant poetry convincing and realistic.

Notes And References

[1]   David Diop. "Contribution au débat sur la poésie nationale" in *Coups de Pilon*, Paris: Présence Africaine, 1973. pp.72-73.

[2]   Translation: "une expression violente d'une conscience raciale aïgue".

[3]   Translation : "He would soon understand that what constitutes the Negritude of a poem is less the theme than the style, the emotional warmth which gives life to words, which changes speech into words."

[4]   Trans. (French version in bracket).

[5]   According to Senghor "son humour cingle comme un fouet" ("his humour bites like cane").

6 "Contribution ..." in *op. cit.* p.70. Trans. "Literature is the expression of a changing reality; its point of departure is this reality which it captures and expands from its budding phase and helps to mature ... It is therefore indispensable for the poet to draw from the best of himself what reflects the essential values of his country. This is what makes his poetry national ... It is essential for him to speak from the root from which he has sprung; whatever comes after this is just additional to his authentic self ".

7 *Op. cit.* p. 75. Trans. "I shall be leaving for Guinea at the beginning of next week with Abdou Mumuni, Joseph Ki-Zerbo and four other African teachers. As I have indicated in my writing, there are instances when whoever is aspiring to be an intellectual must no more be contented with wishful thinking or with a mere declaration of intentions but should give to his writing a concrete reality and effect. It was only the issue of my family that forced me to hesitate a bit for some time. But after a careful reflection, this problem did not seem to me to create any impediment to my decision to leave."

8 Bakary Traoré, "Temoignage" in *David Diop : Temoignage – Etudes*, Paris : Présence Africaine, 1983, p.163. "It is from the heart of this mother that he knew Africa and the misery of all the have-nots of the world. It is through the bitter experiences and the spiritual richness of the one, who, for many Africans on exile, offered the reflection of maternal warmth of Africa, that one would be able to understand the vision of the writer of *Coups de Pilon,* the poet of love, the poet of peoples, of the *joie de vivre*, of friendship, of fraternal equality, of the nobility of man."

9 "My dear David, your adolescence has been a long suffering. Your distinction has been your ability to have overcome and dominated the suffering, to have faced difficult studies, to have made these and that, the springboard helping to raise you higher and higher."

[10] See Translation in No. 6.

[11] Transl. "Ce cri traversé de violence, ce chant guide seul par l'amour" in 'A ma mère'.

[12] The title of each poem in the collection also has deep connotations. Most of the titles are very symbolical and strongly summarise the theme(s) developed in each poem.

[13] In "Contributions ..." in *Coups de Pilon*, p. 72.

[14] Diop's word in "An Interview (imaginary) given by David Diop to Lenrie Peters" in *Hommage à ...* p.138.

[15] "Je suis né pour briser à coups de pierres dures, la carapace tenace de nos faux paradis."

[16] In Iwiyé Kala-Lobè, "Ensemble Avec David Diop, Mon frère", in *David Diop: Hommage-Etudes, op. cit.*₁. p. 86.

[17] *Ibid.*

Bibliography

PRIMARY REFERENCES

David Diop. *Coups de Pilon.* Paris: Présence Africaine, 1980.

David Diop. *Hammer Blows*, (Bilingual) by Simon Mpondo and Fjnk Jones, London: Heinemann, 1973.

David Diop. *Hammer blows and other writings.* Bloomington: Indiana University Press, 1973.

L. S. Senghor. *Anthologie de la nouvelle poésie nègre et malgache d'expression française.* Paris: P.U.F. 1948.

Critical Works on David Diop

Adama Sow Diop. "David Diop: *Coups de Pilon*, Notes de lecture, *Notre Librairie*, no 81, Oct-Dec. 1985.

Enid R. Rhodes Enid H, "David Diop: Poet of Passion", *L'Esprit Créateur*, 10, 1970.

Paulette Trout and Ellen C. Kennedy, "Profile of an African Artist: David Diop: Negritude's angry youngman", *Journal of New African Literatures and the Arts*, Spring and Fall, 1968.

Présence Africaine (ed). *David Diop: Témoignages – Etudes*. Paris: Présence Africaine, 1983.

Ruth Simmons. "La Pertinence de la poésie de David Diop pour les jeunes Noirs aux Etas-Unis", *Présence Africaine*, No 75, 3e trim. 1970.

S. Ade Ojo. "David Diop: The Voice of Protest and Revolt", *Présence Africaine*, No. 103, 1977.

S. Ade Ojo, *"Coups de Pilon"* in *Dictionnaire des Oeures Littéraires de l' Afrique Noire Francophone*. Sherbrooke: Editions Naaman, 1983.

S. Ade Ojo. " L' humanisme de David Diop", *David Diop: Temoignages - Etudes*. Paris: Présence Africaine, 1983.

Simon Mpondo. "David Mandessi Diop: An assessment" *Présence Africaine*, No. 75, 3e trim 1970.

3

IMAGES AND SYMBOLS IN TCHICAYA U TAM'SI'S POETRY

Joseph Obinaju

INTRODUCTION

Tchicaya U Tam'si is no doubt one of the most prolific writers Africa has produced to date. Unfortunately, his works, especially his poetry, have not been given enough attention by scholars and literary critics alike. The major reason for this paucity of critical essays on him has been that the poet, in the opinion of many, has chosen to be "difficult", "incomprehensible" or to use the commonest tag attached to his work - "hermetic". Madam Kesteloot actually said of his poems: "poésie difficile que la poésie de Tchicaya qui a hérité de Césaire..."! Gerald Moore, lending his voice, talks of the "oblique nature" of U Tam'si's oeuvre, its "exigencies" and the difficulties presented by the surrealist elements in his style[2]. As for Robert Bajart, one needs to be a "genius" to understand U Tam'si who has "voluntarily" chosen to be hermetic[3]. But the poet himself in his many interviews and discussions on his poetic mission insists thus: "Les clefs sont sur la porte". For him therefore, his poetry is neither difficult nor hermetic. On the contrary, it is one of the easiest to read and understand if only the reader would be "patient" to read in-between the lines, putting the punctuation marks where necessary[4]. This view is equally very sympathetically expressed by Jean-Michael Devesa who recently opined thus: "... Tchicaya n'est hermétique que pour ceux qui ne veulent rien entendre et se ferment d'avance à ce que le poète avait à coeur de partager"[5].

Thus, it is clear that the major problem lies in scholars and critics not being patient enough to get at the roots of Tchicaya's poetry. Consequently, many have not as yet been able to decode his language effectively so as to discover the numerous possible access routes to what the poet did between 1955 and 1980.

This difficulty probably accounts also for the paucity of information that is available on U Tam'si's works in general. Those interested in the poet and his works, would agree that there are very few articles and research works informative enough to guide the reader who is nonetheless eager to understand and enjoy the poet's creative efforts. This chapter is therefore an attempt to help the anxious reader battle through the world of images and symbols which at a glance make U Tam'si appear difficult to read and understand.

With Tchicaya, the first thing the reader needs is patience. This is necessary because there is a patterned choice of images and symbols to suit the black/white dialectics which form the nucleus of his writings up to 1962. From this time to 1980, one finds these images and symbols metamorphosing in line with the new historical verities evident in his post-independence writings. In other words, the dominance of the theme of social commitment, or the Black/ White and the Black/Black dialectics which condition the evolving drama of the poet's consciousness, make his images and symbols assume a very multifarious, striking and confusing nature for the non-initiate. In fact, Leopold Sedar Senghor aptly describes them in his preface to *Epitomé* as "images touffues, changeantes tournantes..."[6] Some of these include: jackal, thief, bloodsucker, vampire, which, by the process of symbolisation, represent the white man and colonisation whose unfortunate victim the black man happens to be. But before the details, who really is Tchicaya U Tam'si?

THE POET

Tchicaya U Tam'si[7], for those who may not have heard of him , is a Congolese, from the then Congo Brazzaville, today La République populaire du Congo. He was born in 1931 to a well-known political figure - Jean Felix Tchicaya - in a small town called Mpili. As was the case for most sons of influential blacks within the colonial set-up, he had his early education in France where he came face to face with the stark realities of racism. The resultant anguish and his revolt turned him into a school drop-out. He even fell out with his father at a stage for bringing him to Europe. And to show his anger, he quit their home to take care of himself, doing several odd jobs like serving as a restaurant porter, a warehouse-man and a farm hand to survive. It was in the heat of these tribulations that he published his debut collection of poems titled, *Le manuvais sang* (1955). Since then, Tchicaya has left an impressive record as a writer with eight poetry collections, four novels, three plays and a collection of short stories[8] which cut him out as one of Africa's most prolific writers to date, even as he is no more.

Before he died of cancer in 1988, he lived in Paris and worked with UNESCO in its Department of Education and Cultural Affairs for Africa. As a public figure, he had also contributed to major international conferences and colloquia the world over, on Negro arts, culture, language and literary advancement in Africa.

DIALECTICAL IMAGES

From the foregoing, it is evident that the poet's age and literary activities root him firmly in the all-important period when blacks the world over were struggling against the odds of colonial domination and oppression. In fact, the devastating effects of imported and tailored values under the colonial system forced blacks at that time, between 1920 and 1960, to constitute a world view of their own based on "relative" principles as opposed to the "absolutism" in Western thinking. In this conflictual situation, it stands to reason that the poet should, consciously or otherwise, join his social group - the oppressed blacks. This is evident in the myriad of images and symbols called in to play in his writings up to independence, i.e., 1955-1960, before further historical verities turned him away from his fellows in later poems.

As a partisan of modern poetry where in principle, the poet must strive to elevate persons and things beyond 'immediate comprehension', U Tam'si seems to enjoy the lavish use of images and symbols. Most of these are chiefly dialectical and embedded in figures of speech such as metaphors, metonymies, synecdoches and so on which help the poet to "evoke" without being obliged to name things directly. This way, it becomes possible to effect symbolic transpositions of real and lived socio-historical situations, as dictated by the Black/White relationship during the colonial era and the Black/Black relationship after independence. This trend is very evident in U Tam'si's premier collection titled: *Le mauvais sang* published in 1955. In this collection, the poet refers to himself as "Ombre saclette" and later as "enfant public" possibly in Paris. These are some of the choicest metaphorical interpretations of his anguish and nostalgia as an oppressed and an abandoned Negro.

With this inference, it is possible for the patient reader with a good historical sense to recognise a variety of metaphors and other figures of speech that symbolise the "White" or "Colonisation" as well as those that represent defiance or resistance of the blacks sometimes represented in the poet's personal attitudes. Let us look at a few examples here:-

A   'le vent chacal ricane aux portes ...." (ms:29)
     (the jackal wind is scratching at the doors ...)

     "L'ouragan déferle et la flamme survient" (ms:35)
     (Hurricane breaks out and fire erupts)

     "vint la cruauté la saveur aux lèvres" (ms:46)
     (Came cruelty with savour on its lips)

     " les chacals se sont tus pour m' entendre chanter" (ms:146)
     (the jackals kept quiet to hear me sing)

B   "...si la chair est roc c'est plus besoins de pleurs" (ms:37)
(... if the flesh is rock then no further need for tears)

"Je suis l'acier trempe, le feu des races neuves" (ms:43)
(I am the hardened steel, the fire of new races)

"je suis le Bronze, l'alliage du sang fort ..." (ms:45)
(I am Bronze, the alloy from strong blood)

In the cited verses, 'vent chacal', "ouragan" 'flamme' 'cruauté' and 'chacals' are diverse metaphorical ways the poet has chosen to best represent the whites and colonisation without necessarily calling them by name. In the same vein, "roc" "acier trempe", "feu" and "Bronze" symbolise the strength and the resistance of the oppressed Negro who refuses to be cowed by colonial brutality. What is true of the poet here, is that he intentionally exploits the process of symbolisation as against direct meaning. This is to be expected since poetry demands real economy of words for which symbolisation is well known. Since according to Tzvetan Todorov, the relationship between the symboliser and the symbolised is arbitrary or unnecessary[9], this arbitrariness provides enough room for the poet to manipulate his thoughts using metaphorical, metonymic, synecdochic and allegorical images and symbols among others. And his preference for metaphorical images stems from the fact that as 'condensed comparisons, metaphors are the best symbolisers' and help very much in cutting long stories short. This is what happens in the association between "flamme" and colonial invasion and that between "chair" and roc. "Colonial in vision" and "roc" are the nearest periphrases in the on-going Black/White dialectics to recreate the sense of the words "flamme" and "chair" when these are used metaphorically.

The reader who is sufficiently aware of the poet's dialectical leaning and backed up by a good knowledge of this "motivation" process would notice then that, as U Tam'si's visionary instincts flow from one collection to another, in rhythm with the conflict, his rich baggage of images and symbols drawn from floral, faunal, socio-historical and scientific sources among others, are intensified, opposed and polarised to ensure their fidelity to the Black/White dialectics in the first instance. This is how in *Le mauvais sang* le "fouet' and "lettre rouge", respectively symbolise the slave masters and the slave whose back, already bent by the crushing weight of slavery, trembles and bleeds with `red zebra' markings. In the three other collections up to independence: *Feu de brousse* (1957), *A triche-coeur* (1958) and *Epitomé* (1962), metaphorical and other images and symbols are also stockpiled and file past in quick succession in the same polarised manner. In *Feu de brousse*, the whites are successively assimilated into "fauves", "sangsues", "poisons apathiques", "hyènes" whimpering behind small huts before finally metamorphosing into "vampires". And as one would expect from this "Flight of vampires", typical of surrealist writing, the Congo, the poet's home country, and indeed Africa, are sent into a state of desolation. This sad event is transposed (mediated) by the poet in the ensuing verses where the "trees" - i.e., black families, tribes and countries - are constrained to take on leaves other than theirs. In other words, these families, tribes and countries in Africa superimpose on their traditional values, the imported and tailored values of the colonial masters. This is particularly true of the Francophones, governed by the infamous principles of assimilation. So we read in "Le Vol Des Vampires".

> The wind had dog's teeth and here are the winds these same winds have brought to the trees other foliages plucked the parrots perfumed the jackals while waiting that another mother may give birth to a child with three heads and without legs perhaps to continue the desolation on the savannah" (Fb.:67).

From the above, other symbols such as "parrots" and "jackals" remind us of the fate of both the strong and the weak, the very vocal and the bootlickers among the leaders of the blacks then who were either chastised or rewarded according to their degree of resistance or collaboration with the masters[10]. Considering a bit further the surrealist images and symbols at play here, it will be noticed that the anticipated monster-child with "three heads" and "no legs", presents the poet as a prophet foretelling in 1957, what would come to pass in 1960 with the emergence of "three" Congos

Congo Brazzaville, Congo Kinshasa and the secessionist Katangese republic. These were originally one and the same people but now separated by the activities of the colonialists. In this same collection, the resistance of the oppressed blacks to colonial invasion represented here by the "jackal wind" and the "vampires", is evoked in equally rich metaphors. For instance, to fight for their freedom, the souls of the blacks turn to "silex", while the poet as their mouthpiece tranforms himself into a monster: "je suis un monstre", says he in the poem *"Le vertige"*. He also becomes god of the armies: " je suis dieu des armées," before lashing out at the oppressor: "Voici ma chair de bronze". This bronze-like body is later transformed in rhythm with the defiant attitude of the poet, to all the hard and resistant objects one can imagine: cuivre, zinc, pierre, and even the "poisson coelacnth" in order to ensure survival for himself and his oppressed brothers.

EVOLVING IMAGES AND SYMBOLS

THE WIND

It must be mentioned here, that the inclusion of vampires/winds, tree and child in that sizzling poem 'Le Vol Des Vampires' is not an accident. It is in fact a conscious creation by the poet. These three images are the key Tchicayan images, created and sustained in an evolutionary pattern such that in the four collections that cover 1955 to 1962, i.e., from *Le mauvais sang* to *Epitomé* they, according to Michael Dash, "reappear... and at each reappearance, are more or less modified"[12]. With these evolving images and symbols, a sustained account of the binary opposition between whites and blacks is successfully wrapped up without the poet having to go into details. So in *Le mauvais sang*, the poet only gives an insight into what the wind of his imagination looks like. It is, from all indications, an enemy wind, in fact a jackal wind (vent chacal) scratching at the doors. Understandably at this stage, the wind or colonialism which it obviously represents, is still searching for a place to anchor and soon finds one in Africa as *Feu de brousse* recounts. Here, gathering in strength and destructive powers, it acquires "dog teeth" ("le vent a les dents des chiens") and combines its efforts with that of the vampires to devastate Africa as we have seen.

The account in *Feu de brousse* is of course nothing yet for, when this enemy "wind" settles and begins to exploit blacks in *A triche-coeur,* its effects are all the more catastrophic. The blood of innocent blacks is spilled all over the land through slavery and forced labour in the Congo and Central African Republics mainly, and by armed assaults on the protesting masses. And U Tam'si now writes of this wind in the poem, "L'etrange Agonie" (Extraordinary Agony):

> I write that wind in capital of the voracious grass the
> dead sneaking through it sneeze ashamed of their death
> they that do not have light death they have the wheels
> of tractors the weights of buildings the snorting of
> trains the spacing of railway lines on their death and
> in order to humiliate them the fire of their eyes was
> left to burn itself out (Atc:120)

The parade of the dead here in the wind, aided by synecdoches like 'tractor wheels' 'building weights', 'railway spacing' and so on, all object-sources of death, further vivifies historians' and researchers' accounts of forced labour during which black workers got crushed under the painful weight of collapsing buildings or by tractor/train wheels[13]. Like I observed in one of my studies on U Tam'si:

> C'est une véritable "hosties noires" que le poète chante
> et qui fait reconnaître avec L.S. Senghor, que tout le
> long de sa création poétique, la tête du poète est pleine
> d'images. C'est là sa vertu majeure. Dans ces images
> et symboles: vent, arbres, sang, morts, chenilles de
> chars, etc, se lisent les vérités socio-historiques du
> Congo et de l' Afrique de la colonisation[14]

Also in *Epitomé*, which coincides with the climax of colonial exploitation in Africa, the wind displays yet another aspect of its oppressive qualities. Here, already bubbling with courage and force, this same wind "Knocks at each door/that is opened with trembling heart". Then, with a lot of pride and arrogance, it manifests its powers all over the land using its flag of office with its three colours: sky-blue, sail-white, blood-red. And U Tam'si's regrets over this humiliating attitude of the wind is rendered in these rich images and symbols in the poem titled, "Au Sommaire D'une Passion" (The Summary of a Passion):

> How could I rejoice to be born all flesh which is no
> coat of mail nor this wind hammering at every door
> one opens with trembling heart — sky-blue sail-white
> blood-red? I who know nothing of the tree of my life
> my disgrace had three colours. (Ep:31.)

With the 'coat of mail' (côte de maille), the "flag" and the 'tree', there are obvious allusions here to the French colonial administration represented by its "drapeau tri-colore" high up in the wind. Equally indicated in this poem are the capitalist entrepreneurs and the over-zealous black guards charged with recruiting the work force and maintaining law and order in the colonies.

All these sad events had forced the poet to cry out thus in *Feu de brousse:* "coffee bananas cotton tea tapioca/die die whichever cares", while a little later he adds: "I also have memory/of flesh or fruits that were swindled." (Ep:82) Léopold Sédar Senghor, himself an exploiter of images and symbols, aptly summarises U Tam'si's posture in the following appraisal of *Epitomé*:

> The summary of his passion, here is what explains
> the title of this collection: **Epitomé** the Negro
> sufferings and firstly that of the crucified Congo, at
> the turn of the century, or at the crossroads of the
> Congo-Ocean, and again the dead and the wounded
> during the recent uprising in Leopoldville, that is what
> Tchicaya laments[15] ... (my translation).

Senghor's testimony is probably one of the most conclusive on the ravages of colonisation (the wind) for it coincides with this poetic outburst again from the anguished poet: "see how laxative scoundrels descend/on constipated savannahs" (Ep: 42). Here as usual, "laxative scoundrels" as symbols of oppression, stand for the parasitic colonial masters, while "constipated savannahs" conjure the image of stiffled and suffocating black countries under colonial domination.

At the same time as we note the evolution of the "wind" as a symbol of oppression in U Tam'si's poetry, it would be of immense benefit to see what the poet makes of the "tree" and the "child" which are symbols diametrically opposed to the "wind".

ORPHAN-CHILD/TREE

The first important thing to note here is that the child in U Tam'si's pre-independence poetry is chiefly represented as the "orphan" while the black race is represented by the "tree - the popular "arbre généalogique" he so desperately keeps searching for from *Le mauvais sang* to *Epitomé*. The second note is that the "orphan child" and the "tree", as dialectical symbols, complement themselves in the struggle against the oppressor - the wind. In fact, the story of the orphan's loss of identity cannot be fully comprehended if one fails to grasp the progressive struggle between the "wind" and the orphan's "tree of life"! The orphan's anguish, despair and rage sometimes rise and fall in consonance with what the poet discovers in his search for this "tree" from 1955 to 1962.

In more concrete terms, therefore, the child that is noticed in *Le mauvais sang* is actually an unhappy child who, in more ways than one, is a "double" of the poet. The child, like the poet, is quickly declared a public child, without parents and so an orphan. The wind did in fact say of him in the poem ,"Entendu Dans Le Vent" (Echoes in the Wind):

> I see you with neither father nor mother,
> nor brother...
> And they are neither dead, there, ... nor living
> nor dead! (ms:34).

If the orphan's parents and relations are neither "dead" nor "alive" there could be only one explanation. Slavery and colonisation have so incapacitated these beings that they are no longer able to free themselves from bondage. In recognition of this ugly situation, with the attendant frustration, the orphan (the poet?) cries out thus in *Feu de brousses*:

> Mistake! I was born in the egg of stiffled empires!
> my father knew how to be a brother convict,
> that is why there is so much tare on my lands. (Fb:89)

Later, he summarises his pitiable situation in these images and symbols: " the forest has reclothed me with darkness/without the idea of what makes up the family" (Fb:91).

These devastations are indeed so total that by 1958 as one flips through the pages of the third collection, *A Triche-Coeur*, these trees of life (arbres de génie) now completely transformed, have no single trace of the orphan's family members on them as the following account in the poem *"L'Etrange Agonie"* (Extraordinary Agony) shows:

> Then
> One young idiot opened for me her sex to piss upon my
> already purulent pain god alone knows how I enjoyed and
> coming back on my path more valiant I met nothing but
> trees which carry fruits one of the other trees all the same
> but not one member of my family on their branches.
> (Atc:121.)

Consequent upon this realisation that he could in fact be "a man without history" as the oppressor had asserted, who suddenly "one morning came up black/against the light of setting suns" the anguished orphan dies of "rage" in the "guts of wind". This death symbolises the loss of hope for freedom for his social group represented by the tree. But this is where something remarkable happens in the poet's psychological/spiritual adventure for which he should be given credit. Here, like Sisyphus, like his predecessor Aimé Césaire, he refuses defeat because he knows that his people - the Congo and Africa at large - want to be free: "mourir non/ je comprends que mon Congo/veuille vivre libre" said he in *Feu de brousse*. Turning the table therefore against the oppressor-the wind, he resuscitates the orphan to continue his search up to the fourth collection, *Epitomé,* which marks the apogée of this duel. Here again, the orphan's search for "l'arbre généalogique" almost comes to nought which makes the child (the poet?) laments: "O my absurd ancestry!/Down from which tree? What flowers will that tree/let fall, before the funeral bell?"/—(Ep:21). However, we are quickly intimated with what the "tree" this time around can do. In fact, the tree that one meets in *Epitomé,* conceptualised and realised between 1960 and 1962, is no longer docile and subservient. It is indeed a stubborn tare which,

> ... at the top of a hill lift like a candle a branch of blood the branch carries a green leaf at its tip image of yellow and soft flame against the light with demons hooting at it. (Ep:21).

As could be deciphered from those heart-rending, surrealist verses, against the orphan's despair and laments, occasioned by faded and falling flowers (fleurs fanées), symbolising dead and dying members of his social group - the blacks - the poet juxtaposes other images and symbols of hope and victory against the oppressor. The images and symbols at issue here are those of the "branch of blood " with a "green leaf" at its tip. These evoke the imminent bloody battle between the oppressor and the oppressed with the "leaf" as the first sign of victory for the latter. This victory is again certified by the image of yellow and soft flame against the light signaling the passing of the blacks from the dark ages of slavery and colonisation imposed by the now incapacitated "demons" - les "djins" - or the whites, to freedom. Obviously, U Tam'si's conception of the tree in *Epitomé* raises to a higher pedestal the view held by his homologue, David Diop, himself another avowed freedom fighter of the "Negritude-aggressive" type. In his poem, "Afrique", he saw in the tree the image of a new Africa that would emerge from slavery and colonisation into independence.

Thus, without having to go into details, thanks to these evolving images and symbols, the poet succeeds in giving an in-depth account of the polarised forces at play in the "universe police de la colonisation". Beyond this, mention needs to be made also of what has come to be termed the "ambivalent" images in U Tam'si's oeuvre. These also lend their helping hands in the satisfactory explanation the reader must have in order to enjoy the poet's verses.

AMBIVALENT IMAGES AND SYMBOLS

Ambivalent images and symbols in U Tam'si's poetry are those images and symbols borne out of some deep psychological disequilibrium that the poet suffered in life. Lovers of Tchicaya U Tam'si know that he had to contend with a family scandal surrounding his birth. He also has this nagging feeling of frustration and sometimes hatred for agents of slavery, colonisation and even neo-colonization whose scandalous romance with his people caused his feelings to degenerate into what psychologists term "approach-avoidance" reactions. "Approach", because these images and symbols like the sea and river, the woman, Christ and his black brothers are persons and things that he ordinarily cherishes. " Avoidance", because of their dubious roles and collaboration with the white man in changing his destiny and that of the black race. So, we have running through his collections, as is the case for dialectical images, the following: water (river, sea, ocean), woman, Christ, blacks, as ambivalent images and symbols.

WATER

This symbol, which easily encompasses rivers, seas, oceans, is one of the sources of joy and happiness for the poet probably because his people, the Bakongos, are very close to the sea. Thus, one finds commendable references to water and its related images; "... the seas rebounding were dressing me up in corals..." (ms:27) and in *Feu de brousse* he affirms " this river which lives in me repopulates me (Fb:595). But as one looks through *A Triche-coeur*, the sea becomes something frightful and even resentful for the poet as it now chooses to ally with slave masters and colonial masters. Indeed, it was the waters (rivers, seas, oceans) that served as route for carting away millions of innocent blacks to America as slaves and they also brought in the colonial masters at a later date. Whence regrets such as these in *A Triche-coeur*;

> make of my hand a vertical to sound at the low water
> mark of a simple love the river that I lead to the sea
> the sea that leads me to death (Atc:113).

In the poem *"L'étrange Agonie"* (Extraordinary Agony) he indicts the waters this way:

> my voice striking the bush in ecstasy then came
> numberless to me with three centuries of death which
> had pissed upon my country's sickness the water of
> the river swells and I rejoiced swallowing all my
> sadness here I am again before the sea, the sea now
> only obeys the slave masters not a wave sings the time
> is void with sadness not a lady bird the sea does not
> even move not one bather ... I have lived long without
> memory (Atc:125).

There are obvious allusions here to the three centuries of slavery symbolised by "three centuries of death" and "my country's sickness". And the poet does not forget the complicity of the waters which offered themselves willingly as routes for perpetrating this crime against Africa! So much is the poet's disappointment and suspicion that in *Epitomé* he even queries the river thus: "sea, are you also hiding away the missing tree of my life?" (Ep:36). Water in all its ramifications, therefore, is both a symbol of sadness and joy, a source of life and death as the poet remembers Emmett Till lynched and drowned under the waters by callous racists in America: "He was killed under the waters", says he in *Epitomé* (Ep:92). In *Arc musical* produced some years beyond *Epitomé*, in 1969, U Tam'si reflects further on the water question and gives this verdict; "I like the sea very much". But this is only : "when it is resting/ from the tumults of its abyss—" (Am:117). It is, therefore, clear from these excerpts that water as symbol occupies some important space in the poet's creative consciousness, as it saves and destroys, as colonialists' ally; mixing hope with despair for the black man!

WOMAN

The woman as symbol presents almost the same pattern of mixed feelings as the waters in the poet's life, probably because of his somewhat scandalous birth. It does look like something sordid and disappointing happened at the poet's birth, for we are told by Professor Moore, a credible critic of the poet, that Tchicaya never knew his mother, nor her whereabouts until he died[16]. Is he then the result of some of these "accidents" in love affairs? This is possible for he talks with so much regret about this in "Le Mal," one of the key poems in *Le mauvais sang*. In the said poem, he says: "They spat upon me, I was still a child". He also refers to himself as "enfant public" - a public child - belonging to nobody in particular and remembers again that: "They spat upon him" because of something incestuous or illicit in his parents' union (ms:31). In *Feu de brousse*, he makes this far-reaching confession on himself, his mother and his family: under *"Le Forcat"* a symbolic title reminiscent of his vicissitudes in life: "my mother has never had/ preconceived ideas about love/that is why my sisters/do not like me/it's even a pattern" (Fb:89). This regret buttresses his earlier notice of this scandal and the need to cleanse it somewhere in "Le Vertige" (Vestiges):

> I am the flesh of those carrying me I understood my
> source as the flame of some sex whose objection need
> be cleansed. (Fb:64)

These revelations and the disappointment they occasion tend to dampen the poet's happiness sometimes vis - à - vis the woman whom he otherwise cherishes as one of nature's most wonderful creations. For example, "Sammy the pagan" to whom *A triche-coeur* is dedicated, is one woman that is always on the poet's lips. He loved her very much and was loved in return. So faithful were they that somewhere in *Feu de brousse* he insisted, probably against pressures, to drop his loved one; "O my expedients/.../ no, leave me alone to love Sammy" (F6:72). And he recollects; "Sammy's hair were smelling mist and amber/we dreamed to the point of bursting our memories/.../but our love/a basket of crabs" (Fb:84).

The poet's misgivings over this uneasy love, richly symbolised by "basket of crabs" is later re-echoed in another regret over this "Sammy the pagan".

> I had wanted to die for the one who has promised me
> love my two hands have since become the two trays of a
> balance with which to weigh my shadow and hers (Fb:93).

The "basket of crabs" symbolising the conflicts and misunderstandings (Fb:93) experienced in love has finally led to the poet abandoning this love as shown above. In *Epitomé*, he talks also of some love escapades with women, this time in Paris:

> I have the finger nails of a woman in my flesh I bleed
> so that she can enjoy love (Ep:25).

But almost immediately, he is frightened by this woman's hold on him and longs to be separated from her and her impressions, so as to remain faithful to his cause and to his people. So he screams: "But hide the image of her god from me/This Fakir whose grins dampen my spirit". (Ep:25)

Faced with the betrayals of the Church during the Congolese crisis, U Tam'si again reflects on Sainte Anne of the Congo - the grandmother to Jesus Christ and the "Protectrice" of the Catholic Church and finds her "hardly saintly". For him, she is stone-hearted, very wicked and therefore can kill even with her sex! To show his resentment at her complicity with the colonial masters, he promises her "Litany in rags" (Atc:123) which he achieves in *Epitomé*, in the section titled: *"Au Sommaire D'Une Passion"* (The Summary of a Passion). The woman, for all he cares, is a double-edged sword. She can give life, provide love and happiness, protect and the like. But amidst all this, she is also a devil incarnate when it pleases her, for she can deceive, hate and destroy. Little wonder then why in *Le ventre* (1964) he warns man to beware of: "his folly/with women who [always] destroy him" (Vt:123).

CHRIST AND CHRISTOLOGICAL IMAGES

One striking thing about U Tam'si is that he is often difficult to place as a devout Christian or as a non-believer. He moves very easily from one to the other as his fancy dictates. For example, in *Le mauvais sang*, he sees Christ as the most spectacular among men for redeeming the souls of "all the sinners" on earth (Ms:47). He is thus tempted to compare his mission as poet to that of Christ the redeemer whose travails on earth come quite close to his own travails. As mortals, they have both been loved and betrayed and so he writes in *Epitomé*,

> Christ I laugh at your sadness oh my gentle Christ
> Thorn for thorn We have a common crown of thorns I
> will be converted because you tempt me ... (Ep: 61).

Pursuing this relationship further he adds;

> Am I just your brother They have already killed me in
> your name was I guilty of my death... In kissing your
> cross my mouth was stained with blood (Ep:62)

In these verses taken from a section of *Epitomé* titled *"Le Contempteur"* "(The Scorner), U Tam'si is meditating on Christ and his religion and mixes his admiration and love for him with hatred and admonition as he discovers that this sacrificial lamb is after all not as "clean" as he supposed him to be. For example, during the Congolese crisis of 1960-1964, the "Church of Christ" played a very dubious role, allying with the colonialists instead of saving the innocent blacks from oppression. The poet as an uncompromising moralist finds this unacceptable and blames Christ for it since the Church belonged to him[17]. It is no surprise then when he goes pounding and barraging the poor Christ with insults and accusations such as these;

> Walk on this road of my people where I limp You will
> tell me in which Egypt my people groan My heart is
> no desert speak oh Christ speak ... (Ep:63).

Later he queries, as he contemplates on Congolese sufferings:

> You do nothing The Congo divides its pain Ah Christ
> how dirty you are to ally with the bourgeois ... Say
> what wine shall I drink for lying to my people ... For
> the Eucharist I begged wine leaven and salt I was the
> wandering Jew to betray you who have betrayed me
> They have already killed me in your name betrayed
> and sold.

In this poem which cannot be cited in full for want of space, lots of images and symbols touching on Christ and the Church abound to impress upon the reader the real significance of Christ and Christianity. Thus one finds here and there, christological images and symbols such as; the burning bush, Egypt, crown of thorns, jubilate, Eucharist, Judas, St Joseph, Saint Anne, Mary Magdalene, pascal lamb which all revolve around the lives and times of the Jews, Christ, and the Catholic Church which for him has failed the black man. So disappointing in fact is the church in Africa that the poet wastes no time in letting Christ know what pain and anger he feels as he punctuates; "Christ I hate your christians" "Your temple is full of merchants who sell your cross Christ" (Ep:61). To buttress this feeling, he opts in another section - Promenade"- in *Epitomé*, "To be a pagan at the pagan renewal of the world..." (Ep:121).

Because of this ambivalence of the poet's emotions across a number of collections, Gerald Moore had to remark that:

> Every important symbol evokes a polarity of moods,
> and to measure this polarity it is necessary to read
> Tchicaya in long stretches at a time.[18]

It is, therefore, advisable not to seek to jump verses or sections in reading U Tam'si, since the full meaning of his mission as a poet is achieved by some harmony between the different sections of the collections and between one collection and the rest from 1955 to 1978, when he stopped writing poems, his mission of liberation and humanism having been realised.

ALLEGORICAL IMAGES AND SYMBOLS

One other captivating aspect of Tchicaya's imagery is the dearth of allegorical symbols that pervade his works especially the later ones. These symbols, which are "indices" to real historical, social, political, religious and other events of some sort[19], abound from *Epitomé* to *Arc musical* as the poet contemplates the unfolding socio-political drama in his country - the Congo. And, in line with the dynamism which characterises his writing, there is a shift of emphasis in these later poems from the "Other" to "Self," that is from the "whiteman" to the "blackman". This shift comes as a result of the betrayals and the brutality of the new leaders - Africans - who, as independence is achieved, now arrogate to themselves more rights and privileges than the colonial masters had. Side by side with this, the poet discovers too, to his utter chagrin, that the world is increasingly becoming unsafe for man because of anarchy and wars caused by lack of compromise among nations and races. Faced with this new awareness, U Tam'si's poetry now further evolves, inventing new images and symbols - allegorical ones mainly to catch up with the new situation. Thus, in *Epitomé*, as he contemplates with deep sorrow, the massacre of blacks in the Congo and Africa at large, he notes: "... 1908/Then 1959[20]". These two verses are actually pregnant with historical and political facts which cause him to chastise Christ the more:

> Christ I spit at your joy, The sun is black with negroes
> who suffer with jews searching for the leaven of their
> bread What do you know about New Bell At Durban
> two thousand women at Pretoria two thousand women
> at Kin also two thousand women at Antsirabe two
> thousand women What do you know about Harlem
> (Ep:65).

As presented here, the allegorical symbols at play are those of dates, names of towns, the figures and women. They all fuse into one to adequately highlight the suffering of the Congolese and the blacks in the diaspora. The death toll of "two thousand" and the use of "women" are chiefly symbolic, representing the refracted versions of true historical accounts that depict the social injustices perpetrated against the masses by colonialists, neo-colonialists and their black agents. This is particularly true of Congo Kinshasa and Pretoria, to take just those two examples. In the Congo, violent clashes between the supporters of Kasavubu, Lumumba and Moise Tshombe in the late fifties and early sixties produced a lot of casualties, including Lumumba himself, while white on black and black on black violence occasioned by the supporters of the late Mobutu Sese Seko and Etienne Tshissekedi or those of the apartheid regime, Zulu Inkhata and the African National Congress (ANC) in South Africa, have equally given rise to thousands of dead men, women and children. This experience is probably why in *Le Ventre* (1964), the poet renews his resolve to keep fighting for man the world over as the symbols below depict:

> *I shall never stop abusing negro jew white cuban!*
> (Vt:104)

But the issue of betrayal must be adequately addressed before extending the fight to the whole human race. Engulfed now in black/black dialectics, he remembers Lumumba's assassination and refers to him as Le "ventre" trahi (Vt:15), le "martyr" (Vt:17) and "Le Congo" since Lumumba had said of himself "Le Congo c'est moi" (Vt. 19). In the same collection, allegorical symbols like "Ventres blancs" dans "Un ban de ventres blancs ... sur le Stanley pool" (vt:14) refer to the massacre of the whites by the Congolese revolting black soldiers in July 1960. "L'antichambre de l'évêque de Kin" (Vt:21) symbolises the role of the church in the Congolese disaster of 1960-1964, while the "dollar" (Vt:23) represents the major but negative role played by the Americans in the same crises[21]. In all this, the poet does not forget that his black brothers are the key actors and so he laments; "Kitona or Kamina/Congolese! Blood blood blood/flows with the funeral tambourines" (Vt:39).

This lament is of course matched with verbal violence; insults and abuses he rains on his "brothers of negro obedience". For him, they are "baboons", "jackals", "Jews" and some are even "prostitute ministers" all in *Le ventre*. And in *Le pain ou la cendre* (1977) the leaders are "Hired assassins", "Blood thirstymen" and "Puppets" (vt:163-164). It is interesting to note here how mobile some of Tchicaya's images and symbols can be. This quality makes some of them change camps at will. For example, in the beginning, the poet had used symbols like "Jackals" "blood suckers", "rogues" to describe the whites. In the present black/black dialogue, he applies the same treatment almost to his counterfeit black brothers as shown here because for him the status quo still prevails and this means there is exploitation or man's inhumanity to man everywhere.

FROM IMAGES AND SYMBOLS TO UNIVERSAL HUMANISM

From what has been said so far, it becomes possible and even necessary to repeat, at least in part, what Jean-Paul Sartre observed about Aimé Césaire: "rien n'est gratuit ici; pas d'écriture automatique". [22] Like Césaire for whom he had a lot of respect and admiration, there is evidence of the stylistic choice of expressing himself uniquely in images and symbols which portray him as difficult or hermetic. But his poetry, in the main, retains its internal logic and its primary obsession which is, for him as for Césaire, testifying for the oppressed blacks in the Diaspora. The two poets in fact have some deep penchant for this defence of their social group as the images and symbols highlighted here show . In the case of Cesaire for example, this defence is so intense that anger becomes an important emotional springboard for his reaction against white domination Thus, with an "internal tension and an eruptive violence which translate his mood of defiant rebellion", he lashes out in surrealist pattern; "My desire, a hazard of tigers, surprised, armed with sulphur[23]"

The remarkable thing about U Tam'si, though, is his faith in man's triumph, the moment all agree to work together. This is no surprise for, as an avowed humanist, he prefers "collectivism" to "individualism" among men whatever their race and colour. This logic is what gave rise to the exemplary "pardon" he granted the white man in *Epitomé* [24] before going ahead in *Le ventre* and *Arc musical* to re-echo the "Universal humanism" so dear to Leopold Sedar Senghor. So in *Arc musical*, as he further regrets the chaos in his country referring to the Congo and Lumumba as "île fragile" and "île cernée de sang" (Am:107), he made sure that he let the reader into what the new world of his imagination could be in *Le ventre* : "The world remade in my image/shall be with eau de cologne" (Vt:107). This world, made of the set-smelling perfume - eau de cologne - symbolises universal love, peace and unity in diversity which the poet accepts as the best way forward for mankind. And those conversant with U Tam'si and his poetry would agree that this optimism climaxes in *Arc musical* where the poet actually attempts a poetic remoulding of the world after the biblical tower of Babel. This appears in the section titled "Epitaph:"

> I predict a babel in inoxydizable metal or of crossed blood Mixed with the dregs of all raw! After the red man, After the yellow man, After the black man, After the white man. There is already the bronze man, The only alloy with soft fire, Already very possible but in wait (Am:109).

Here, the allegorical symbol "Babel" symbolises the new world of the poet's desire, built by people of diverse races and colours and therefore of diverse tongues. The other very important symbol "the bronze man (l'homme de bronze), stands most probably, for the new man, born out of the blending of the different shades of men as depicted by the adjectives: red, yellow, black and white. Such a man, equal in strength and resistance to the bronze metal, would be better able to address the problems of pollution, corruption and racial discrimination inherent in the old world[25]! And as if to guarantee this new venture, the poet transforms himself into the "echo" of fresh bodies and later to "God": "Je suis Dieu" says he in the poem "Marines" (Am:125). In this godly outfit, he remembers his departed black brothers, resuscitates them in their families so that they can partake fully in the celebration of this new world without hatred and oppression. This is how the symbols "arbres" and their resurrection greet the reader in *Arc musical* especially as they are:

> *All fruit trees among vanilla and thyme*
> *up to this sea without secret abyss*
> *(Am:129).*

Let me mention here that U Tam'si, just like Cesaire, is very much in love with floral and faunal images as the treatment thus far has shown. This is because he personally loves nature and celebrates it. Thus here, "fruit trees" (arbres à pain) as one of the most recurrent vegetal symbols in his poetry, allude to the fertility of black families, once sterile and dead under colonial oppression. The 'vanilla' and 'thyme' also as vegetal symbols represent the beauty of such families because as odour-rich plants they cannot but transfer their qualities to the trees around them. As for "Sea" (mer) and secret abyss" (abysses secrets), these by the mobility referred to earlier in this chapter, now represent the new and vast world, without surprises and lies for the poet! And as this "Civilisation de l'universel" is achieved, U Tam'si foresees and foretells absolute peace for his fellow black brothers and for the new man in his last collection, *La veste d' antérieur...* (1978) where he says:

> We shall dust our souls We shall dry our
> fat Everything shall be greenish water shall
> divide heaven and earth we shall have a
> home under roofs without silence or simply
> of mud if pardon is achieved (VST:9).

CONCLUSION

With the closing remarks above which are almost biblical in outlook, the reader would agree that U Tam'si's poetry is one in which theme and style fuse perfectly into one to maximise its expressiveness. From *Le mauvais sang* (1955) to *La veste d'antérieur...* (1978) images and symbols of all sorts; metaphors, metonymies, synecdoches, ambivalent, allegorical and surrealist images among others, indicate an evolution in the poet's psychological-cum-spiritual adventure. As a brutal moralist, it is clear here that all the juggling the poet does with images and symbols of his heart's desire is to bring to the limelight the key issues at stake in a world torn to pieces by excessive polarisation and dichotomisation, especially as it concerns blacks and whites. And as he sues for peace, he does so in rich images and symbols that do not fail to impress upon the reader, the need for all of mankind to work together to achieve universal civilisation, for as he put it in one of his interviews:

> I picture civilisation as being like rivers, all flowing
> into the sea to become a universal civilisation.[26]

In fact, to restate what we said in an earlier study on U Tam'si and his poetry, it would not be too wrong to opine that:

> What makes thematic and stylistic unity the charm of
> U Tam'si's works is its continued aspiration according
> to what Professor Irele said of Aimé Césaire, towards
> the "Absolu" a new order where all is diluted; without
> hatred, without oppression, just Man and Man only![27]

This search for an ideal world, woven around very rich floral, faunal and biblical images and symbols among others, where Man, reinstalled in nature, according to Irele, in an immediate union, finds the "rock" without 'dialect', the "leaf" without "guard"; fragile water without 'Femur', is what the poet achieved in *Arc musical* after more than twenty years of serious search for a deep apprehension and appreciation of the "self" and of the "universe." And this could be considered as his greatest legacy to humanity.

Let us hope that this treatment, which may not have been very exhaustive, still provides an opportunity for many more readers and lovers of U Tam'si to explore his poetic universe, using it to sanitise the human race that is still at war with itself today as depicted by the many ethnic, tribal and international conflicts that plague it.

Notes and References
Preliminary Note:

Because of the need to expose U Tam'si much more to readers with little or no knowledge of French, translations of the poet's verses have been mostly used here. And except otherwise stated, all such translations are by the writer. References are, however, to the original texts.

1. Lylian Kesteloot. *Anthologie négro-Africaine.* Verviers: Les Nouvelles Esditions Marabout, 1978, p.309.

2. Gerald Moore. *Tchicaya U Tam'si: Selected Poems.* London :Heinemann, 1970, pp. ix-x.

3. Read: "Tchicaya U Tam'si interviewed by Edris Makward—", supplement to *Cultural Events in Africa,* No. 60, 1969, pp. ii, iii.

4. *ibid,* p. ii.

5. Jean-Michel Devesa. "Tchicaya U Tam'si, écrivain hermétique" in Jacques Chevrier (éd.) *L'Afrique Litteraire: Hommage A Tchicaya U Tam'si,* No 87, 1995, p. 39.

6. Léopold Sedar Senghor. "De la poésie bantoue à la poésie négro-africaine" in Tchicaya U Tam'si. *Epitomé.* Tunis: S.N.E.D., 1962, pp. 9-10.

7. "Tchicaya U Tam'si is the poet's pen name and means "Petite feuille qui parle pour son pays". His real name is Gérald Felix Tchicaya.

8. U Tam'si's writings include:

   ### i) POEMS

   Le mauvais sang (1955), *Feu de brousse* (1957), *A triche-coeur* (1958), *Épitomé* (1962), *Le ventre* (1964), *Arc musical* (1969), *Le pain ou le cendre* (1977), *La veste d'antérieur suivi de Notes de veille* (1978).

   ### ii) NOVELS/SHORT STORIES

   La Main sèche (1980), *Les Cancrelats* (1980), *Les Méduses ou les orties de mer* (1982) *Les phalènes* (1984), *Ces fruits si doux de l'arbre à pain* (1987), *Légendes africanes* (1969).

iii) PLAYS

Le Zulu (1977), *Le Destin Glorieux Du Maréchal Nnikon Nniku Prince Qu'on Sort* (1979).

9. Tzvetan Todorov. "Sémantiques" dans *Sémantique de la poésie.* Paris: Seuil, 1979, p. 20.

10. For a further account, read C.H. Kane. *L'aventure ambiguë.* Paris: Union Générale d'Editions, 1961, pp.59-60.

11. The "poisson coelacanthe" is a type of bony fish whose ancestors date back to 300 million years! This explains their capacity to survive and the poet's choice of it as symbol for himself and his race in the on-going Black/White dialectics.

12. Michael Dash. "Feu de brousse" in *Dictionnaire des oeuvres littéraires négro-africaines.* Sherbroke: Editions Naaman, 1983, p.203.

13. Read Marcel /soret, *Histoire du Congo.* Paris: Berger-Levrault, 1978, pp.162-163.

14. N. J. Obinaju. "Titres et phrases en exergue dans la poésie de Tchicaya U Tam'si", in E. O. Anyaehie (ed.) *The Language Professional 1.* Okigwe: FASMEN Communications, 1997, pp 169-170.

15. L. S. Senghor, *op. cit.,* p. 11.

16. Gerald Moore. *Twelve African Writers.* London, Hutchinson University Library for Africa, 1980, p.149.

17. For details, read J. N. Obinaju. "Les Oeuvres poétiques de Tchicaya U Tam'si: de la critique de l' "AUTRE" à la critique de "SOI" (1955-1980)". Doctoral Thesis, University of Port Harcourt, 1988, pp.92-132.

18. Gerald Moore. *Tchicaya U Tamsi: Selected Poems.* p.x.

19. Edmund Reiss. *Elements of Literary Analysis.* Cleveland & New York: The World Publishing Co. 1967, pp 28-29.

20. J. N. Obinaju. "Les œuvres poétiques de Tchicaya U Tam'si", pp 80-81.

21. Ibezim Chukwumerije. "The United States and the Congo Crises of 1960-1964," in *KIABARA; Journal of the Humanities,* Vol, II, Harmattan Issue, University of Port Harcourt, 1978, p. 87.

22. J. P. Sartre. cf L. S. Senghor. *op. cit.,* p.10.

22. Abiola Irele. "Aimé Césaire: An Approach to his Poetry" in *Introduction to African Literature.* Harlow, Essex: UK Longman Group Ltd, 1982, p. 71.

24. N. J. Obinaju. "Tchicaya U Tam'si et la clémence d'Auguste ou un nouvel humanisme universel —" in *Neohelicon* Vol. XXIV, No. 1, Budapest, 1997: pp.324-325.

25. N. J. Obinaju. "Tchicaya U Tam'si et le nouvel humanisme universel—", in *Neohelicon,* Vol. XXV, No. 1, Budapest, 1988: pp.354 - 355.

26. G. D. Killam. *African Writers on African Writing.* London: Heinemann, 1973, p.155.

27. N. J. Obinaju. "Metaphors and Dialectics in the Poetry of Tchicaya U Tam'si" in E. N. Emenyeonu (ed.) *Literature and Black Aesthetics.* Ibadan: Heinemann, 1990, pp 127-128.

Bibliography

POETRY WORKS

Césaire, A. *Cahier d'un retour au pays natal.* Paris: Présence Africaine, 1983, ed.

Diop, D. *Coups de pilon.* Paris: Présence Africaine, 1973.

Senghor, L. S. *Poèmes.* Paris: Editions du Seuil, 1964.

U Tam'si, T. *Le mauvais sang suivi de Feu de brousse et A triche coeur*. Paris: l'Harmattan, 1978.

—— *Epitomé*. Tunis: Société Nationale d'Edition et de Diffusion, 1962.

—— *Le ventre, Le pain ou la cendre*. Paris: Présence Africaine, 1978. ed.

— *Arc musical; précédé de Epitomé*. Honfleur: P. J. Oswald, 1969.

— *La veste d'antérieur suivi de Notes de veille*. Paris: Nubia, 1977.

OTHER WORKS

Dathorne, O. R. *African Literature in the Twentieth Century*, University of Minnesota Press, 1974 -75.

Goldmann, L. *Le dieu caché*. Paris: Gallimard, 1952,

Guiraud, P. *La stylistique (Que sais - je)*. Paris: P.U.F., 1979

Kane C. H. *L'aventure ambiguë*. Paris: Union Générale d'Editions, 1961.

Kesteloot, L. *Anthologie négro-Africaine*. Verniers: Les Nouvelles Editions Marabout,
1978.

Killam, G. D. *African Writers on African Writing*. London: Heinemann, 1973.

Obinaju, J. N. "Les œuvres poétiques de Tchicaya U Tam'si: de la critique de l' "Autre" à la critique de "Soi" (1955- 1980)". Doctoral Thesis, University of Port Harcourt, Nigeria, 1988.

Reiss, E. *Elements of Literary Analysis*. Cleveland & New York: The World Publishing
Company, 1967.

Rimbaud, A. *Poèsie. Une saison en enfer. Illuminations.* Paris: Gallimard, 1973.

Sartre, J. P. *Qu'est-ce que la littérature?* Paris: Gallimard, 1948

Soret, M. *Histoire du Congo,* Paris? Berger-Levrault: 1978.

Ziegler J. *Main basse sur l'Afrique.* Paris: Seuil, 1980.

4

NEGRITUDE AND AFRICAN WORLDVIEW: SENGHOR'S POETRY AND RITES OF PASSAGE

Adebo Adejumo

INTRODUCTION

A lot of Africans believe that their continent, Africa, is the cradle of civilisation. As an old continent, it possesses a rich cultural patrimony which is the object of many studies, some of which are rich anthropological discoveries. Others are romanticised, mythical and subjective representations. An exploration into various ideas that constitute an African worldview will divert attention from the focus of this study hence it is a lot more pertinent to limit it to the perception of a Negritude exponent.

A worldview that involves a glorification of the African past and a feeling of nostalgia for the harmony of traditional African society inspired the literature of Negritude initially, with the literature subsequently reinforcing this worldview. Negritude, for the purpose of this study, is seen from its cultural standpoint. It is seen here mainly as the search for and rediscovery of the values of the African past that are capable of uniting Africans of the continent with those of the diaspora. In essence, Negritude is a cultural patrimony built on the African worldview that emphasises a revalorisation of the rich African past usually referred to by the exponents of Negritude as "Un retour aux sources". Scholars of African past such as the late German critic, Janheinz Jahn in *Muntu* and John V. Taylor in *The Primal Vision* have discussed at length the African worldview.

What the exponents of Negritude seek from the past is not just its glorification, they need proofs to debunk a myth of a cultural "tabula rasa". Egyptology served as a useful study in this realm. Cheikh Anta Diop emphasised the values of Egypt as proof of Black African origin of civilisation with claims of inventions in Mathematics, Astronomy, Religion, Arts, Writing, Architecture and Science in general. A people without a history does not have a future. The dual yoke of the Negritude writers therefore, was to prove that Africa had a past to be proud of and with it to re-invigorate the continent and the diaspora.

The various rites of passage that have survived in the African society, while serving as a link with the past, could contribute meaningfully to a future cultural development. Senghor's attachment to them is an indication that he recognised their durability and their value to the modern African society. His constant and enduring reference to them in his poetry is testimony to their significance; it also constitutes the source of our attachment to the poetry. It enriches the poetry, while drawing lasting attention to the place of Negritude values in modern African poetry in French.

INITIATION RITES

Initiation as a religious practice is part of the cultural heritage of Africans. Leopold Sedar Senghor, as well as many other poets of French-speaking Africa and the diaspora, invite their readers to experience, however vicariously, this African rite. This cultural practice is not peculiar to Africans: Romans shed their "toga virilis" when they needed to separate "boys from men". If the process of acculturation has had its toll on Senghor, escape from alienation caused by assimilation was secured mainly by nourishing his thoughts with African forms of inspiration. Senghor escapes from Western Judeo-Christian-cum-technological civilisation into African rhythm, metaphor, his form of sensibility and his Serer values, all of which are reflected in his writings.

Initiations occur in both rural and urban centres. In the latter, freemasons exist. Senghor's father-in-law, Governor-General Eboué was one. Many sects and messianic movements modelled after Western practices are highly developed in the spiritual realm. Senghor brought initiation rites to bear in his poems such as "Elégie des Circoncis" and "Chant de l'Initié" with rich lexical contributions and terms taken from initiation practices. Examples abound,[1]

> "j'ai consulté les Initiés de mamangètye" (p. 179)
> "que gronde le tambour des initiés (p. 194)
> "je dois régler le ballet des circoncis (p. 136)
> "Circoncis je franchirai l'épreuve (p. 1940)

Several references are made to secret Mossi societies such as the high priests of Poeré and Bénin.

Initiation rites are evoked in Senghor's poetry, such as the evocation of the practice of circumcision. It is quite easy to slip into an ethnographic assessment of the use of the rite of circumcision in Senghor's poetry and pass value judgements. It was once defined as "une remise en ordre, par la gloire, du monde compromis et confus"[2]. This rite of passage "snatches" the young adolescent from the vagaries of childhood, from the smothering protective world of maternal care and allows him access to a virile fraternal world, which is more in consonance with the realities of life. All within a week marked by days and nights of tough experiences, adolescents of the same age group are camped at a location normally at quite a distance from the village with intent to prepare them for a future life. Usually dancing and singing are part of the activities. There is a particular night of anguish that is spent at the foot of a sacred tree, around bonfires that symbolise a departure from their past life of ignorance. As the drums sound rhythmically, the adolescents dance frenetically as they wait for the mystic to appear in form of an awesome lion:

> "Au pèlerin dont les yeux sont larmés par le jeune et les
>   cendres et les veilles
> Apparaît au soleil-levant, sur le suprême pic, la tête de
> Lion rouge
> En sa majesté surréelle". (p. 195).

The rites of passage from ignorance to the essential, the enlightening discovery of sex and the access to adolescence form another stage of their development through initiation.

> "Dansons au refrain de l'angoisse, que se lève la nuit du
> sexe dessus notre ignorance dessus notre innocence" (p.201)

The flow of blood (from circumcision) is, in the words of the poet, of the colour of dawn and that with which the adolescents are purified

> "Je vous lamente Eaux lustrales pour l'expiation.
> Que la nuit se résolve en son contraire,
> que la mort renaisse vie, comme
> un diamant d'aurore
> comme le circoncis quand, dévoilée
> la nuit se lève le mâle, soleil!" (p. 207-208)

Senghor's expression, "plus-que frères", expresses the bond of fraternity of these young men.[3]

The departure from the world of childhood usually confounded with mother's milk comes to the forefront as a primary necessity. It is concretely formalised through a change in lifestyle, change of language and later, culture. This departure, which Senghor calls "arrachement de soi à soi" (p. 138), is a stage that leads to memories, arouses a nostalgia for the rebirth of childhood innocence:

> Soyez bénis mes pères, qui bénissez l'Enfant prodigue!
> Je veux revoir le gynécée de droite;
> J'y jouais avec les colombes, et avec mes frères les fils du
> Lion.
> Ah! de nouveau dormir dans le lit de mon enfance
> Ah! bordent de nouveau mon sommeil les si chères mains
> noires
> Et de nouveau le blanc sourire de ma mère. (p. 51-52)

This rupture is often associated with signs. These are signs that guide Toko Waly in explaining "les signes que disent les ancêtres" (p. 36), that "ta main me guidait par ténébres et signes" (*ibid*). Initiation into the proper world of the adolescents is through signs of recognition. They guide even in New York so that the "initiated" do not miss the tracks that lead to the Africa of princes and princesses. Signs are linked in Senghor's world to senses; they act as true means of protection in the progression towards the knowledge of the African world. His joy reaches ultimate limits when he can shout out, "J'ai compris les signes de la Tribu" (p. 204) conveying a feeling that Senghor expresses in this form:

> Et nul besoin d'inventer les sirènes,
> Mais il suffit d'ouvrir les yeux à l'arc-en-ciel d'Avril
> Et les oreilles, surtout les oreilles à Dieu .... (p. 117)

PILGRIMAGE AND STRUGGLE

Senghor's poems are rich in images of pilgrimage to sacred ancestral sanctuaries. In the ethnic hierarchy, an important place is given to the ancestors' "pèlerinage par les routes migratrices, voyage aux sources ancestrales" (p. 192). An observation of African spiritual practice reveals that access to the supreme divinity is through intermediaries. Rituals form an integral part of this access. Senghor uses this procedure as a theme, for example, the theme of purification in "Que m'accompagnent Kôras et balafong VIII" where the desert is the land of purity. Pilgrimage in this poem is undertaken without concessions to Western civilisation in order to regain the riches and honour of his race (teddungal):

> Or nous ayons marché tels de blancs initiés.
> Pour toute nourriture de lait clair,
>   et pour toute parole la rumination du mot essentiel.
> Et lorsque le temps fut venu (—) je proférai le mot
>   explosif teddungal! (p. 109)

Initiations involve struggles, some of which are symbolised by fights with wild animals. Examples abound in "L'homme et la Bête" and "Le chant de l'initié". Most often, even when defeated, the initiated must get up and renew the struggle by following the rough road. He must march successfully through this difficult path marked by experiences such as climbing inaccessible rocks, facing the hostility of the bullies, surviving the stormy Eastern winds, the cunningness of scorpions, chameleons, the wild laughs of monkeys and all the weirdness "comme peau de panthère zébraient la nuit" (p.108). It is after successfully overcoming the tests of the demon forest that he enters triumphantly into the clearing and liberty of the savannah which prepares him for a revelation.

The revelation, in form of cries, trauma, shocks, evil/demons, and so on, is both brutal and sudden. An analysis of these manifestations will portray the interference of the dead in the present world. Flying objects like comets or frightening birds are images that add colour to the terror: "Si l'aigle se jettait soudain sur nos poitrines, avec un cri sauvage de comète!... (p.187).

REBIRTH AND FEMININITY

Rebirth and femininity form a theme akin to initiation in which images of mother earth are linked with the rapacious nature of the eagle in "Chant d'ombre":

> L'aigle blanc des mers, l'aigle du Temps me ravit
> au-dela du continent (...)
> C'est le cri sauvage du Soleil levant qui fait tressaillir
> la terre
> Ta tête noblesse nue de la pierre, ta tête au-dessus
> des monts, le Lion au-dessus des animaux de l'étable
> Tête debout, qui me perce de ses yeux aigus.
> et je renais à la terre qui fut ma mère   (pp. 40-41).

A certain truth dawns on the poet, one that helps to open his horizons and reveal itself in form of a painful and a vertiginous state. In "le grand déchirement des apparences" (p. 109), Senghor salutes the gift of this essential truth even when it was leading to annihilation:

> Salut Dompteur de la brousse,
> Toi Mbarodi! Seigneur des forces imbéciles (p.101).

With Senghor, the initiation itinerary involves intermediaries like women. Women occupy an important place in his poetry, they are for example, the gate to beauty and grace, the entrance to primordial time. The poet attributes to love immense qualities: "je n'ai pas goût de magie: l'amour est ma merveille' (p 206). Feminine images such as rivers add to the beauty of his poems; the river Congo is portrayed like a lover:

> ...dont l'huile fait docile mes mains, mon âme
> ma force s'érige dans l'abandon, mon honneur
> dans la soumission. Et ma science dans l'instinct de ton
> rythme (p. 102-103)

The revelation of feminine qualities, images of women, as conflicting as life and death or sometimes inexplicably mysterious is a stage in the itinerary of the African. "Chant de l'initié" contains images of feminine beauty and death. It is a death that is symbolical of rebirth and beauty.[4] She is compared to the sun of the new world, she is the Ethiopian who is as incorruptible as gold, who is the image of purity, of crystal and of diamond:

> "le ciel de ton esprit, le pays haut de ta prestance, la nuit
> bleue de ton cœur
> Me seront fêtes à la fin de l'initiation.
> Tu es mon univers (p. 139).

The idealised woman becomes real, the poet becomes impatient before her beauty:

> Je chante ta beauté qui passe, forme que je
> fixe dans l'Eternel
> Avant que le Destin jaloux ne te réduise en
> cendre pour nourrir les racines de la vie (p. 17).

There are very strong ties between mother earth and women's fertility in the African worldview. In "Chants d'Ombre", the face of the African woman appears similar to mother earth.

> "Et je renais à la terre qui fut ma mère" (p. 41).

Also in "Congo", the poet exalts mother earth. The fertility of Africa, the mother, is emphasised when seen in opposition to the sterility of the foreign land where Senegalese sharpshooters died or in "A New York" where the poet regrets the absence of maternal warmth.

MASCULINITY

Masculinity appears in images of the lion and the sun:

> "O Zoulou ô Chaka ! Tu n'es plus le lion
>   rouge dont les yeux incendient le village au lion...
> Tu n'es plus qu'Eléphant
> Le buffle qui brise tout bouclier des branes." (p. 128).

Governor Eboué is presented as the lion that stood on its feet to express negation, to defend the honour of a strong race. Ancestors, so dear to Africans, are lauded in images of the lion:

> "Et pas toi le dernier, Ancêtre à tête de lion,
> Vous gardez ce lieu forclos à tout rire
>   de femme, a tout sourire qui se fane
> Vous distillez cet air d'éternité où je
>   respire l'air de mes pères.

Man's pride, the bastion of African civilisation stands as a cornerstone of Senghor's Negritude. Race pride in opposition to race hatred is instilled by Senghor's roots as it was expressed earlier on by Langston Hughes on 23 June, 1926, when he said, "We younger Negro artists, who create now, intend to express our individual dark-skinned selves without fear or shame"[5]. The Rennaissance that became known as Negritude drew its source from the peculiarities of African culture whether in the continent or in the diaspora.

Finally, women can only give the poet approximations of their beauty; here lies the object of the search:

> "Tu seras la même toujours et tu ne seras pas la même.
> Qu'importe? A travers tes métamorphoses, j'adorerais le
>   visage de Koumba Tâm (p.187).

THE AFRICAN HERITAGE

In addition to women, other intercessions envisaged in Senghor's poetry are the black race and the African past. These aspects of the

African worldview are epitomised in Kaya-Magan, the "first person" who unites day with night. Nature, which introduces man to the perception of cosmic rhythm, leads to a promise when it blends with sexual drive and dances. However, what plays the major role of intercession is the word. In the conception of the Griots, or, as Senghor calls them, "Maîtres de la parole", the word is in itself real if not surreal. Words are capable of restoring the surreal:

> Et le lait m'en faillir au visage (p. 84).

Similar to the energy generated by incantations, words could be explored, they could destroy a world of mere appearances and they could also be creative.

> "Seigneur, entendez bien ma voix. PLEUVE !
> il pleut (p. 208).

The poet knows the limit of the power of utterances:

> "les mots s'envolent et se froissent au
> souffle du vent d'Est comme les monuments
> des hommes sous les bombes soufflantes"(p. 115).

Revelation is examined as the ultimate result of initiation. Different types of interpretations are possible: the double lesson of initiation which involves participation in the cosmic rhythm of love as illustrated by an imagination of germination, fertility, renaissance, dawn, natural cycles on one side, and an end to the antagonisms of the real world which is embedded in the total perception of our time and space, on the other.

> Mon empire est celui des proscrits de César,
>   des grands bannis de la raison ou de l'instinct
> Mon empire est celui d'Amour, et j'ai faiblesse
>   pour toi femme
> (…) Car je suis les deux battant de la porte,
>   rhythme binaire de l'espace, et le troisième temps
> Car je suis le mouvement du tamtam,
>   force de l'Afrique future (p. 105)

Initiation, in the ordinary sense of it, is an insertion into the community, it is at a symbolical level, an interpretation into a world where mystery becomes brightness. The sun becomes an imagery of the last act of initiation. Initiations are not only limited to purification, they serve as a stepping stone for animist fusion with the world:

> Princesse, nos épaules roulent sous les vagues, nos
>   épaules de feuilles tremblent sous le cyclone
> Nos lianes nagent dans l'onde, nos mains s'ouvrent
> nénuphars et chantent les alizés dans nos doigts de filaos.
>   (p. 144).

CONCLUSION

Past and present, life and death, love and hate, today and tomorrow, "Africa of the future" and "Africa of the empires" "My country of salt" and your country sing in unison": cultural blending (métissage), an idea close to Senghor's heart, finds a place in this messianic immanence of the world. The initial unity that is promised is thus recovered. This explains why Senghor said that the world of the child (Royaume d'enfance) is not only important at the beginning of his life but also at the end.[6]

Ceremonies form the high mark of African life, they may be those of firstfruits, harvests or traditional rites such as circumcision. The rhythm of life in Africa and the diaspora is marked by ceremonies accompanying rites of passage. Children and adults, men and women, the living and the ancestors, all play different roles in traditional African lives and in Senghor's poetry. In order to express the happiness of African community life both in the Continent and in the diaspora, Senghor sings in poems that illustrate initiation rites. Senghor's commitment to Africa is illustrated in several ways through poems that feature initiation rites. They, in turn, carry a message of rebirth, hope, brotherhood, a message of life in accordance with the psychology of Black Africans and in consonance with their worldview. Senghor's poetry, conceived in the notion of Negritude, serves as a means of attaining the heights of a humanity; both new and superior.

Notes

1. Léopold Sédar Senghor. *Poèmes*. Paris: Editions du Seuil, 1984.Further references to this work in the chapter will be by insertion of the relevant page(s).

2. G. Durant. *Les Structures anthropologiques de l'imaginaire*. Paris: Bordas, 1969, p.193.

3. For a more detailed account of initiation rites, see Camara Laye. *L'Enfant noir* and Massa. M. Diabaté. *Comme une piqure de guêpe*. Paris: Préssence Africaine, 1980.

4. Ethnic Serer, Senghor's roots, is patriachal; notwithstanding, there is a lot of room made for a matriachal society in Senghor's poetry.

5. See Langston Hughes' article in *The Nation* of June 23, 1926. See also Mercer Cook's " Afro-Americans in Senghor's Poetry" in Janice Spleth (ed.) *Critical Perspectives on Leopold Sedar Senghor*. New York: 1993 p.83 for a comparison of "The Weary Blues" by Langston Hughes and "A New York" by Sen   ghor.

6. Léopold Sédar S. Senghor. *La Poésie de l'Action*. Paris: Stock, 1980, p.45.

Bibliography

Blachère, J-C. *Les écrivains d'Afrique noire et la langue française*. L'harmattan, 1993.

Diakhaté, Lamine. *Lecture de lettres d'hivernage et d'hosties noires de L.S. Senghor*. Paris: Les Nouvelles Editions Africaines 1996.

Diop, Chiekh Anta. *Nations nègres et culture*. Paris: 1954.

Guibert, A. *L.S. Senghor*. Paris: Présence Africaine, 1962

Irele, Abiola. *The African Experience in Literature and Ideology*. London: Heinemann, Ibadan, 1981

Kesteloot, Lilyan. *Comprendre les Poèmes de L.S. Senghor*. Paris: Les Classiques Africains, (1986).

Marquet, Marie Madeleine. *Le Métissage dans la poésie de L.S. Senghor*. Paris: Les Nouvelles Editions Africaines, 1963.

Ndiaye S. *L'image dans la poésie de L.S Senghor, expression de l'âme africaine*. Dakar: 1960.

Nkashama, Ngandu P. *Négritude et Poétique*. Paris: L'harmattan, 1992.
Présence Africaine. *Hommage à Léopold Senghor*. Paris: Présence Africaine, 1976.

Présence Africaine. *Léopold Sédar Senghor et La revue "Présence Africaine"*. Paris: Présence Africaine, 1996.

Senghor, Léopold Sédar. "La négritude métisse" préface à Edouard Maunick. *Ensoleillé vif*. Paris: Ed. Saint-Germain-des-Près, 1976.

Spleth, Janice (ed.) *Critical Perspectives on Léopold Sédar Senghor*. Colorado Springs: Three Continents Press, 1993.

Tidjani-Serpos, Noureini. *Aspects de la critique africaine*. Paris: Silex et Abidjan. Ceda, 1987.

THE NOVELS

5

THE SIGNIFICANCE OF THE CYCLICAL TECHNIQUE IN THE NOVELS OF MONGO BETI

Cletus Ihom

A characteristic feature of Mongo Beti's narrative technique is the presentation of itinerant or "unstable" characters who manifest the tendency to "wander" between the rural and urban centres. This narrative technique is adopted by the author because of its aesthetic importance as it can be observed that Beti takes advantage of the so-called instability of his characters in order to produce a "double movement" in his presentation. This double movement confers a cyclical structure to Beti's narrative which is characterised by an emigration of a major character from the rural area, his sojourn in the urban centre and eventual return to the village and vice versa. Our intention in this work is to highlight the significant effects, which Beti seems to produce through the cyclical technique, which occupies a fundamental position in his fictional world. We propose to analyse the significance of the cyclical technique through a study of Beti's three pre-independence novels namely, *Ville Cruelle* (1954*), Le Pauvre Christ de Bomba* (1956) and *Mission Terminée* (1957). We shall highlight the cyclical technique as a phenomenon of replacement and compensation, the double image of the milieu in Beti's fictional universe and the initiatory voyage and the author's use of satire as a literary process of demystification and revolt.

In Beti's fictional universe, the cyclical technique is reflected through the oscillations of the major characters between the rural and urban centres for various reasons. In *Ville Cruelle,*[1] (Beti's first novel written under the pen name of Eza Boto) for example,

Banda, the hero of the novel, decides to leave his village, Bamila, because of the deteriorating conditions of life in that village. In fact, Beti presents Bamila as an incarnation of misery, a ferocious jungle that has been utterly abandoned by the colonial administration. In Bamila, tradition tends to impede all initiatives aimed at individual growth because of the attitudes of impertinent old men whose primordial preoccupation is to safeguard their pre-eminence. Above all, Bamila is an egocentric village where there is complete absence of African hospitality.

Obviously, Banda, whose dream is to ameliorate his life, does not conceive any hope of progress at Bamila. He therefore considers himself detached from this village and ends up migrating into the town (Tanga), where he hopes to live a better life. However, his expectations about town life are equally shortlived because of the manipulations of the monstrous colonial ideology which renders town life even more "cruel" than village life.

Rejected thus by a mercantile civilisation which has no room for weak people like him, Banda returns to his village; but incapable of making any meaningful living here because of his alienation, Banda now dreams of a more significant evasion which will take him to Fort-Nègre, an imaginary ideal town.

Banda's movement is symbolic and confers an open or cyclical structure to Beti's narrative and can be graphically represented thus:

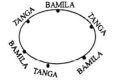
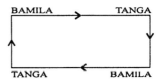

The significance of Banda's cyclical movement can be first and foremost appreciated in the context of the phenomenon of replacement and compensation which Beti uses to open the " vicious circle" to enable his characters to go in search of new possibilities in order to fulfil their dreams. Thus, in *Ville Cruelle*,

Banda's oscillations between his village (Bamila) and the town (Tanga) give him several possibilities of substituting what he loses at every stage of his itinerary. If he leaves Bamila as a result of a rupture with his girlfriend, he is compensated at Tanga where he meets and falls in love with Odilia, a girl that his authoritative mother also loves. If he loses his cocoa at Tanga, he is at the same time compensated by the discovery of some money by the side of the dead Koumé, Odilia's brother. In the same manner, Odilia who loses her brother Koumé, finds another replacement in Banda whom she eventually marries. Odilia equally replaces Banda's imaginary little sister and his deceased mother.

This phenomenon of substitution which confers a cyclical effect to *Ville Cruelle* enables Banda to explore new horizons and to escape from the pessimism which is characteristic of the colonial situation. In fact, the novel ends on an optimistic note as a result of the manipulation of the cyclical technique.

Furthermore, Banda's cyclical movement enables Beti to invoke a double image of the milieu in his fictional universe: the village and town are depicted as autonomous, geographical entities and places torn by contending social and historical forces. According to Simon Gikandi who reflects on Chinua Achebe's writings and the poetics of location, Beti does not, however, seek to represent the African reality as a "Utopian counter to European heterotopias", in order to avoid valorising the romantic image of Africa to counter the Western projection of the continent as a savage space.[2] According to Gikandi, by providing us with an "ingenious but paradoxical, deployment of space", Beti has succeeded in countering the "heterotopic representation" of the African in the colonial texts. In other words, Beti has succeeded in simultaneously representing, contesting and inverting the standpoint of colonial texts on Africa. The cyclical technique thus enables Beti to make his fictional universe an "epistemological presence", according to Gikandi, "one defined not only by the process of time, but also by an ensemble of spaces."[3] Beti's attempt to reflect the everyday reality of the African colonial situation through Banda's successive journeys and his refusal to idealise the African village or town, justify Gikandi's observations about the significance of his technique.

In his book, *La Littérature Africaine et sa critique*, Locha Mateso also reflects on the narrative technique that is structured on the itinerary of the hero and postulates a "triadique" structure of this type of narration. According to him, the hero is first of all camped in his African village or town where he begins his evolution in harmony with the purity and innocence of traditional life. However, this seeming paradisiacal harmony is soon perturbed as a result of the intrusion of some external force, Europe or western civilisation. The hero consequently finds himself in a state of psychological imbalance, which causes his departure for the European town in Africa or even Europe. Here, he undergoes a traumatic shock as a result of the conflicting values, which he confronts. The third stage of his journey, according to Mateso, corresponds with his return to his country of origin or village. Mateso concludes that equilibrium is restored at this stage and it takes the form of a real or symbolic triumph of authentic values.[4]

In Beti's novels, as we have seen with Banda's journeys, the cyclical technique is structured on a voyage which depicts a "movement" through a "milieu" and terminates on a kind of "open ending" because of the hero's tendency to start the journey afresh. This technique, which also presents a triadique structure postulated by Mateso, is symbolic because the beginning of the journey corresponds with the psychic state of the hero. Also, the significance of this presentation is to show the conflicting aspect of the society, which forces the hero to undertake the voyage. The milieu corresponds with the totality of experiences the hero is subjected to and the end represents the consequences of the reaction of the hero who becomes aware of the true position of things. Furthermore, the spatial and temporal divisions recognisable in Beti's cyclical technique are characterised by significant stages, each of which represents the acquisition of new knowledge. What is more significant is the fact that the cyclical technique enables Beti to adopt, at the beginning of his narrative, a simple linear structure which consists of the representation of a unique action and a principal character who does the narration. This linear structure, however, eventually turns out to be pluridimensional or "homoautodiegetic", according to Genette,[5] in the sense that the principal character is part of the history which he narrates and, at the same time, he is the hero of the narrated history. This is true of *The Poor Christ of Bomba*[6] and *Mission to Kala*[7] which present a unique action respectively and which have narrators who are also heroes of the narrated stories. The significance of this narrative structure can be further appreciated through an analysis of the narrative techniques of the two novels in question.

In *The Poor Christ of Bomba*, the linear action is structured on a cyclical tour made by Reverend Father Drumont in the company of Denis, a young acolyte and Zachary, a catechist, to the hinterland of Tala, a region attached to the Catholic Mission of Bomba. It can be observed that this tour is significant because right from the beginning, the novel poses a conflict which Father Drumont has to resolve by undertaking a tour in order to reconcile with the people of Tala whom he has abandoned for the past three years. The tour takes place in a temporal duration of fifteen days and is characterised by a journey across different villages, which make up the region of Tala and a return to the Catholic Mission of Bomba. It is Denis who carefully takes note of everyday events and all the conversations to which he is a witness in the course of the two-week tour.

In fact, the novel takes the form of a "diary" in which Denis carefully takes note of all the missionary activities of Father Drumont and the reactions of the indigenes with regards to these activities.

However, Bernard Mouralis observes that, because of his abject naivety, which makes him incapable of grasping the underlying significance of situations and integrating them into a coherent vision, Denis is not an "omniscient" narrator. According to the critic, Beti takes care to present Denis in such a way that he only narrates what he has actually seen or heard, refusing to draw possible interpretations or judgements from his (Denis') observations. When Beti happens to present Denis' personal observations, they are usually aimed at projecting or even exaggerating Father Drumont's points of view. Mouralis goes further to explain that the adoption of a narrative technique through the intermediary of an adolescent who is visibly favourably disposed towards missionary activities and who is contented with merely seeing without condemning, is in conformity with Beti's intention. This technique makes it possible for the author to place himself at an "ironic distance" from his protagonist's observations and to address a "caustic satire" against missionary activities in Africa.[8] In fact, it is through the cyclical technique that Denis and Father Drumont are progressively led to make new discoveries or face new experiences and thus, to see the world from a different perspective. The cyclical journey through the hinterland therefore turns out to be a confirmation of the "insincerity of the evangelisation project" which he hopes to accomplish in Africa.[9] Presented as a stereotype of the white colonialist right from the beginning of the narration, Father Drumont is utterly blind to African reality after twenty years of proselytisation in Africa. The journey across the hinterland thus gives him the opportunity of becoming conscious of his personal weaknesses and to discover that his missionary activities have been hitherto based on misconceptions. On the whole, the cyclical journey of Father Drumont enables Beti to reveal the limitations of Christian evangelisation in the context of the African reality of the period.

Reflecting on the significance of Beti's narrative technique in *The Poor Christ of Bomba*, Thomas Melone posits that Denis' narration provides a disguise for the "subversive author" that enables him to address very sensitive issues with relative impunity. According to the Camerounian critic, through the deontology of the journalistic profession of his narrator, Beti appears as a kind of "patron" who seeks to guarantee the objectivity and the sensible nature of information and to force the authorities to protect and guarantee the respect for certain liberties in the exercise of the journalistic profession.[10] Melone's observation is very significant if one considers the period during which Beti wrote *The Poor Christ of Bomba,* a period characterised by press censorship, arbitrary arrests and incarcerations of those whose writings were considered inimical to the interest of the colonial administration.

Like *The Poor Christ of Bomba, Mission to Kala* presents a linear structure which centres on Jean-Marie Medza's journey to the village of Kala in order to recuperate Niam's wife who has run away from the matrimonial home. The novel also presents a homoautodiegetic structure because Jean-Marie is not only the principal narrator of the story, he is also the hero of the novel.

In *Mission to Kala* the cyclical journey from Vimili to Kala is symbolic because it makes it possible for the hero-narrator to become conscious of his factitious life as an intellectual and a town dweller, a life which makes him a social misfit in the context of the African society. This journey is significant especially if Medza's pretentiousness and preconceived ideas about the so-called bushmen of the countryside, are taken into consideration before he becomes aware of the insufficiency of his intellectual status and his deficiencies vis-à-vis the African rural peasantry. As Eustace Palmer observes:

> Jean-Medza comes to Kala with preconceived ideas about
> the people, but he will gradually be forced to change them
> and to discover his inferiority in many ways.[11]

In fact, parallel to the pretentiousness and the so-called superiority of Medza, Beti places the simplicity and the apparent ignorance of the peasants, which constantly remind Medza of his inferiority. Thus, Beti manipulates his narrative technique in such a way that the naivety of the peasants is a kind of "mirror" in which Medza's borrowed personality is constantly reflected.

It is particularly due to the difficulties that he encounters in an attempt to make himself understood by an illiterate audience before whom he is the guest speaker that Medza becomes aware of the futility of his western education. His vanity and, above all, the distance, which separates him from his people, become glaring. According to Judith Gleason,

> In the course of his journey, Medza makes a self-
> evaluation of his personality. He discovers that,
> compared with the village kalans, he is wanting in
> many respects .... Medza discovers that these country
> boys enjoy a freedom he himself will never be able to
> recover.[12]

These are late discoveries but very pertinent ones and Medza returns home a rebel against the patriachal system represented by his father, and everything that the colonial school symbolises and becomes a vagabond in search of individual freedom and an authentic African personality.

According to Bernard Mouralis, Medza's cyclical journey also enables him to discover that in the African traditional society, the behaviour of the people is "programmed" in such a manner that the individual is not considered as an "autonomous being" with a distinct personality from the rest of the community. According to the critic, this aspect of the African traditional society constitutes a kind of oppression because of the refusal to allow its members the possibility of satisfying their individual aspirations.[13]

Thus, at the end of his journey, Medza, like the marginalised young peasants of Kala, refuses to play the role, which the society expects of him but rather becomes a wanderer. Because of his decision to abandon his new wife and to live an unstable life which is completely alien to his community, Medza seems to invent another system of cultural values. His position is significant because it conforms with Beti's symbolic technique which seems to emphasise individual freedom and to denounce those annihilating aspects of tradition which impede the progress of the African societies.

Commenting on the narrative technique of *Mission Terminée*, Thomas Melone postulates that, through the technique of "topological displacement" with its legendary rhythms and picaresque evasions, Beti seeks (once more) to disguise himself and to distract public attention from the main sensitive issues raised in his novel. Melone concludes that, through the process of dissimulation, Beti is able to raise fundamental questions about the colonial situation without running any risks. He is also able to make fun of the colonial administration, express explosive ideas on the bush life and anticipate the accession of the Kala peasants (just like the catechumens of Tala in *The Poor Christ of Bomba*), to a revolutionary consciousness.[14]

On the whole, the adoption of the cyclical technique enables Beti to introduce his readers to the problems of Africans. To the outsiders, Beti presents African customs and beliefs based on everyday life. He makes an appraisal of the colonial situation by drawing a parallel between the colonial actvities and the reactions of Africans to the colonial enterprise. For the Africans, Beti insists on cultural originality, laying emphasis on the multiple mutations arising from the colonial situation. He is thus made to condemn a retrogressive tradition which tends to frustrate individual and collective aspirations.

More significantly, in Beti's narrative structure, the cyclical technique corresponds to a process of psychological and political conscientisation which allows the hero to grasp the truth or have a better understanding of the colonial situation. In this regard, the cyclical technique has a pedagogical significance in the sense that it uplifts the hero from a "zero degree" of human experience, according to Melone, to a "psychological enrichment" as a result of his confrontation with the new changing world.[15] Thus, the cyclical technique constitutes not only a theme but also a technique which more often than not controls the profound structure of Beti's fictional aesthetic.

In conclusion, right from his first novels up to the last ones, Mongo Beti has manifested a constant obsession with "rewriting" everyone of his novels. This obsession to start his works all over again is an important element of Beti's "intellectual revolution" which envisages the establishment of a new socio-political order that will ensure a people's liberty, justice and happiness. The cyclical or open technique thus enables Beti to represent the complete physiognomy of the African world that can be accessible at every moment to a global apprehension.

Notes

[1]   Mongo Beti (under the pen name of Eza Boto). *Ville cruelle*. Paris: *Présence Africaine*, 1954.

[2]   Simon Gikandi. "Chinua Achebe and the Poetics of Location: the uses of space in *Things Fall Apart* and *No Longer At Ease*", in Abdulrazak Gurnah. *Essays on African Writing: A Re-Evaluation*. London: Heinemann, Abdulrazak Gurnah Edition, 1993, p.3.

3   Simon Gikandi, *ibid.* p.3

4   Locha Mateso. *La Littérature Africaine et sa critique*. Paris: A.C.C.T et Editions Karthala, 1986, p. 342.

5   Gérard Genette. *Figures III*. Paris: Editions du Seuil, 1972.

6   Mongo Beti. *Le Pauvre Christ de Bomba*. Paris: Editions Laffont, 1956.

7   Mongo Beti. *Mission Terminée*. Paris: Buchet/Chastel, 1957.

8   Bernard Mouralis. *Comprendre l'oeuvre de Mongo Beti*. Paris: Editions St Paul, 1981,   pp. 41-43.

9   Bernard Mouralis. *ibid.* p.45.

10   Thomas Melone. *Mongo Beti: L'homme et le Destin*. Paris: Présence Africaine, 1971, pp.259-260.

11   Eustace Palmer. *An Introduction to the African Novel*. London: Heinemann, 1972, p.148.

12   Judith Gleason. *This Africa: Novels by West Africans in English and French*. N. Y.: North-Western Press, 1965, pp.136 and 156.

13   Bernard Mouralis. *ibid.* p.50.

14   Thomas Melone. *ibid.* pp.264-265.

15   Thomas Melone. *ibid.* p.270.

6

POLITICAL DISILLUSIONMENT AND AESTHETIC EVOLUTION IN THE NOVELS OF ALIOUM FANTOURÉ

Tar Adejir

> "S'il n'y avait rien eu à abattre,
> à combattre, la littérature n'eut
> pas été grand-chose."
>
> – Simone de Beauvoir

The African writer has always been forced by circumstances of the political and social situation around him to be combatant. The problems against which he wrote during the colonial times have, with the coming of independence, simply changed the people creating them and not their nature. The colonial system, manned by Europeans has been replaced by a system manned by "the man of the people" or the man in uniform, all of whom are more ruthless than the foreigners. As the police officer in *Le Cercle des tropiques*, Sept-Saint Siss puts it to Malekê,

> vous êtes plus cruels entre vous, que ne le sera jamais un toubab à votre égard. Croyez-moi, le venin ne vient pas de l'extérieur. Vous sécretez vous-mêmes votre poison (*CT*,116).

There is therefore no gainsaying the fact that most, if not all, African writers do not hold strongly to the notion of "art for art's sake" and thus were not found wanting when the clarion call to arms came a second time. Fully aware of their duties and responsibilities towards their society on the continental and national levels, they took up the weapons very readily available to them, their pens.

As Jean-Paul Sartre had put it, every writer

> sait que les mots ... sont des "pistolets
> chargés." S'il parle, il tire. Il peut se taire,
> mais puisqu'il a choisi de tirer, il faut que
> ce soit comme un homme, en visant des
> cibles (Sartre, 1948, p.31).

And it is not targets that are in short supply for the African writer, what with colossal political, economic and social mismanagement, leading to the institution of totalitarianism, that has become the bane of almost every country on the African continent.

Alioum Fantouré, the Guinean writer, came on the literary scene in 1972, fourteen years after the painful, but hope-inspiring, independence of his country. In his mid-thirties when he published his first novel, *Le Cercle des tropiques*, Fantouré must have had the time to think over the events lucidly before deciding to answer the call to arms. Only twenty years old when Sekou Touré of Guinea answered "NON" to the French Community, he, like any young man of his age and time, must have had hopes for a bright future for himself, his country and the African continent. What followed independence seems to have been summed up in the previously quoted speech by Sept-Saint Siss, with the "permanent plot" syndrome and the attendant imprisonment and execution of opponents and purges of allies that came to characterise the Guinean political scene under Sekou Touré. In a post-Sekou Touré era interview, Alioum Fantouré sums up the situation in these terms:

> Le drame de la Guinée a été de croire en un être qui
> avait peur de ses compatriotes.... Quand un leader
> commence à avoir peur de ses concitoyens, il fait une
> sorte d'appel à la force, pour créer un carcan: "vous
> ne m'aimez pas, eh! bien, je vous oblige à m'aimer"
> *(Fantouré,* 1987, 123).

Let us say at this point that "Les Marigots du sud", "Ce-pays", "Sahel-Atlantique" and "Sahel-Maritime", the fictional countries in *Le Cercle des tropiques (Le Cercle), Le Récit du cirque....(Le Récit), L'Homme du troupeau du Sahel (L'Homme)* and *Le Voile ténébreux (Le Voile)* are not individually or collectively, Guinea. Their setting, in both time and space, fits quite a number of African countries. In this way, Guinea is therefore found in all of them as the country does not escape the conditions prevalent at any given moment of the history of the African continent. Besides, Fantouré, as a Guinean writer, must have been inspired to write primarily by the conditions that prevailed in his own country more than anywhere else. Mouloud Mammeri, an Algerian writer, had rightly remarked that:

> du point de vue littéraire, on ne parle bien ou n'apporte d'expérience authentique que sur les êtres et les choses dont on a une intime connaissance....Je crois profondément aux valeurs universelles et je crois aussi que le meilleur citoyen du monde est d'abord celui qui est profondément ancré dans un coin de cette terre (*Mazouni,* 1969, 220).

That Fantouré very much had Guinea at the back of his mind when he started writing is borne out by the fact that he had to keep strict anonymity (pen name and no pictures) for a while as a writer. His first two novels are situated in totally fictitious countries, somewhere "sous le cercle des tropiques". There are no landmarks in these novels to tie them to any particular country on the African continent. In *Le Récit*, even time is blurred. The temporal setting is simply referred to as "Ce-temps". By this, the past and the future seem to have been obliterated. It is only in *L'Homme* and *Le Voile* that both the time and space of the fictional universe become recognisable, most especially in relationship with the realities of the continent.

The writer's desire to conceal his identity as well as the anonymity of time and space in his first two novels marks his intention to avoid reprisals resulting from what he may have said. He had remarked in the already quoted interview that:

> A cause de mon livre, si j'étais rentré dans ce pays[1], on m'aurait arrêté, on m'aurait assassiné .... je ne [voulais] pas qu'on me cite pour écraser d'autres personnes (*Fantouré,* 1987, 124).

In this study, we are going to see how the writer has used his novels to examine the development of events in the post-independence Africa in general and in Guinea in particular. We shall also determine how these developments affect the aesthetic presentation in his novels. As much as possible, we shall avoid tying the fictional universe in the novels to Guinea. However, we shall not shy away from doing so where we feel such events as presented in the novels are specific to Guinea.

We shall begin our study with *L'Homme* and *Le Voile,* the last two novels on our corpus, and shall end with the first two novels written by the Guinean writer: *Le Cercle* and *Le Récit* in that order. Our seemingly unorthodox method of beginning from the middle is quite logical if we take a look at the internal chronology of the novels. After the presentation of what the writer calls "l'angoisse du futur, l'angoisse de l'intolérance" in his first two novels, Fantouré seems to have gone back, to put it in Achebe's words, "to see where the rain began to beat us". Fantouré is quite liberal with the use of analepse in his narrative technique and the last two novels are thus presented as analeptic to the first two. The setting in time of *L'Homme* and *Le Voile* is roughly between 1938-1956. Guinea, the first West African Francophone country to gain independence, is just about two years from the famous "NON". It is around this time that Manguai Africounah, the protagonist in *Le Voile* is condemned to "sept années d'interdiction de séjour au Sahel Maritime et en Afrique occidentale' (VT, 157). Like Jonah in the whale, Manguai remembers, not God but his country, from the "profondeurs de son désarroi." He tells us that his incarceration and subsequent banishment have made him one with his country:

> Désormais, je n'ai plus de forme   Je ne suis que ma terre natale
>   Dont   L'avenir se nomme.
> Liberté - Espoir (*VT*, 138)

In more than one way, this novel thus introduces *Le Cercle* published thirteen years before it[2]. In this novel, there is perpetual opposition between good and evil, represented by two political organisations: "Le Club des travailleurs" and "Le Parti Social de l'Espoir" respectively. Hope and liberty, nascent in *Le Voile,* seem to have fallen into the wrong hands in the post-independence era. The "Parti Social de l'Espoir" brings no hope and the "place de la Liberté" in post-colonial Les Marigots du sud has become the execution ground for the hope of the country - the youth.

L'Homme and *Le Voile,* from all indications, are the first two volumes of a trilogy entitled "Le livre des cités du termite"[3]. As is characteristic of a trilogy, the main characters in one novel reappear directly or indirectly in the subsequent novels. Manguai; Sassi and Lamine-Dérété thus play important roles in the two novels, and in that order. We shall, however, concentrate on the roles of the first two characters. Both intellectuals, they, in more than one way, help us to see how the political tyrants of the post-independence Africa had developed over the years from colonial times.

Manguai, for example, is known to have an astonishing capacity:

> de jouissance et d'amour de la vie, de haines et de
> revanches, de travailleur et d'organisateur, de courage
> et de lâcheté, d'altruisme et d'égoïsme, d'opportunisme
> et d'ambition (*HT*,103).

Assoumani, a member of Manguai's "Unité Tsé-Tsé," tells the latter to his face:

> Tu es du genre qui ne connaît pas le partage de
> responsabilités. Tu veux tout penser, tout
> prévoir, tout ordonner, tout juger, tout
> sanctionner sans jamais accorder aucun respect
> à toute autre opinion que la tienne (*HT*, 78).

He concludes on a note of sadness that, "Des types comme toi pourraient être dangereux tôt ou tard pour les pauvres Africains comme nous" (*HT*, 79).

Sassi, on the other hand, is described as someone who "espérait toujours plus, en voulait toujours plus, en arrachait toujours plus. Il n'aidait personne sans voir ses propres intérêts" (*HT*, 216).

Appropriately, later in life, the same Manguai becomes a trade union leader while Sassi takes to politics. We would like to point out at this point that Manguai most especially has some affinities with Sekou Touré. Manguai in Malinke means "son of a chief".[4] It is a known fact that Sekou Touré claims to be descended from Samory Touré. Manguai, like Sekou Touré, was expelled from a colonial school just before the outbreak of World War II. The fictional character and his real-life counterpart started their union activism as civil servants and were both dismissed for it. Manguai, however, never went on to become a politician. He thus can be said to represent the unionist side of Sekou Touré, while Sassi is to be seen as his political side at their early stages, with all the faults (most especially) and strong points.

In *L'Homme* Manguai cringes so much before the colonial officer that he is later reproached for it by his people in *Le Voile*: "Tu es un *horo* et tu as été plus servile qu'un esclave, car l'ordre que tu exécutais était donné par les toubabs" (*VT*, 55). One can justifiably say that, given the situation in which he found himself at the time, this judgement is rather too harsh for Manguai. Sassi, however, roundly condemns his attitude to the Africans when he deals with them. Ruse and deceit are evident in his actions:

> Tu as lutté pour être le bon génie de l'Afrique,.. Bien qu'en réalité d'après ton comportement, tu pourrais bien être Manguai-le-Diable qui mènerait tôt ou tard les enfants du Sahel vers un nouvel esclavage, à moins que ce ne soit un nouveau charnier. Tu es trop ambitieux, trop dur avec les autres (*HT*, 152).

This comment was provoked by the fact that what Manguai thinks of himself became easily visible through his own behaviour. He believes that he is going to be the future "défenseur des travailleurs africains" (*HT*, 123). In an internal monologue, we discover, however, that Sassi had judged him quite rightly. Manguai sees himself as a leader who would use the people to serve his own interests:

> je lèverai une armée de chômeurs que je constituerai comme support derrière moi...Je deviendrai un poids lourd africain afin de mieux *dicter ma loi* aussi bien aux colons qu'aux autres indigènes. Je massacrerai la

> gueule de ceux qui refuseront de se laisser sauver par
> moi... Ce qu'il faudra, c'est *la manifestation des*
> *travailleurs* casés dans les emplois mal rénumérés.
> J'exciterai à la révolte et aux insurrections les victimes
> des travaux forcés d'hier et les chômeurs
> désespérément misérables de demain... Il faudra faire
> attention à toucher à un de mes cheveux (*HT*, 124).
> (Emphasis added.)

Later in the novel, when Manguai feels threatened by Sassi both as
the head of the "Unité Tsé-Tsé" and as the future union leader, he
is quite categorical on what he has to do to the latter: "De nous
deux, il y aura toujours un de trop au Sahel" (*HT*, 152).

By an authorial intrusion, Fantouré comments on this attitude
by making a statement, part of which he had reproduced in the
already quoted interview: "Il n'y a jamais un enfant de trop sur une
terre natale, jamais, sauf pour l'envahisseur intérieur ou le tyran"
(*HT*, 153). Sassi's attitude towards Manguai, however, seems to
espouse Fantouré's idea of co-existence and tolerance: "Nous
n'avons pas la même conception de la vie, mais avons la même
terre... Autant se tolérer" (*HT*, 205). Fantouré confirms this view
when he states in an interview that:

> Le nom même que j'ai choisi, "Fan", veut dire "bon",
> "tolerant"; dans aucun de mes livres, on ne trouvera
> quoi que ce soit qui puisse pousser à l'intolérance,
> non seulement dans mon pays, mais ailleurs (*Fantouré*,
> 1987, 124).

The postscriptum to *L'Homme*, proleptic to the events in *Le Voile*,
allows us to catch a glimpse of what had become of the two even
before we read about them in the latter novel. Whereas Manguai
had followed his chosen career with disastrous results, Sassi has
become a successful politician, within the limits of the colonial
situation.

In *Le Voile*, Fantouré turns his searchlight on Manguai whom he
presents as a young African in search of his roots. Significantly,
his full name is given as Manguai Africounah: Manguai, the African.
He is thus a sort of incarnation of the African youth at the
crossroads between the Western and African ways of life. The

desperation and frustration that he has to face under the colonial system are those of the African youth in general at that period in time. Such an existence can hardly advance one's personal ambitions if one had such a lively and independent mind like Manguai. It is not surprising therefore, that the novel opens and ends on his failures. Dismissed from the civil service when he was really looking forward to "un salaire convenable à la fin du conflit mondial, en souvenir de [sa] bonne action durant la guerre", he ends up being banished for seven years from his country, Sahel Maritime, and indeed French West Africa. Between these two events, Manguai has more or less been obliged by circumstance to "remonter en amont pour retrouver la part essentielle de [lui-même]." He therefore goes back to his roots on both physical and spiritual levels. This "remontée en amont" seems to be the expression of a wish on the part of the writer for the African youth. Even if he knew that the youth of his country had changed, he is quite shocked when he came back to Guinea to discover the extent to which this change had become the bane of the society. The post-Sekou Touré youth:

> n'avaient aucun respect des valeurs [traditionnelles],
> parce qu'ils ont eu la liberté d'agir contre les parents,
> pour un système établi. On a tué en eux le futur. Or le
> passé prépare le futur, mais si on n'a aucun héritage,
> qu'on attend le présent au jour le jour, on est coupé du
> futur (Fantouré, 1987, 123).

The greater part of the novel, *Le Voile*, deals with Manguai's efforts to come to grips with his past. The moment he goes back to his ancestral Timbuctu, he realises to what extent he is cut off from his people: "j'avais commis plus qu'un crime. J'avais failli à l'esprit de mes ancêtres et m'étais coupé de mes racines" (*VT*, 49), he notes. It is because of his being cut off from his roots that he makes a mistake that almost costs him his life: he chooses the poisoned dish out of the two presented to him in a way that only a total stranger to his ancestral traditions would have done! He is later told that:

> Dans la main gauche, celle du coeur et de la vie, se
> trouvait la nourriture saine; dans la main droite, le

> poison. Conformément au respect de l'esprit de nos
> ancêtres et de Faro, tu aurais dû prendre le don du
> coeur. Mais tu as préféré celui de la main droite, celle
> du matériel. Tu as fait le choix d'un étranger qui
> ignorait tout des traditions millénaires de notre terre
> (*VT*, 53).

His stay in his ancestral home is quite salutary to him. After proving his innocence in his actions to his compatriots during the "Troupeau du Sahel" affair, by the "jugement de l'eau", he tells us that his obsession is "de réapprendre à vivre selon ma tradition ancestrale. Enfin exister pour les miens" (*VT*, 83). Before he sets out to look for the "livre des ancêtres" which the elders of Timbuctu had ordered him, he is told among other things that "Il faut se méfier des sauveurs, quels qu'ils soient, ils finissent toujours par échapper aux normes morales de l'humaine condition" (*VT*, 86). After the quest, from which he comes empty-handed because the "livre des ancêtres" was all the time in Timbuctu, the journey being just a subterfuge for his self discovery, he is told that "*L'espoir De L'homme, C'est Aussi L'homme. On ne Peut Pas Le Servir En Le Detruisant Ou En L'alienant De Son Droit D'etre*" (*VT*, 90). (Emphasis in the text.) These two statements are politically charged and seem to be target directed.

Manguai's experience at his ancestral home seems to prepare him for the difficulties that he later faces at the hands of the colonial administration. His experiences during his quest had taught him, among other things, "*La Simplicite De Ceux Qui Se Savent Mortels*" (*VT*, 87) (Emphasis in the text). He is now in a position to judge situations with a lot of lucidity. Hence, he has to be literarily blackmailed by Lamine-Dérété, who later abandoned him, into participating in the strike that ended with his banishment.

In his problems with the colonial authorities, one of Manguai's most sure allies is Sassi. The truce entered into in *L'Homme* seems to be holding. This truce seems to be a promise of co-operation between trade unionists and politicians, an alliance that was used effectively during the anti-colonial struggle. The events in *Le Cercle*, however, take a different turn. Does this mean that Fantouré questions the very much-talked about co-operation between the two social organisations during the colonial era?

If chronological indices are rather scanty in *Le Voile,* they are practically inexistent in *Le Cercle.* In the first novel, however, we have the impression that the story ends somewhere in the mid-fifties: African deputies have been elected into the French National Assembly and this took place in 1956. This is just a few years before the "soleils des indépendances" in the Francophone and Anglophone countries (1957-1963). The fictional universe in *Le Cercle* is set at its initial stage, a bit earlier than where *Le Voile* ends. By its internal chronology, as we have already stated, *Le Voile* introduces *Le Cercle.*

Le Cercle is divided into two parts: "Porte Océane" and "Le Cercueil de zinc". Each deals with pre- and post-independence periods of Les Marigots du sud. It is perhaps not by chance that the name of this fictional country resembles that given to Guinea at an earlier time in her history: Les Rivières du sud.

If it can be said that *Le Voile* serves as an analeptic introductory novel to *Le Cercle,* no traceable link can be made between the two, either from the point of view of their setting or of their characterisation. *Le Voile* introduces *Le Cercle* by the fact that the events presented in the first novel occur in time before those presented in the latter work. It is unthinkable that even Sassi, the selfish politician, could have metamorphosed into the monster, that is, Baré Koulé. Perhaps, it could be more acceptable that there is some resemblance between Manguai and Monchon or Malekê, and this to a greater extent than all the names starting with "M".

There is a greater point of divergence in the direction of events in the two novels. The co-operation between the trade unionists and the politicians that one looks forward to in *L'Homme* and *Le Voile* has failed to materialise. There is the bitter fight between "Le Club des travailleurs" and "Le parti Social de l'Espoir", a fight between good and evil. As it is sometimes the case in real life, good temporarily triumphs as Baré Koulé is overthrown by the Army. However, a few months later, the prominent actors in the struggle for the end of Baré Koulé's rule are mysteriously assassinated, with the exception of General Baba-Sasessi. It is a revolution doomed to failure for not carrying the grassroots of the society along with it, Fantouré seems to be saying.

If *L'Homme* and *Le Voile* are the presentation of the making of future African leadership from among the youth, the first part of *Le Cercle*, "Porte Océane", presents an adult who is being groomed by the colonial business interests to rule for their continued exploitation of the country. Neo-colonialism, as Nkrumah called this situation, thus becomes entrenched in "Les Marigots du sud" in the second part of the novel, "Le Cercueil de zinc." It is the same subject matter that is being treated in Fantouré's second novel, *Le Récit*. The preparation of a man for such a take-over seems to have been planned for a long time. Arrested for illegal cattle trafficking, a "colon" had laughed at Capitaine Henri's efforts to defend the right of the colonised Africans when he told him that:

> Après la guerre... le gouvernement ne changera rien
> au traitement des nègres. Au contraire, il encouragera
> les colons à mieux exploiter les colonisés pour
> reconstruire le pays [la France] détruit par la guerre
> (*HT*, 247).

The colonial exploitation of Africans in the pre-independence era, as described in "Porte Océane," differs from that described in *L'Homme* and *Le Voile* only in details. Bohi Di is the principal narrator through whose eyes we see most of the action in the novel. Born a peasant, this "fils de la terre", according to the meaning of his name, sees events from the point of view of the oppressed. It is in this manner that we move from the oppression and exploitation of the peasantry in the countryside to that of the city dwellers who are preyed upon by all sorts of swindlers and political demagogues as well as unscrupulous businessmen. It is through Bohi Di's naivety that we first come into contact with Baré Koulé's men and subsequently the man himself. From that point on, Baré Koulé dominates the narrative and the political scene of "Les Marigots du sud". Known to be the candidate of the "corporation fruitière"(5) for the leadership of the country, he is said to be ruthless in getting what he wants. Halouma, his principal hatchet man ominously warns Bohi Di, who wants to escape his crutches, that Baré Koulé, alias "Messi-Koï ne recule devant rien" (*CT*, 67). He prepares and executes his diabolic "folie des marchés" with precision to the extent that he easily implicates Monchon, the leader of the "Club des travailleurs" in the affair. Unsure that even the warped colonial justice would do what he wants done to Monchon, Baré Koulé gets him assassinated. Thus decapitated at a crucial stage in the anti-colonial struggle, and with a strong resistance from the colonial system itself, the opposition to Baré Koulé loses ground easily as the latter instals his "messie-koique" system and rule over the country.

Significantly, the section of the novel treating the independence era opens by telling us that "La nuit tombait sur Les Marigots du sud" (*CT*, 125). The opposite is supposed to have been the case. It becomes evident that Fantouré would have us believe that the foundation for independence has been laid on a very shaky political leadership, from the times of Manguai and Sassi through to Baré Koulé. The inhuman and sadistic Guide in *Le Récit* is the summation of these past leadership experiences.

Baré Koulé's title, "Messie-Koï" (Messiah-King), is meant to suggest a certain affinity with the people. It is ironical that they see him for what he is: a false god. When we hear about him for the first time, his "disciples" await his arrival at the foothill of Mount Koulouma. This recalls the fact that Christ (the Messiah) would appear on the Mount of Olives during his second coming. Mountains in Fantouré's works, unlike in the Christian religion, however, are closely associated with the tyrants of the post-independence era. In *Le Cercle,* it is Mount Koulouma while Mount Dounouya (life) ironically houses in its flank the lair of the monster that is the Rhinocéros Tâcheté, with its myriads of death cells.

Baré Koulé, like the false god that he is, does not appear on the Mount Koulouma but at its foothills. Young Bohi Di clearly sees through his falsehood when he tells us that:

> Le Maître ne se décidait pas à se montrer au milieu de
> notre cour de miracles. Il se faisait attendre, désirer.
> Il prenait son temps comme tout chef qui n'a rien
> d'autre à offrir que du bluff (*CT*, 69)

After independence has been granted to Les Marigots du sud, Baré

Koulé is therefore "salué comme un nouveau dieu par ses compatriotes" (*CT*, 127).

Published when Sekou Touré was well entrenched and all-pervasive in Guinea, *Le Cercle* uses a more direct narrative style in its narration. It can be said that Fantouré was aiming at a wider audience, most especially in his home country. Even though this was his first work, he avoided the simple linear narrative style, making use of analepse quite freely to advance the story. Perhaps it is because this was his first work that, at times, the relation between fiction and reality, as far as Guinea is concerned, is much more thinly veiled here than in the other novels. A few examples of this will suffice. Sekou Touré was known for his long speeches. That is the most important, and perhaps the only talent of the New Master of Les Marigots du sud, Baré Koulé. Bohi Di tells us that "Le Messie-Koi parlait dur et net. C'était la seule chose qu'il faisait avec virtuosité" (*CT*, 130).

It is the political organisation and control of Guinea by Sekou Touré that comes in for closer attention and comparison by Fantouré. The single party system which has become quite rampant in sub-Saharan Africa, had spread its tentacles throughout Guinea. The militia was the favourite instrument of fear and oppression. The "permanent plot" syndrome meant any one was liable to be picked up and imprisoned, tortured and killed at will. Halouma, whose name means thê "hyena", Baré Koulé's head of the militia, does not mince words when he tells Malekê that "Il n'y a qu'un seul parti dans ce pays, tout le monde y adhère de gré ou de force" (*CT*, 146). He later adds that "Désormais toute tentative de résistance au Parti sera puni de mort" (*CT*, 148).

Unlike Baré Koulé, Sekou Touré had not been groomed to take over power in order to protect foreign business interests. They have ended up doing the same thing, according to Fantouré: "le pays est hypothéqué au profit des membres du Parti" (*CT*, 157). The activities of the militia and political officials are such that the peasants see them as the "nouveaux colons", who give no hope to anyone: "Nous sommes trop exploités pour pouvoir espérer" (*CT*, 138). The situation has become so bad that Malekê declares: "depuis le jour de l'indépendance, nous sommes des condamnés à mort en sursis" (*CT*, 146).

The "permanent plot" syndrome was used to eliminate enemies as well as to purge bothersome allies. It is in this manner that Halouma tastes his bitter pill of implicating enemies in plots in order to eliminate them. More importantly, however, Fantouré takes a hard look at the role of the militia in an oppressive state. Manguai has stated in *L'Homme* that he understood, while in the army, why "la plupart des régimes totalitaires ont l'armée pour matrice, il n'y a pas d'arme humanitaire, ni d'armée humaniste" (*HT*, 50). In a totalitarian regime, the militia is a military organisation that sometimes supersedes the regular army and police in importance, training and equipment, and if not in numerical strength.

In *Le Cercle*, Malekê regrets the "mollesse de l'armée" over the years. He angrily tells Colonel Fof, in the course of a face-off between the Red Cross and the militia:

> Préparez-vouz à enterrer les corps des morts de la Croix-Rouge, puisque vous ne servez qu'à cela . . .
> Vous assistez passivement à l'agonie de la nation et vous prétendez être le garant de sa sécurité (*CT*, 206).

When the militia become hunted and killed in an organised "folie", they turn to their natural allies, the police and the gendarmerie for protection. The reaction of the two security organisations is quite revealing of how they take their emasculation by the militia:

> Les policiers impuissants depuis l'indépendance s'en moquaient; quant à la gendarmerie, avertie par une consigne générale, elle avait rejoint ses cantonnements dès le début du déferlement de la masse sur la ville (*CT*, 241).

Sekou Touré is said to have remarked after the Portuguese invasions of Guinea in 1970 that

> Every soldier who opposes the militia is an immediate
> or potential recruit of imperialism which seeks to
> establish neocolonialism within the armed forces
> everywhere; also every soldier who opposes the militia
> is in fact opposing the democratic revolution
> (Adamolekun, 1976, 146).

Such a speech could easily have been made by Baré Koulé.

Messie-Koï's régime suddenly comes to an end through a military coup. Before we have time to rejoice, we realise that we have the case of "the King is dead, long live the King!" As Baba-Sanessi announces the military takeover, "Le Messie-koï s'écroule sur une nappe rouge" (*CT*, 251), Bohi Di announces almost gleefully that "la plaisanterie était terminée, le cirque Messie-koï ferme ses portes" (*CT*, 250). These two statements require some comments. One can say that Baré Koulé is finally drowned in the blood of the people, which is represented by the "nappe rouge." The same colour stands for danger, the immediate danger threatening the newly found freedom as the announcement of the mysterious death of the most active participants (except Baba-Sanessi) in the struggle against oppression in Les Marigots du sud reveals.

The "plaisanterie", that is Messie-koï's rule is, therefore, not over. The circus doors that are supposed to have been closed resemble those in *Le Récit* that close on the spectators to oblige them to watch the sombre play/film throughout the night. Appropriately, Fantouré's second novel is entitled, *Le Récit du cirque de la Valleé des Morts*. The action takes place in a playhouse with the stage being covered by "Le Rideau de l'indifférence" which is made of "un tissu de velours rouge". Could it be that the red table cloth over which Baré Koulé had collapsed was simply taken away to make the curtain?

Le Récit, pervaded with the presence of Death, the "Vainqueur des Vainqueurs de toute existence" (*RC,* 127), as he boastfully calls himself, seems to have taken over from where *Le Cercle* ended. It has a post-independence setting with an analeptic account of the birth of the "Culte du Rhinocéros-Tâcheté" going back to an indeterminate time in the past. The novel also indirectly links up with the "colonial novels", *L'Homme* and *Le Voile* through the enigmatic character Afrikou (Manguai Africounah?). This character is not clearly seen to be definitely identified. We see him only as "une ombre qui se déplace. On devine une forme mais rien ne dit que c'est un être humain" (*RC*, 60). He announces that he is going to play the role of the new

> guide de ce spectacle du Récit du Cirque de la Vallée des Morts... Je suis partout sur ce continent, cette terre saignée par des souffrances millénaires... Je suis Afrikou... N'oubliez pas (*RC*, 60).

Manguai Africounah has it as ambition to lead people. Could we assume that this is his spirit come back from the dead to guide the living through the spectacle that is life in post-independence Africa? The spirit nature of Afrikou is strengthened by the fact that he is "partout sur ce continent", as he puts it. Elsewhere, we are surprised at his astonishing intimate knowledge of the forbidden "Vallée de Morts", as he takes Fahati through it and then disappears into thin air. Whatever we make of him, his nature heightens the oniric presentation of events in *Le Récit*.

If, as Fantouré states in *L'Homme*, "Il est vrai qu'en Afrique, la réalité dépasse souvent la fiction" (*HT*, 282, 283), then one cannot choose an "ordinary" way to present it in a work of art. When you reach a certain level of violence, Dib tells us, you can describe it only:

> par des images, des visions oniriques. Ce sont les seuls projecteurs capables de jeter quelque lumière sur de tels abîmes (Dib, 1962, 191).

Hence the way he wrote *Qui se souvient de la mer* and *Cours sur la rive sauvage*. Hence Picasso's *Guernica*. It is in the same vein that Fantouré has written *Le Récit*.

Onirism in *Le Récit* is perceivable not only in the narrative style but also in the spirit nature of the characters. An onomastics of their names is quite revealing in this light.[5]

Action in *Le Récit* takes place in the limited space of a playhouse. We catch the play when it is going into the second part. When it finally opens, this "étrange personnification de la mort" (*RC*, 12) makes his appearance. He is so hideous in his appearance that people make for the doors which had since been locked. We are thus in a way condemned to watch the play/film throughout the night in spite of the horror that it sometimes inspires. When the doors finally open, "La lumière d'une journée ensoleillée / éclabousse les spectateurs" (*RC*, 150). The word "éclabousse" contrasts with what "une belle journée ensoleillée" stands for in the usual sense: hope. We are not disappointed when we come to understand that the envelope that the spectators are given as they leave the playhouse simply enjoins them to do what is expected of them: RETOURNEZ A VOTRE INDIFFERENCE.

The playhouse is very much representative of the country in question in *Le Récit*, Ce-pays. We learn that it is here that "l'homme a eu l'honneur de construire tout le long de ses frontières une zone infranchissable des Marécages Insalubres" (*RC*, 32), and where "les citoyens ont fini par ressembler à des fauves et des reptiles d'une réserve naturelle" (*RC*, 32). Time, and therefore progress, have stopped for Ce-pays, just as the clocks were stopped after Mihi Moho's death on the stage of the playhouse.

The paucity of actors in the play/film, sometimes necessitating the participation of the spectators like in the traditional story telling session, recalls the paucity of the number of people who really participate in running the affairs of the country. In fact, the country is administered by the "Conseil de 13", a number that is usually associated with ill-luck.

Oppressed, exploited and brutalised, the citizen-subjects of Ce-pays have slumbered into indifference. It is this indifference that really irks the writer and to which he comes time and again. The novel opens with the "rideau de l'indifférence" and closes with the injunction: "RETOURNEZ A VOTRE INDIFFERENCE" in the form of a cross. Indifference is thus the cross the people seem to have chosen to bear, going as far as resisting any one who would have them do otherwise. When Mihi Moho tries to shake off their torpor by telling them some home truths, "Les spectateurs exigent son expulsion de la salle" (*RC*, 19), whereas they are ready to accept Fahati's insults without reacting. Unable or unwilling to react to Mihi Moho's assassination on the stage, Saibel-Ti calling them "bande de lâches" and "Messieurs et Mesdames de l'indifférence aux Atrocités" (*RC*, 25), says that "ce ne sont pas des injustices dans les sociétés de notre époque qu'on doit combattre, c'est l'indifférence qu'on devrait attaquer" (*RC*, 25). It is this indifference to their plight that leaves them out in the cold as spectators and not makers of the history of their country. It is also this indifference or lack of reaction that has made it possible for their leader, Fahati, to refine the method of oppression into an art form. Called "une étrange personnification de la mort" right from the beginning of the novel, Fahati is really the angel of death. In his final moments, when he finally sees the master he has been serving most of his life, he easily recognises him: "Cette chose me ressemble comme un autre moi, mais elle m'est étrangère" (*RC*, 136), he tells us.

Fahati, the oppressor had been led by Afrikou, then Death, on a journey into his past inner self so as to discover the absurdity of an existence such as the one he had led as "tyran et l'envahisseur intérieur". "Un jour comme un autre" therefore, Fahati, alias "le Guide", alias "le Rhinocéros-Tâcheté," but whose name means "the deceased" (because he is dead to his people), "installé à jamais dans ses propres déjections", dies at the foothills of Mount Dounouya (life), not far from the River Faha (Death), in "la Vallée des Morts", in the middle of "la nature en révolte" apparently against the presence in its midst of such an amorally and physically monstrous person. Afrikou's lament that "pour quelques êtres, diriger un pays, c'est d'abord organiser l'assassinat d'un peuple..."(*RC*, 97) could be a fitting epitaph on his tombstone. To do this he had turned the Rhinocéros-Tâcheté, a "symbole de l'innocence" from the beginning, into "une chose du Mal au service d'un pouvoir destructif" (*RC,* 76), that is the masters of the "Communauté des intolérances".

It is only in this novel that Fantouré makes a clean break with the traditional style of writing that was hitherto prevalent with African writers, Fantouré included. In this work, prose, poetry, theatre and cinematographic techniques are combined to create a certain intensity of expression and to heighten the tension in the atmosphere as the story unfolds. Some of the "chapelets" are nothing more than play/film sketches, complete with stage directions. Multiple narrators are used to present events from different perspectives. Fahati's journey into his own past, for example, is initially narrated by Afrikou from the point of view of someone who wants to bring a tyrant face to face with his past misdeeds. Later, Death takes over and his interest seems to be to find out what motivated Fahati to destroy human lives the way he did. Midiohouan sums up Fantouré's style and its effects by telling us that by this anticonformist style, the reader is:

> introduit dans une atmosphère particulièrement oppressante, faite d'angoisse, de violence et d'horreur.... *Le Récit du cirque...* est aussi l'incitation à la révolte et à l'action. Au-delà de la dénonciation de la dictature et de ses turpitudes, au-delà de la profonde amertume qui se dégage du roman, on note chez l'auteur le refus de se laisser écraser par la fatalité et gagner par le désespoir face à l'Afrique des "indépendances", qu'il exprime à travers une écriture insurrectionnelle qui, en amenant chaque protagoniste à reconnaître et à assumer sa part de responsabilité, vient lever "le rideau de l'indifférence" en vue d'indiquer le moyen de briser le "cercle infernal" du totalitarisme (Midiohouan, 1984, 23, 24).

Fantouré seemed to agree with this point of view when he said in an interview that "je mets dans mes livres l'angoisse du futur, l'angoisse de l'intolérance et le refus de baisser la tête, même si je dois mourir" (Fantouré, 1987, 124). The style adopted here rightly fits the subject treated.

Throughout the works of Fantouré, each social and political system and organisation is presented in a way that best describes its nature. The African traditional system, as presented in *Le Voile* most especially, and of which we catch glimpses here and there in the novels, is enigmatic and mysterious. In a way, the expression that we have used principally to qualify the tyrannical situations of the post colonial era, "en Afrique la réalité dépasse souvent la fiction", can be used in a more positive sense here. The very title of the novel, *Le Voile ténébreux*, is indicative of the extent to which this world could be mysterious to the non-initiates. The colonial system is much easier to understand: there are the oppressors on the one hand and the oppressed on the other. The narrative technique used in presenting this system is much more straightforward, with a lot of words of violence used to situate this world in relationship with its nature. The post-independence system is suppressive and oppressive to the extent that the writer's style heightens tension in the atmosphere and, consequently, space and time become blurred as is the case with the second part of *Le Cercle* up to *Le Récit*.

If some African writers, to quote Jean-Louis Joubert, have crossed "le rideau de cocotiers et voyagent sans frontières" (Joubert, 1990, 9), Fantouré, after *Le Récit,* seems to have taken the reverse direction. Firstly, the subject that he wrote on (the plight of young aspiring African leaders under the colonial system) does not go well with the style in *Le Récit*. This style is more likely than not to discourage most African readers where a reading culture is yet to take root. Genet had warned the Moroccan writer, Tahar Ben Jelloun:

> à être simple, à ne pas mépriser le lecteur. . . Il faut
> donner des repères au lecteur, ne pas le perdre dans le
> labyrinthe d'une recherche strictement personnelle, de
> type psychanalytique (Ben Jelloun, 1990, 42).

The statement above is in no way a condemnation of the way Fantouré wrote *Le Récit*. The subject treated in the novel chose its own style.

Fantouré uses imagery quite frequently in his novels, most especially in those that treat the traditional and the oppressive post-colonial societies respectively. It is in this way that water and earth take on symbolic meanings that permeate almost all the four works in question here.

Fantouré's birth place is Forécariah, a coastal town. This is perhaps one of the reasons that make water so important in his novels. *Le Récit,* excepted, all the fictional countries in the other novels contain the water element: Les Marigots du Sud (*Le Cercle*), Sahel-Atlantique *(L'Homme)* and Sahel Maritime *(Le Voile)*. In

Le Récit, however, the one geographic feature no citizen of Ce-pays can ignore is the River Faha which, in some regions "est sève de vie, d'espérance, dans d'autres, simple cours d'eau destiné à faire disparaître des crimes perpétrés contre les peuples..." (*RC*, 111).

Associated with water is mud, which is a combination of water and earth. In the right proportions, this combination is essential to life. In excess, it produces something that can be quite a nuisance, if not life-threatening. The insidious manner in which mud penetrates places and abodes, destroying physical beauty and happiness is thus comparable with that in which tyranny destroys moral beauty and happiness in a society. Significantly, the mud episodes feature more prominently in the narratives on the post-colonial era. In *Le Cercle,* Bohi Di dreams of a stream of mud invading the country. Seated on a raft and totally indifferent to the destruction and death around him, a fat man eats away, getting fatter and fatter until he bursts. In *Le Récit,* Mihi Moho comes on stage to tell how an African leader establishes his authority and tyranny over his people. After gaining full membership of the "Club... de la mauvaise foi, du sadisme, du cynisme, des intérêts matériels et idéologiques" (*RC*, 22), such a leader, in spite of the noises he makes about liberty and anti-despotism, immediately opens up:

> les vannes souterraines de la boue qui
> polluera les institutions humaines de [sa]
> société pour ne laisser la place qu'aux
> marais et à la jungle (*RC*, 22).

Like the fat man in Bohi Di's dream, he, the dictator in *Le Récit* surveys all this mess "du haut de [sa] tour, prêt à inonder toute zone- tempête quelle qu'elle soit" (*RC*, 22). It is only then that his "liberté de chef incontestable commencera réellement" (*RC*, 22).

Even where tyranny has not risen to levels comparable with that in *Le Cercle* and *Le Voile*, the mud image is still used as a hindrance and thus oppressive. In *L'Homme,* rainfall in the Nimba region makes the ground quite muddy to the extent that it obliterates the hoof marks left by the cattle in search of which Manguai and his team have been recruited. In *Le Voile,* after eating the poisoned food, Manguai finds himself prisoner in what is evidently a mud house until he purges himself of "lèse-tradition".

Fantouré's choice of names is not made in a haphazard manner. We have explained the meanings of some of them before. The writer's very "nom de plume" is quite significant too. If "fan" means "bon", "tolérant", then 'Fantouré' simply means the good tolerant Touré, thus easily distinguishable from the one who ruled Guinea with an iron hand up to the early 1980s.

Notes and References

1   Fantouré refers several times to Guinea in this interview as "Ce-pays," the name that he gave to the fictional country in *Le Récit du cirque...*

2   In a less dramatic way, *L'Homme du troupeau du Sahel* ends with a postscriptum which is a summary of *Le Voile ténébreux*, published six years afterwards.

3   I am aware of the fact that the third volume of this trilogy, *Le Gouverneur du territoire*, has been published. I was, however, unable to lay my hands on it.

4   See Alu R. Uganden. "The Evolution of Pessimism in the Works of Alioum Fantouré." Diss. Ahmadu Bello University, Zaria, 1983: p.20.

5   The name of the enterprise and the product that it exports - bananas - makes one think of Les Marigots du Sud as a "banana republic."

6   Faha means Death, Fahati – the deceased, Afrikou – Africa, Dounouya – Life, Kikée – the moon, mirror and Saibei-Ti – the Writer. See A.R. Uganden. "The Evolution of Pessimism...": p. 20.

Bibliography

Adamolekun, Ladipo. *Sekou Touré's Guinea.* London: Methuen, 1976.

Adebisi, Raufu A. "Themes and Historical Reality in the Works of Four Guinean Writers." Diss. Ahmadu Bello University, Zaria, 1988.

Aire, Victor O. "Le Renouveau technique dans le roman africain: Mudimbé et Sassine." *Bulletin of the School of Oriental and African Studies,* XLVIII, 1985: Pp.536-543.

Blair, Dorothy S. *African Literature in French.* London: Cambridge University Press, 1976.

Dib, Mohammed. *Qui se souvient de la mer.* Paris: Seuil, 1962.

Fantouré Alioum. Interview. "L'exil: une forme de présence." *Notre Librairie,* No.88/89 (1987): Pp.122-124.

Joubert, Jean-Louis. "Une décennie parmi les livres." *Notre Librairie,* No.103 (1990): Pp.6-11.

Mazouni, Abdallah. *Culture et enseignement en Algérie et au Maghreb.* Paris: Maspero, 1969.

Midiohouan, Guy Ossito. *L'Utopie négative d'Alioum Fantouré.* Paris: Silex, 1984.

Morgenthau, Ruth Schacter. *Political Parties in French-speaking West Africa.* London: O.U.P., 1964.

O'Toole, Thomas E. *Historical Dictionary of Guinea.* New Jersey: Metuchen, 1978.

Uganden, Alu R. "The Evolution of Pessimism in the Works of Alioum Fantouré." Diss. Ahmadu Bello University, Zaria, 1983.

7

SOCIO-POLITICAL CONSCIOUSNESS IN THE NOVELS OF YVES-EMMANUEL DOGBE

Raymond Elaho

> "Un homme qui a peur de crever comme un
> rat ne peut pas être totalement sincère
> s'il se contente d'écrire des poèmes sur
> les oiseaux. Il faut que quelque chose de
> l'époque se reflète, d'une manière ou d' une
> autre, dans son oeuvre."
>
> - Jean-Paul Sartre

Novelist, poet, short story writer and literary critic, Yves-Emmanuel Dogbe was born on 10th May 1939 in Lome, the capital of the tiny West African country of the Republic of Togo. Although relatively unknown in Anglophone literary circles, Dogbe is one of the most prolific and outstanding African writers of his generation. To date, he has published not less than twenty works comprising four novels, six books of poems, seven critical essays and three books on mysticism. His latest book titled *L'Essentialisme est aussi un Humanisme* is due to appear any time from now.

We have chosen to write on Dogbe in order to fill the yawning gap in the study of African literature by bringing his works to the attention of the Anglophone reading public. Like many writers of his generation, Dogbe is a committed writer à la Sartre. But unlike some African writers, he does not seek publicity. That probably explains why his works have passed unnoticed for a long time. He believes that the writer must make himself relevant to the society in which he lives. He has demonstrated this in virtually all his works – particularly in his novels. In other words, Dogbe's novels contain a high level of socio-political consciousness, as will be seen from a close study of his four novels to date – *L'Homme de Bê* [1], *La Victime* [2], *L'Incarcéré* [3] and *Le Miroir* [4].

But before we go on to analyse these novels, it is pertinent to say a word or two on what we mean by socio-political consciousness. Socio-political consciousness in a work of art is the deliberate concern of an artist – in this case a novelist – with the happenings in the society in which he/she lives. It is a form of commitment or engagement.

The notion of commitment in a work of art is so well known that one hardly needs to dwell on it at length here. However, since there are so many definitions of the term, we would like to state that it is the Sartrian definition that is of interest to us here. According to Jean-Paul Sartre,

> Je dirai qu'un écrivain est engagé quand il
> cherche à prendre la conscience la plus lucide
> et la plus entière d'être embarqué, c'est-à-
> dire quand il fait passer ... l'engagement de
> la spontanéité immédiate au réfléchi. [5]

What Sartre is saying in effect is that the writer must make a conscious and deliberate effort at influencing his society.

Dogbe, like Sartre before him, has never hidden his burning desire to influence the society in his works. He is consciously and fully aware of his responsibility to society. Hear him:

> Je dirai qu'un écrivain est engagé. Le rôle de l'écrivain
> dans la société contemporaine (ou tant de problèmes
> se posent) doit être de <u>sensibiliser</u> les gens à la nature
> réelle des problèmes qui les préoccupent, en <u>mobilisant</u>
> les forces pensantes pour réfléchir et dégager des
> solutions ....[6]

Indeed, sensitise (sensibiliser) and mobilise (mobiliser) are Dogbe's favourite expressions in his quest for solutions to the numerous problems confronting the African society in particular and humanity in general. As one critic rightly observed in a recent work, Dogbe is conscious of the fact that "les sociétés s'enfoncent dans des maux dont elles sont elles-mêmes productrices."[7] It is precisely because of these social vices that Dogbe has taken it upon himself to be the mouthpiece of the oppressed in his novels.

Dogbe's first novel, *L'Homme de Bê*, was first published in 1965 when the author was only twenty-six years old. This short satirical novel which could pass for a novelette is the story about money-lending business (le prêt à usure) which was and still is one of the greatest vices in the Togolese society. Dogbe revealed that his aim was to condemn this social vice having been inspired by his reading of Shakespeare's *The Merchant of Venice*.[8]

Bada Dansou, the 60-year old money lender, is presented as a heartless and ruthless man, who is bent on having his "pound of flesh" from any of his clients, who is unable to pay back in time, the money borrowed from him at a very high interest rate. He is a man with "un coeur qui se nourrit de scélératesse" (p.52). On the contrary, Douto Gavi, another money lender who is 30 years old, is presented as humane, understanding and saintly in his dealings with his clients. He is regarded as a "saviour" by the inhabitants of Bê. There is therefore, the suggestion that even though money lending is bad, it can be performed and given a human face.

Behind the apparent simplicity of the novel lie some serious themes which were to be developed in the later novels of Dogbe. These include the thirst for justice, the value of friendship and the importance of the "inner voice" usually referred to as conscience. Being the first work of the young writer that he was, one can overlook some of the weaknesses of the book which include over dramatisation of the vices and virtues of the protagonists as well as some unnecessary digressions.

One had to wait almost fourteen years to receive Dogbe's second novel which was published precisely in 1979. Unlike his first novel with a rather vague and generalised title, *La Victime*, which is the title of his second novel, is quite revealing. The curious reader, even before opening the book, would want to know who or what is the "Victim" in the novel.

Written when Dogbe was in self-exile in France, *La Victime* treats one of the most burning issues of our time: racism. On the surface, the novel tells the story of a love affair between Pierre Johnson, a young African student who fell in love with a young French lady called Solange Moulino, whom he met for the first time in the African town of Saborou. Unfortunately, his plans to marry Solange did not materialise because of the strong opposition of his lover's racist parents. According to Solange's father, "Il n'y a pas de quoi s'énerver, ma fille: ces gens-là (les Noirs) ne sont pas comme nous" (p.118). In protest against the racist attitude of her father, Solange committed suicide, thus becoming one of the victims of the novel. The other victim is of course Pierre Johnson who was unjustly deprived of the object of his love, Solange.

The second part of the novel deals with yet another topical issue: mixed marriage. Unlike the relationship between Pierre and Solange, which was tragically and abruptly terminated by the death of the latter, the affair between Pierre and yet another white lady by the name Maryse, ended up in marriage. But the attentive reader cannot but be apprehensive about the marriage. There is a strong possibility that it could end up in failure. For apart from the initial objections of Maryse's parents because of the colour of Pierre's skin, the problem of superiority/inferiority complex is evoked by Miss Rosaline Bourgeon, an experienced white secretary who has lived and worked for many years in Africa. As she puts it:

> "Je voudrais, moi, à partir de ce que j'ai observé et entendu autour de moi, donner quelques-uns des éléments qui font que le couple mixte a du mal à réaliser son harmonie. Tout d'abord, il y a les complexes: l'épouse blanche a tedance à se voir supérieure à son mari noir et à se considérer comme un objet de luxe à ses côtés et à lui témoigner peu d'égards par conséquent. Ou bien, c'est le mari noir qui fait du complexe en interprétant les faiblesses de sa conjointe blanche comme étant produites par quelque sentiment de supériorité." (p.233).

According to her, this and other factors are responsible for "tant de victimes dans le mariage mixte" (p.233).

Unlike *La Victime* which treats the themes of racism and mixed marriage, the third novel, *L'Incarcéré*, is primarily a political novel. One cannot agree more with Abalo Kataroh who described the novel as:

> une dénonciation des pouvoirs militaires répressifs, avec leurs systèmes d' embrigadements de Partis Uniques, qui livrent, à cause de la méfiance à leur endroit, une guerre sans merci aux intellectuels.[9]

The novel is indeed intensely militant and combative in tone. This is hardly surprising for it was published barely a year after Mongo Beti, the renowned Camerounian novelist, lashed out at some African writers whom he considered to have shied away from socio-political commitment in their works. Emphasising what the role of the African writer should be, he declared;

> Les espérances politiques de nos peuples ont été le plus souvent soit trahies, soit mystifiées. Pour la plupart d'entre nous, c'est un devoir quasi quotidien de la crier très fort, de stigmatiser les dirigeants noirs qui ont accepté de se faire l'instrument du désespoir de notre continent.[10]

In a similar vein, the Congolese writer, Emmanuel Dongala, stressed the need for African writers to be committed in their writings:

> Quand je vois des innocents arbitrairement arrêtés et torturés autour de moi, quand j'entends un Chef d'Etat déclarer que les états africains ont d'autres problèmes à régler que de régler un problème comme celui des droits de l'homme ...., que peut un écrivain sensible aux problèmes de sa société, sinon prendre sa plume devenue sa seule arme?[11]

It is against this background of the hot debate on the role of the African writer in society that Dogbe published *L'Incarcére* in 1980. The novel was also influenced by his personal experience. Having been imprisoned in his own country for his political views and having escaped to France on self-exile, Dogbe must have no doubt felt the need to write a novel that would reflect his political ideas and his hatred of the dictatorial military regime in his country. The novel is therefore not only socio-political but also autobiographical.

Like Dogbe, Senam, the hero of *L'Incarcéré*, is an African intellectual who, having studied in France for a university degree, felt the need to return to his own country, Sachelle in order to contribute his quota to the development of his fatherland. Unlike his bosom friend, Adri, who dared not criticise openly the repressive military regime in his country, Senam openly denounced the oppression of his fellow countrymen and women. As he put it:

> la peur de la prison ne doit jamais empêcher l'écrivain
> de dire ce qu'il pense, quand il considère que, ce faisant
> il sert les intérêts de la communauté nationale ou
> internationale (p.41).

Not surprisingly, Senam was quickly arrested for what the authorities considered to be his "subversive" views and activities. He was incarcerated as he had earlier predicted, but that did not deter him from continuing with the struggle.

For example, he criticised the government for the large-scale corruption in the country which is characterised by the "détournements des fonds publics." The helpless citizens were arbitrarily arrested and locked up in prison "pour avoir dit du mal du régime et de son parti unique." (p. 123). As Senam's personal experience shows, the prison conditions were horrible and dehumanising:

> Nous avions vu des gars amenés sains apparemment,
> qui étaient devenus fous du jour au lendemain, criant,
> hurlant, divaguant, déchirant leurs vêtements, buvant
> leur pisse, interpellant général, colonel, et autres
> soldats et qu'on finissait par conduire à l'asile de Tsés
> (p.146).

Faced with imminent death in prison, Senam had to escape to Europe on self-exile as the only way to stay alive for the greater struggle ahead. Senam's decision symbolises the tragedy of many African countries today where intellectuals and highly trained professionals who could have contributed to the development of their countries, are forced into exile by the oppressive governments in their countries. It is the problem of brain drain whereby world-renowned writers and intellectuals like Mongo Beti, Wole Soyinka and Dogbe were forced out of their respective countries at one time or the other. As Senam explained to his prison inmates, he escaped:

> Quand on parle de la fuite des cerveaux, on met tout sur le compte de la recherche d'une vie 'facile' de salaires plus elevés en Europe. On ne parle pas, ou pas assez, des conditions d'accueil faites aux cadres et aux intellectuels, en qui les hommes au pouvoir ne voient que rivaux et agitateurs. (p.137)

Unlike some intellectuals who only criticise without proffering solutions to the numerous problems in African countries, Senam recommends an original and African solution to the problems identified:

> Socialisme africain ou démocratie traditionnelle, peu importe en définitive le nom. Ce qui compte ... c'est la pratique socio-politique qui libère le peuple, adaptée à sa nature et à sa tradition culturelle, et fait régner la démocratie en banissant l'arbitraire de quelques privilégiés ambitieux. (pp.170-71)

It is obvious from this analysis of *L'Incarcéré* that the novel is highly committed and uncompromising, a novel written by a man who was himself both a political prisoner in his own country and a political refugee in a foreign land. To a large extent, one can regard Senam as the worthy mouthpiece or *porte-parole* of Dogbe, his creator. As we pointed out elsewhere, *L'Incaréré* is not only "un roman engagé" but "un roman enragé" in view of the very combative tone of the novel.[12] Indeed like Senam, Dogbe sees the writer as "un mobilisateur des masses pour revendiquer leurs droits et défendre des causes justes. . . " (p.198).

Dogbe's fourth and last published novel to date, significantly entitled, *Le Miroir*, continues the Dogbe tradition of committed literature. Unlike the earlier novels whose titles connote living human beings, this one has an object for a title, or so it seems. Everybody knows what a mirror is. In the ordinary sense of the word, a mirror is "a piece of special flat glass that you can look at and see yourself in".[13]

What is *Le Miroir* really about? The publishers of the novel give a very apt summary of the story:

> Elevée par une mère qui a eu le souci de faire d'elle une fille bien, Adèle a fait de brillantes études et a commencé de gagner convénablement sa vie en étant secrétaire dans une société importante. Mais la fatalité va la précipiter dans une chute, qu'elle ne semblait pas préparée à éviter, à supposer qu'elle ait réagi à temps, en écoutant cette petite Voix Intérieure qu'on appelle la conscience, qui dit à chacun de nous s'il fait bien ou mal, et qui a tendance à nous regarder dans le miroir.[14]

Underlined by us, the key words in this résumé which we have quoted at length are "voix intérieure" (inner voice), "conscience" (conscience) and of course "miroir" (mirror). The three words/ expressions could in this context be regarded as synonyms. They show that the mirror in this book is not just a simple object but a symbol of a heroine in constant dialogue (conflict?) with her conscience. This is what gives the novel its moral tone and social relevance.

Like Manon in L'Abbé Prévost's *Manon Lescaut* and Emma in Gustave Flaubert's *Madame Bovary*, Adèle who is the heroine of Dogbe's *Le Miroir*, has many lovers. Is her amorous relationship with as many as six men due to an insatiable desire for sex or money? Or is she simply a victim of circumstances beyond her control? Whatever the reason for Adèle's sexual excesses, it is obvious that Dogbe finds her conduct detestable, particularly her flirtation with another man even after her marriage to Nicolas Mono:

> Elle évite le regard du miroir, car il est accablant à la mesure de sa propre conscience, qui la condamne déjà, sans appel. Y a-t-il des circonstances atténuantes qu'elle est en droit d'alléguer pour sa défense? N'est-elle pas consentante? N'est-elle pas allée retrouver l'homme de son propre gré? (p.164).

Like Emma, Adèle eventually committed suicide, "face à la trahison de l'amour d'un Nicolas toujours si généreux et gentil à l'excès" (p. 179).

A keen observer of the society in which he lives, Dogbe knows that there are many Adèles in our midst. So while condemning through the mirror, the infidelity of Adèle, he nevertheless seems to sympathise with her plight by suggesting that she could still be forgiven by the Almighty Creator:

> "Après une ultime demande de pardon à Dieu, Adèle se couche dans son lit, ou Nicolas la retrouve plusieurs heures plus tard, sans vie, ses deux bras angéliques en croix sur sa poitrine" (p.181).

The socio-political consciousness of Dogbe in the novel is not limited to Adèle's love affair. The whole book is punctuated with references to social, economic and political events in the African society, outside the world of Adèle. The problems of unemployment, corruption, strikes, political instability and military regimes are highlighted. For example, right from the first pages of the novel, the reader is informed that "depuis trois jours, une grève avait paralysé le pays obligeant tout le monde à rester chez soi" (p.14). Political agitations and the corresponding ruthlessness with which they are suppressed by the authorities did not escape the attention of the author:

> Une fois encore, les agitations politiques avaient monté d'un cran et la ville était sens dessus dessous, avec des barricades de voitures calcinées et des pneus enflammés. Les rues étaient prises d'assaut par les militaires et les jeunes qui jetaient des pierres au travers des gaz lacrymogènes (p.15).

We have tried in this study to show that Dogbe is consciously and decidedly involved, through his novels, in the events in society, in this case the African (Togolese) society. This explains why we have adopted a sociological approach in our critical analysis of the novels. As Abiola Irele rightly observes, this approach is "the most apt to render a full account of modern African literature" because it takes into account "everything within our society which has informed the work".[15]

It is perhaps necessary to point out at this juncture that our emphasis on the thematic aspects of Dogbe's novels is informed by the scope of the subject of this essay. It does not in any way suggest that we are unaware of the abundant artistic/stylistic qualities of the novels as works of art. For as Dogbe himself has always pointed out, the writer should be able to create a balance between social commitment and aesthetic beauty in his work.

Talking about aesthetic beauty, Dogbe's novels are always refreshing to read. Some critics have rightly described his prose as poetic while others see Dogbe as a master in the art of creating suspense. Already apparent in his first novel, *L'Homme de Bê*, suspense is amplified in *La Victime* where the reader and even the characters in the novel are kept guessing as to the content of the letter received by Mr. Dokart:

> Spontanément. Il voulut ouvrir la lettre, mais quelque
> chose l'arrêta. Il leva les yeux discrètemeent et
> s'aperçut que la jeune femme avait le regard braqué
> sur lui. Pour ne pas paraître plus lâche et plus couard
> qu'il n'était, il se décida. Les mains presque
> tremblantes, il déchira négligemment. l'enveloppe et
> sortit un papier très blanc plié en deux" (p.57).

Contrary to all expectations, it was the letter recalling Dokart against the blacks.

With *L'Incarcéré*, the aesthetic beauty of the novel is enhanced by the author's ability to use dialogue in exposing the idiosyncrasies and follies of his characters, for example, the long dialogue (confrontation?) between the General, the Minister of Culture, the Security Chief and Senam (pp.109-114). In the case of *Le Miroir*, the personification of the mirror, which elevates it to the status of a living protagonist, contributed to the aesthetic quality of the novel. The tragedy of the heroine, Adèle, is largely due to her refusal to follow the advice of the mirror during the thirty or so times that they confronted each other. It is hardly surprising that the mirror significantly rejects her plea for compassion and leniency in the end (pp.100-101).

We have gone at length to draw attention to some of the artistic qualities of the novels to debunk the view held in some quarters that Dogbe has sacrificed art for message-cum-commitment in his work. For Dogbe who is not only a creative writer but also a literary critic in his own right, it would have been surprising if he did not appreciate the need to strike a healthy balance between content (le pouvoir écrire) and form (le comment écrire) in his novels.

The technical qualities of the novels notwithstanding, Dogbe is best known as a writer who sees his mission primarily as that of an advocate on the side of the oppressed and the wretched of the earth, to use Franz Fanon's expression. In other words, he sees himself as the moral conscience of the people. That is why he sees the novels as "une parole délibérément adressée, sous forme de message, aux autres, à un groupe d'individus ou à tous les hommes.".[16]

That message must take the form of the condemnation of "les bonnes moeurs".[17] And as Tidjani-Serpos rightly observed, "le genre romanesque semble être le meilleur medium … qui permette de parler d'une situation existentielle".[18] It is precisely this socio-political consciousness in Dogbe's novels that we have tried to analyse in this paper.

Notes and References

[1]   Yves-Emmanuel Dogbé. *L'Homme de Bê*. Lomé: Efiyiond Akpagnon, 1989. Though first published in 1965, it is the 1989 edition that we used in this paper.

[2]   Yves-Emmanuel Dogbé. *La Victime*. Le Mée-Sur-Seine: Editions Akpagnon, 1979.

[3]   Yves-Emmanuel Dogbé. *L'Incarcéré*. Le Mée-Sur-Seine: Editions Akpagnon, 1980.

[4]   Yves-Emmanuel Dogbé. *Le Miroir*. Lomé: Editions Akpagnon, 1995.

[5]   Jean-Paul Sartre. *Situations II*. Paris: Gallimard, 1948, p.124.

[6]   Unpublished interview with the author, dated 27/4/85.

[7]   Abalo, Essrom Kataroh. *Yves-Emmanuel Dogbé: L'Homme et L'oeuvre*, Lomé: Editions Akpagnon, 1996, p.100.

[8] Yves-Emmanuel Dogbe, in Preface to the 1989 edition of the book, p.5.

[9] Abalo Essrom Kataroh. *op. cit.*, p.102.

[10] Mongo Beti. Lecture delivered at the University of Wurzurg on 10th July1979.

[11] Emmanul Dongala. "Littérature et Société: ce que je crois" in *Peuples Noirs Peuples Africains*, No. 9, (Mai-Juin 1979): p.62.

[12] Raymond Elaho. "Littérature et Politique: L'Incarcéré de Yves-Emmanuel Dogbé" *Peuples Noirs Peuples Africains*, No. 20, (Mars-Avril, 1981): p.147.

[13] *Longman Dictionary of Contemporary English.* (3rd Edition). Essex: Longman, 1995, p.909.

[14] The editor's résumé on the back cover of the novel.

[15] Abiola Irele. "The Criticism of Modern African Literature", in Christopher Heywood (ed.) *Perspectives on African Literature*. London: Heinemann.

[16] Yves-Emmanuel Dogbé. *Négritude, Culture et Civilisation: Essai Sur La Finalité des Faits Sociaux.* Le Mée-Sur-Seine: Educations Akpagnon, 1980, p.108.

[17] Yves-Emmanuel Dogbé. *op. cit.*, p.109.

[18] Nouréni Tidjani-Serpos. *Aspects de la critique Africaine.* Tome 2 Yaoundé: Silex/Editions Nouvelles du Sud, 1996, p.288.

8

PERSONALITY CULT IN RACHID MOUMOUNI'S *UNE PEINE À VIVRE* AND WILLIAM SASSINE'S *LE JEUNE HOMME DE SABLE*

Tunde Fatunde

"Les hommes forts, les vrais maîtres, retrouvent la conscience pure des bêtes de proie; monstres heureux, ils peuvent revenir d'une effroyable suite de meurtres, d'incendies, de viols et de tortures avec des coeurs aussi joyeux, des âmes aussi satisfaites que s'ils s'étaient amusés à des bagarres d'étudiants".[1]

– Nietzsche

The aim of this article is to examine the relevant concept and theme of *personality cult* in Rachid Moumouni's *Une Peine à Vivre* and William Sassine's *Le Jeune Homme de Sable*. Both novels present the phenomena of the personality cult as the actions of principal and secondary characters in these works of fiction are dictated, influenced, dominated and co-ordinated by one single individual who succeeds in arrogating to himself absolute and indivisible political powers. Such an individual "... combines in himself the executive, the legislative and the judicial functions. That's what we call dictatorship . . . "[2]

The personality cult is a complex and elaborate concept applicable as an instrument of analysis to understand the rationale and various mechanisms portrayed by the major characters in both novels. These individuals create a suffocating and totalitarian atmosphere for people who are perceived to be beneath them. "Personality is that which gives order and congruence to all the different kinds of behaviour in which the individual engages."[3] Such a person takes on an aura of a cult as soon as his body of admirers venerates him through a series of rites centering around 'sacred' or religious symbols. In other words, the personality cult is a set of behaviours which manifests through blackmail and state violence, and confers absolute powers on a person who controls state power.

Nobody is left in any doubt as to the extent to which such a person can exercise these powers. A cultic dimension of the individual's limitless access to all levels of authority is demonstrated by some ritualistic epithets by which he is called. Throughout William Sassine's *Le Jeune Homme de Sable*, the Head of State, a civilian, is simply known as *Le Guide*. In Rachid Moumouni's *Une Peine à Vivre*, the military Head of State is called *Le Maréchalissime*, a pejorative epithet for Field Marshal.

In the works, *Le Guide* and *Le Maréchalissime* make use of specific monopolistic organs as instruments of promoting their egocentric interests at the expense of the entire nation. Professor Wilfrang, Le Guide's foreign ideologue, states at a press conference how his former student came to power:

> . . . il fonda un parti politique qu'il devait animer jusqu'à l'accession de son pays à l'indépendance. Depuis, ce parti est devenu 'le Parti du Lion' et lui-même s'est fait baptiser 'le Guide'[4]

And he goes further to explain how Le Guide became a dictator by linking his personality to that of the lion – the unquestionable and unelected leader in the animal world.

> Je disais donc qu'il se mit petit à petit à ressembler à un lion, dans sa volonté de s'imposer simplement par l'éclat de sa voix, sa loyauté, sa force dans tous les travaux et même dans sa démarche.[5]

Le Guide's towering and asphyxiating character, one of the ingredients of personality cult, becomes more obvious, through the intense propaganda machinery under his total control through the only political party in the country. One of his local sycophants describes Le Guide in the following mystical and cultic terms:

> Le Guide a dit que pour la survie et la grandeur de
> notre cité, tout le monde doit se débarrasser de sa nature
> humaine et de toutes ses faiblesses pour ressembler
> chaque jour un peu plus au Lion de notre invincible
> Parti . . .[6]

The same ideologue does not hesitate to attribute specific religious traits to Le Guide "Vénére soit notre noble lion du désert: que ta pensée et tes actes nous guident, car toi seul sais où nous allons... Prends notre vie et nos biens, car sans toi, nous serions moins que des mendiants."[7]

Moumouni's Le Maréchalissime shares nearly identical attributes with Sassine's Le Guide. The only difference is in the area of priority and attention given to specific organs of power. While Le Guide manipulates the only political party in his country, Le Maréchalissime uses the military to suppress any opposition. A military dictator, Le Maréchalissime shares the views of one of his coursemates from the War College on the importance of the armed forces.

> Je n'aime pas l'armée. Mais mon père est persuadé
> que dans ce pays, il n'y a d'avenir que dans la carrière
> militaire. Il a donc usé des relations dont il dispose au
> Palais pour m'inscrire à mon insu à l'Académie. . . [8]

Without mincing words, Le Maréchalissime gives his potential successor, a lengthy exposé on the theory and practice of the limitless power at his disposal:

> Tu jouiras d'une puissance qui t'effraiera toi-même.
> Au simple ton légèrement haussé de ta voix,
> trembleront tous les murs du Palais, pourtant plus épais
> que ma silhouette. A ton apparition, le soleil intimidé
> se tapira derrière les nuages. Ainsi tu n'auras pas
> besoin de porter des lunettes en verre fumé. S'il te
> chante, tu pourras réfuser la pluie, mettant au désespoir
> nos paysans. Tu auras la possibilité de changer les jours
> du calendrier, troublant nos bureaucrates qui ne sauront
> plus s'ils devront se rendre au travail ou non. Je te
> laisserai même intervertir les dates des fêtes légales,
> sauf celle de mon accession au pouvoir. Tous mes
> généraux, pourtant plus gradés que toi, mouilleront

> leur pantalon à ton approche. Je ne te parle pas de
> mes ministres. Ceux-là devront changer de slip chaque
> fois que tu les regarderas en fronçant les sourcils. Quant
> aux autres, tous les autres, c'est bien simple, devenus
> lilliputiens, ils cesseront d'exister à tes yeux. Il te sera
> impossible de les voir, subitement atteint de la cécité
> du pouvoir. Tu pourras satisfaire tous tes fantasmes, y
> compris les plus fous, et donner libre cours à tes vices.
> Aucune femme n'osera te repousser, pas même les
> jouvencelles que je t'avais interdites. Tu posséderas
> toutes celles qui te feront bander sans craindre les
> scandales. Je te protégerai toujours contre les
> conséquences de tes frasques. Tu seras alors étonné de
> découvrir que la servilité humaine n'a pas de limite et
> que la dignité n'est qu'un mot creux.[9]

His personality cult assumes a frightening proportion when, as a student at the military academy, his instructor describes his predecessor as a *tin god.* "Tu n'auras jamais l'occasion d'apercevoir, même de loin, le commandant. Il est comme Dieu, omnipotent, mais invisible. Notable différence: il n'est pas miséricordieux."[10]

Why have these writers chosen to depict this entrenched personality cult phenomenon in these two novels? The principal reasons are both within and outside the parameters of these fictions. After all, works of imagination are broadly speaking subjective interpretations of our human and objective existence. Ambition, whether inordinate or otherwise, is an integral part of human nature. Ambition, as a process, commences in an obscure form during childhood. "For Freud, the first few years of life are decisive for the formation of personality."[11] Moumouni and Sassine throw some light into the childhood background of their principal characters. According to Professor Wilfrang, Le Guide has, since the age of twelve, taken particular interest in the future of his people[12] – an opaque allusion by Wilfrang regarding Le Guide's childhood ambition of eventually ruling his people. The inference we can draw from the Professor's statement is that some individuals are providentially born to rule. On the other hand, Moumouni gives a lengthy description as to how Le Maréchalissime's childhood environment predisposes him to become an armed survivalist, *at all costs,* which is a major ingredient in the phenomenon of the personality cult. He was born into a nomadic and marauding tribe reputed to live on plundered goods. Moreover, he was left to fend for himself through pilfering because he lost his parents at an early age:

> Je suis né dans une tribu de bohémiens de sinistre réputation. Les plus folles légendes couraient sur eux. On disait qu'ils volaient des nourrissons pour les sacrifier au cours de leurs messes noires, qu'ils jetaient des sorts qui métamorphosaient en crapaud la fiancée imprudente aperçue la veille de ses noces, que le lait qu'ils goûtaient se transformait en vin tandis que se desséchaient les mamelles qui l'avaient fourni. On racontait sur eux tant de balivernes que, dès qu'ils apercevaient leur caravane, les paysans du lieu s'armaient de fusils pour leur ordonner de se détourner . . . Les prédateurs itinérants rencontraient partout l'hostilité des laborieux sédentaires. Ils n'hésitaient pas à employer la force quand ils estimaient pouvoir prendre le dessus. Vainqueurs, ils s'adonnaient alors aux rapines et au carnage. Ils tuaient, ils incendiaient, ils détruisaient et, après avoir festoyé et fait bombance, ils repartaient dès l'aube, jamais las, toujours assoiffés d'horizons nouveaux.[13]

The personality cult is further explained through Jung's theory of the *collective unconscious.* Carl Jung, a Swiss psychiatrist postulates through his theory of the collective unconscious that the entire structure of personality of individuals in all human races is more or less similar and is made up of "the psychic residue of human evolutionary development, a residue that accumulates as a consequence of repeated experiences over many generations."[14] These experiences which Jung calls racial memories or representations are not necessarily inherited. "Rather we inherit the possibility of reviving experiences of past generations. These latent or potential memories depend upon inherent structures and pathways that have been engraved on the brain as a result of cumulative experiences of mankind."[15]

Memories and representations which are collective properties of the society are found in various forms in the personality structure of the individual. In other words, Jung's construct of personality is a blend of accumulated memories of the individual and the structure of the society. The relevance of Jung's ideas to these two novels is in the area of the civil society that perceives and venerates Le Guide and Le Maréchalissime as supreme beings or gods. This kind of mythical veneration of mere mortals as gods by their fellow countrymen and women has been inculcated over several millenia into the collective unconscious of all members of the society as a part of the ancestral and cultural heritage transmitted from one generation to another. Although the concept of the Supreme Being might have undergone slight or dramatic changes, the core or essence of the concept remains intact, i.e., the belief that someone is a supreme being is generally conferred on a person who has absolute authority and arrogates to himself all state powers. Succinctly put, these individuals, who claim to be the spiritual and temporal 'representatives' of God, also indoctrinate their fellow countrymen and women into believing that they, as God's representatives, have the right to dictate the fate of every single individual in the society. Their words constitute the Law and being god-like they are of course, above the Law. Such are the principal traits of Le Guide and Le Maréchialssime who are characterised by the major manifestations of Jung's collective unconscious.

Despite the sadistic and egocentric arrogance of these "supreme" beings and in spite of all the powers that they have appropriated for themselves, Nature still proves to be their formidable nemesis. Indeed, the drought has provoked serious economic problems in Le Guide's country. This makes him gradually unpopular, and he starts to feel that his god-like ability to control the universe is being threatened. Discussing the security implication of the drought with his dreaded Chief of Security, El hadj Karamo, Le Guide expresses the opinion that his citizens are his children and they should be grateful to him for looking after their interests:

> Il faut que mon peuple sente que je veille sur lui . . . Si
> le peuple pouvait savoir combien je souffre pour lui, il

m'aiderait à exterminer tous mes ennemis . . . C'est
moi qui lui aí donné une identité , une réalité. Je suis
son père. Auparavant, il n'y avait rien dans ce pays.
Rien que du sable et du vent. Même les blancs n'en
voulaient pas. Quand ils sont partis, il a fallu partir
complètement de zéro, sans richesse, sans amis et sans
cadres . . . A présent, on me met tout sur le dos.[16]

Le Maréchalissime impresses it upon all his ministers and advisers
that his personal interests are indeed higher and more sacred than
that of the nation. "Vous n'êtes pas assez stupide pour croire que
vous êtes au service de la nation. Ici, on ne sert que Le
Maréchalissime."[17] He goes on to blackmail all those who serve
under his regime. "....Votre collaboration avec un régime militaire
n' a pu que ternir votre réputation."[18]

The unbridled use of state violence is one of the hallmarks of
those imbued with personality cult. Known and imaginary political
opponents and mere critics must be removed at all cost. There is
no limit to the use of state repression. The sledge-hammer is always
at the disposal of such persons to kill a fly. Violence assumes such
sadistic proportions that any trace of humanism has totally vanished
from the minds of Le Guide and Le Maréchalissime. Both of them
rely exclusively on their national security advisers to ensure that
anyone who dares to oppose their iron-fist rule does not escape
alive. In such a situation, the manipulator of state violence attains
at times an incredible level of savagery and barbarism. Tahirou, a
classmate of Le Guide, who later became one of the critics of the
regime simply had his head chopped off! Another opponent's lips
were locked up with a strong padlock. Holes were inserted into his
lower and upper lips through which the padlock was passed. A
more sinister use of violence was put into practice when a lioness
was let loose on the people of the city and the animal indiscriminately
killed innocent citizens after the successful poisoning of Le Guide,
Professor Wilfrang and another dignitary of the regime. The
explanation for such a move by one of Le Guide's supporters is
equally sadistic:

> La lionne ne s'attaque qu'à ceux qui n'ont pas la
> conscience tranquille... il ne faut pas tuer la lionne
> parce qu'elle est nécessaire à la purification de la cité
> et qu'il faut commencer à lui livrer tous les traîtres
> démasqués ... Cette lionne nous aidera, j'en suis sûr,
> à séparer les bonnes des mauvaises graines de notre
> société. Elle ne tuera que les gens incapables de se
> défendre. Et qu'avons-nous à faire des gens incapables
> de se défendre contre seulement un animal? Grâce à
> cette lionne et à notre soleil, nos concitoyens
> apprendront à ne compter que sur eux-mêmes; au bout
> de cette nécessité, ils découvriront le prix de la véritable
> indépendance sur laquelle le Guide veut bâtir une
> société solide et juste, de cette solidité et de cette justice
> que seuls savent renforcer des hommes disciplinés et
> ingénieux.[19]

The daily elimination of imaginary opponents acquires a habitual
undertone with Le Maréchalissime. Nobody is spared. The more
people he eliminates the better. And he shows no compunction for
his inhuman and sadistic acts:

> Retranché dans mon antre, je m'appliquais à déjouer
> les projets de complots en mettant à la retraite anticipée
> les jeunes officiers non encore corrompus, à monter
> de faux complots afin d'emprisonner les jeunes
> officiers encore libres et non mis à l'étranger, à exiler
> à l'étranger ceux assignés à résidence, à assigner à
> résidence ceux encore libres, à l'exception d'une
> poignée d'inoffensifs qu'il me fallait garder comme
> instigateurs des futurs complots et boucs émissaires
> des mécontentements populaires à venir. Le sort des
> hommes n'était plus que fil entre mes doigts, et tous
> ignoraient en s'endormant s'ils se réveilleraient
> condamnés ou promus. Je commençais à tisser la trame
> à la tombée de la nuit et mon travail ne s'achevait
> qu'au matin. Mes yeux ne supportaient plus la
> luminosité diurne et il me fallut porter des lunettes
> teintées. Cela décupla la terreur que j'inspirais et ceux
> qui me croisaient se figeaient soudain, n'osant se
> détourner ni continuer leur chemin, car il ne faisait
> pas bon se rappeler à mon souvenir.[20]

Conversion of state resources by these dictators to satisfy their egocentric needs is a recurrent issue in both novels. Such a phenomenon is perhaps expected in the sense that the resolution of material problems confronting the citizens is never considered the priority of both dictators known for their egocentric habits and uncontrolled greed. In Le Guide's country, incessant drought which has ruined the farmers cannot be wished away by mere recognition of the problem by state officials, while the situation remains unaddressed. Instead, dignitaries close to the corridors of power are busy stealing and selling millet to drought victims; millet sent to the country by relief agencies as food assistance. State kleptomania by various government officers was encouraged by Le Guide and Le Maréchalissime. The principal beneficiaries of this policy was first and foremost the Chief Security Officer. Le Maréchalissime, whose country is an oil-producing state, does not hesitate to put government revenue earned from the sale of crude oil at the international markets, at the disposal of his close aides. However, Le Maréchalissime's kleptomania has a sinister dimension. In order to boost his dwindling popularity, periodic public executions of some selected kleptocrats are organised as a symbol of his anti-corruption crusade:

> Laisse-les s'enrichir, insistait le Maréchalissime. Ils sont bien connus de mes services, qui entretiennent sur eux des dossiers aussi imposants que ma panse. Ils sont trop obsédés par l'argent pour penser à autre chose. De toute façon, ils ne forment qu'un cheptel de gras moutons promis au sacrifice. De temps à autre, faisant mine de lutter contre la corruption, j'en jette un en pâture à la vindicte populaire. Cela ne manque jamais de faire baisser ma côte d'impopularité. [21]

Absolute power which corrupts absolutely manifests itself in a situation where state powers are in the hands of a single individual without the existing mechanism of checks and balances as suggested by Montesquieu – the 18th century French philosopher.

Where there is oppression, sooner or later, there is bound to be resistance. It is this possibility of resistance that compels Le Guide and Le Maréchalissime to spend so much of the state resources in installing an 'efficient' security apparatus. The fear of rebellion by the people gets to a paranoid stage where the presidential guards in both novels are better equipped and catered for than the regular 'republican' army. In spite of all these security measures, resistance to oppression was prevalent. Oumarou, son of Abdou, Le Guide's right-hand man, planned and executed successfully the elimination, by poison, of Le Guide and some of his close collaborators. As for Le Maréchalissime, he has to contend with incessant revolts both within the civil society and the armed forces. Drawing inspiration from Carl Jung's collective unconscious, one could also say that oppression as thesis and resistance as anti-thesis have always existed as part of ancestral heritage passed from one generation to another in all human societies. The synthesis which is the death of the dictators ushers in another possible era of freedom.

One of the strong aspects of Sassine's novel is the penetration into the complex rebellious psyche of Oumarou. As a child, he always felt that he was not loved by his wealthy father and his submissive and deeply religious mother. Moreover, he was deeply disturbed by the incessant physical violence to which his father subjected his mother. In reply to questions by Oumarou as to the reasons for her physical and mental degradation, his mother would simply reply that Allah, the Almighty has ordained that women should serve and obey the men. The common sight of numerous children of poor people begging for alms traumatised Oumarou to the point where he disguised himself as a beggar and joined these mendicants. He was, however, discovered and reprimanded by his father's friends and sent home. Despite such reprimands, he went back to the streets begging for alms. The social injustice in the midst of abundance and the cruel manner in which his mother was treated feed Oumarou's rebellious instincts which are given a legitimate philosophical support by Tahirou, the principal of the secondary school who was equally rebellious. Tahirou's anti-establishment attitude greatly reinforced Oumarou's anger against an unjust world order. This sense of solidarity against injustice further estranged Oumarou from his father:

Il s'éloigna davantage de son père, occupé à agrandir
ses affaires, et dont les activités toujours plus prospères
permettaient si mal à son fils de jouer un rôle de petit
"orphelin". Chaque colis qu'il recevait à l'école lui
apparaissait comme un acte de dénonciation paternelle
de sa condition de privilégié. Il le partageait aussitôt
après avec un air coupable.[22]

There are two interrelated theories on personality to explain
Oumarou's incessant rebellious nature from childhood to adulthood.
The first is Erik Erikson's psychosocial theory of development.
According to Erikson, each individual undergoes, broadly, eight
unequal stages of development. And in one of the stages, especially
at childhood, a particular recurrent event which might at first appear
in the form of what he calls dramatic ritualisation could develop at
adulthood into a sense of guilt for the individual. "The child actively
participates in play acting, wearing costumes, imitating adult
personalities, and pretending to be anything from a dog to an
astronaut. This early stage of ritualisation contributes to the
dramatic element to be found in rituals (such as drama as a ritual of
its own) throughout the remainder of its life. The inner estrangement
that may ensue from this stage of childhood is a sense of guilt". [23]

Another theory of child's psychology that is relevant to the
explanation of Oumarou's behaviour is that of Karen Horney's
anxiety theory which is defined as:

the feeling a child has of being isolated and helpless
in a potentially hostile world. A wide range of adverse
factors in the environment can produce this insecurity
in the child ... The insecure, anxious child develops
various strategies by which to cope with its feelings of
isolation and helplessness. It may become hostile and
seek to avenge itself against those who have rejected
or mistreated it."[24]

In other words, the two theories help, to explain why Oumarou's
rebellious attitude was a carry-over from his childhood.

The final process of the synthesis which should manifest itself
through the dawn of a new era (i.e., a free and democratic society)
is absent in the conclusive parts of both novels. It is the right of any

writer to exercise his freedom of expression by ending his work the way he or she chooses. Two important issues are, however, present at this stage: the troubled conscience of Le Guide and Le Maréchalissime, and the complex philosophical issue of death as the final arbiter of all dictators. Despite their iron-cast mind, both dictators betrayed a natural sense of guilt, – albeit very temporary or in passing. This betrayal is a demonstration of the fact that no matter the level and quality of bestiality inherent in a tyrant, he still has a residue of humanity existing in him. The most evident sign of a guilty conscience of his crime against humanity comes up when Le Guide experienced insomnia:

> Le spectacle de mon peuple en train de souffrir me déprime et m'empêche de dormir... un jour vient où l'on est obligé de se reposer. C'est à ce moment-là qu'on commence à grossir de quelque part. Alors on prend l'habitude de soigner ses insomnies en cultivant la confortable confusion entre responsabilité et fatalité, entre mal et malheur. [25]

As a result of constant surveillance of the presidential palace, key members of the presidential guard and those of the armed forces, Le Maréchalissime also lost sleep. Insomnia is part and parcel of his personality disorder which doctors could not cure but could diminish occasionally. "Tu n'arrives plus à dormir et tes insomnies résistent à tous les traitements." [26]

Death is presented by the two novelists as an inevitable *deux ex machina* and a 'solution' to the ravaging problems inflicted on the society by Le Guide and Le Maréchalissime. The former dies of poisoning while the latter ends up in front of a firing squad. The few moments of guilty conscience manifested by both of them were moments when they felt that death, the ultimate equaliser, would also catch up with them. The inevitability of death in human affairs, hanging like the sword of Damocles, over both the oppressed and the oppressor in the two novels has a philosophical dimension termed *existential psychology* by Medard Boss, a Swiss psychatrist. Existential psychology, otherwise known as *dasein*, rests on three planks. First, human beings are free to choose the way they want to live and are broadly responsible for their existence. They can, however, decide by themselves to transcend their physical environment and their physical bodies. Second, one phenomenon they cannot overcome is guilt, because according to Boss, "Man's existential guilt consists in his failing to carry out the mandate to fulfill all his possibilities."[27] And thirdly, another phenomenon which man cannot transcend is the dread of Nothingness. According to Boss, an essential component of death is *nothingness*. This is "... a presence within Being of non-Being." It is always there, fearful, uncanny, and beckoning. To fall into nothingness is to lose one's being, to become nothing. Death is the absolute Nothingness, but there are other less absolute ways by which non-Being can invade Being – alienation, isolation from the world – for example. The extent to which the possibilities of existence fall short of fulfilment is the extent to which non-Being has taken over Being.[28] In other words, death in a way contains a damage control element that checkmates further destruction that could have been committed by individuals clothed in the dreadful personality cult garment. Death, by the same streak of ironical fate, also terminates the lives of those liberators, who are committed in the two novels, to repair the damage caused to humanity by these two prominent tyrants. The essence of Death, as a leveller and equaliser of both the oppressor and the oppressed, is brought to the fore by Ahmedou, Oumarou's friend."Tu ne sais même pas qui tu es; tu es un jeune homme de sable : à chaque coup de vent, tu t'effrites un peu et tu te découvres autre. Un jour, il ne restera rien de toi."[29]

Notes and References

1 Quotation by Nietzsche, cited in preface to Rachid Moumouni. *Une Peine à Vivre*. Paris: Stock, 1991.

2 Ola Vincent, quoted in *Nigerian Tribune on Saturday*, (Ibadan), 15 August 1998: p.2.

3 S. Calvin Hall and G. Lindzey. *Theories of Personality*. New York: John Wiley and Sons, 1978, p.8.

4 William Sassine. *Le Jeune Homme de Sable.* Paris: Présence Africaine, 1979, p.35.

5 Sassine, p.36.

6 Sassine, p.16.

7 Sassine, 20.

8 Rachid Moumouni. *Une Peine à Vivre*. Paris: Stock, 1991, p.52.

9 Moumouni, p.91-92.

10 Moumouni, p.27.

11 Hall and Lindzey, p.54.

12 Sassine, p.35.

13 Moumouni, p.16-17.

14 Hall and Lindzey, p.119.

15 *Ibid.*, p.119-120

16 Sassine, p.69.

17 Moumouni, p.267.

18 *Ibid.*

19 Sassine, pp.155, 157-158.

20 Moumouni, p.125.

21 Moumouni, p.84.

22 Sassine, pp.164-165.

23 Hall and Lindzey, p.95.

24 Hall and Lindzey, pp.176-177.

25 Sassine, pp.70-71.

26 Moumouni, p.212.

27 Hall and Lindzey, p.329.

28 *Ibid.*

29 Sassine, pp.180-181.

9

BEYOND DISILLUSIONMENT: THE CONCEPT OF CHANGE AND DEVELOPMENT IN THE NOVELS OF HENRI LOPÉS

Aloysius Ohaegbu

INTRODUCTION

Literature expresses life personally lived or shared with others in the society; this life may be good or bad for the writer and the society. The good writer is by nature a very attentive observer, a thinker and critic. He has a responsibility to himself and to the society whose interests he must defend. This is what the French existentialist writer, J.P. Sartre alludes to when he says:

> Puisque l'ecrivain n'a aucun moyen de s'évader,
> nous voulons qu'il embrasse étroitement son époque;
> elle est sa chance; elle s'est faite pour lui et il est fait
> pour elle[1]
>
> (Since the writer has no means of escape, we want
> him to embrace his time closely; it is his lot: it is
> made for him and he is made for it).

Events which affect the human condition in the society produce in the writer vibrations which push him to create or recreate the realities of life in that society and by so doing arouse the consciousness of his people to the realities of their existence. Because he cannot remain indifferent to the problems which run counter to individual and collective well-being, and because his dream world is humane, he denounces the ugly in the society,

169

castigates evil and pricks the consciences of those responsible for the contradictions in his society; he takes this posture to force change and development.

The Congolese novelist, poet and essayist, Henri Lopés is a good example of the African writer who has taken pains to articulate in his works the problems which have continued to plague post-independence Congo Brazzaville in particular, and Africa in general, problems which threaten the foundations of post-independence Africa, its development and that of man in it. He has published *Tribaliques*[2], a collection of eight short stories most of which raise issues of nation-building which are developed in his novels among which are *La Nouvelle Romance*[3], *Sans Tam-Tam*[4] and *Le Pleurer-Rire*[5]. The present study is based on these three novels.

The critical reception of Henri Lopés' works is favourable. Critics are unanimous in their views that he treats problems of contemporary Africa, that he expresses his "disillusionment" over post-independence Africa, his anguish over the "betrayal" of post-independence African leaders. Others call his works "militant". These critical opinions are correct; but they do not appear to me to go far enough because they tend to mistake the smoke for the fire, or the symptom for the disease.

In reality, beyond the expression of disillusionment over, and of indictment of post-independence Africa, which literary critics have too often celebrated, the concept of development is central in Henri Lopés' novels. It is this desire for development, which sustains his creative imagination and constitutes the essential unity and message of his works. For him, this development must come through a revolution propelled by the people's awareness of their condition and their resolve to move the society forward. By development, we mean change for the better. This change implies the economic advancement of the state, the advancement of science and technology needed for the production of the modern amenities considered vital to the promotion of the living standards of the people, the equitable distribution of available resources among the citizenry. We also mean the education of the people so that they can be useful to themselves and the society in which they live, moral upliftment and the abolition of certain traditional practices, which impede self-actualisation.

Whether it is in *La Nouvelle Romance, Sans Tam-Tam* or in *Le Pleurer-Rire*, the reader is fed with such words as "change", "evolution", "revolution", "progress" and "development" which bring to us images of physical, material and moral metamorphoses which characterise the novelist's concept of development. The feeling of betrayal, planlessness, wastage, abandonment, mediocrity and outright decay hangs over the fictional universe which Henri Lopés presents to the reading public; these are suggestive of the novelist's desire for a revolution which would usher in a new era – that of positive development of his people and the society.

The narrator in *Le Pleurer-Rire* laments that "since independence nothing has changed"; Wali, the heroine in *La Nouvelle Romance* calls independence "colonisation readjusted" where "a handful of the privileged" rely on ancient and outmoded customs and practices to exploit their people, especially women.

CULTURE AND MENTALITY

Culture is a distinctive aspect of people's identity; it also helps social integration and organisation. But it is dynamic and not static and that is why it has to adapt itself to the changing times. Blind attachment to culture in spite of the changing times and society pulls development back and forces people to live a primitive life out of tune with the modern world which is controlled by education, science and technology.

An attentive reading of the novels of Henri Lopés reveals that male chauvinism, ethnicism, excessive drinking and dancing, superstition and reluctance to work hard are some of the cultural traits which hamper the development of the individual and the society. These traits belong to traditional or ancient Africa and have to be reformed or completely abolished in order to make room for the emergence of modern Africa, for, as long as post-independence Africa valorises these habits, so long will social, cultural, political and economic progress remain a dream.

Traditional African culture tended to over-limit the rights of the woman in the society; her preoccupation was child-bearing, house-keeping, obeying every command of her husband without too much complaint, cooking and serving the entire family and visitors, farming. Gatse, the central character in *Sans Tam-Tam*, presents the travails of his mother in these terms:

> mère était toujours enceinte, partageant sa vie à
> s'occuper du dernier nourrisson, à recommencer
> chaque jour la cuisine et à cultiver le manioc dans
> les champs voisins.[6]

> (Mum was always pregnant, her life divided
> between taking care of the last baby, each time
> beginning kitchen work each day and cultivating
> cassava in the neighbouring farms).

In *La Nauvelle Romance*, Wali recalls with horror the sufferings of her own mother and other famished women in the farms, under the sun and the rain, tilling the ground, turning and re-turning it, while her father and the other men would be resting in the village square, drinking and discussing futilities. This is the image of ancient African society. Wali cannot understand this culture and this mentality which relegate women to the background and force them to do the hard labour in the fields, thus imposing on them the suffering which God meant for the males. Using the technique of irony, Wali expresses her unpleasant surprise over the victimisation of women by men:

> Peut-être qu'un Dieu en avait ainsi décidé. Pourtant
> c'est bien à Adam qu'il avait dit de gagner son pain la
> sueur de son front. Et voici que depuis des siècles,
> c'était Eve.[7]

> (Perhaps a God has decided it that way. However, it
> is Adam that he told to get his bread by his own
> sweat. And for centuries now it has been Eve).

At the end of the novel, Wali abandons her chauvinistic husband, leaves for Paris to acquire higher education and prepares her plans for a total social revolution which she hopes would sanitise the rapport between man and woman and correct the injustices of the past. This ending is very indicative of the revolutionary intent of Henri Lopés' work and points to the fact that the novelist is calling for the abolition of certain traditional practices and mentalities so that real development will take place in the post-independence society.

Also in *Le Pleurer-Rire*, we are told that Tonton, the president, dissolves his cabinet because he saw in a dream a plot that would overthrow him, and surrounds himself with men from his own ethnic origin - again an unprogressive mentality based on pure belief in superstition. In *Sans Tam-Tam*, Lopés makes a ridicule of his people's over-indulgence in drinking and dancing while the government spends so much money in hiring foreign experts to sustain the economy, and public functionaries "burn salaries which their real work does not merit". Tonton of *Le Pleurer-Rire* hires jets to attend the meeting of the Organisation of African Unity so that he can be recognised by his colleagues, while his people are dying of hunger, ignorance and disease. In *Sans Tam-Tam*, Gatsé tells his friend, a senior government official, and members of the ruling party that:

> Il ne faut pas prendre l'ascenseur dans les pays où
> l'on ne peut encore le réparer.[8]
>
> (There is no need to make use of the elevator in
> countries where nobody is yet capable of repairing it).

Henri Lopés is not only making a mockery of the illusion of grandeur of post-independence African leaders, but he is also condemning their mentality of mindless waste of tax-payers' money and at the same time making allusion to the need for scientific and technological development. But science and technology, in the modern sense, can only be acquired through schooling, through the development of the intellect. As long as post-independence African leaders neglect the education of the youths, so long will scientific development elude the African continent, and the road to modernisation closed.

Cheikh Hamidou Kane has rightly observed in his *L'Aventure ambiguë* [9] (Ambiguous Adventure) that if Western European countries conquered and colonised Africa, it was because of the superiority of their technology over that of Africa. Thanks to the towering personality of the Grande Royale, the Diallobe saw the need to relax their over-attachment to ancestral culture and wisely decided to send the young Samba Diallo to the whiteman's school to learn how to "tie wood to wood" and "how to conquer without being right".

INTELLECTUAL DEVELOPMENT

Nature has endowed man with a reasoning faculty. The great philosophers, Protagoras and Plato, have rightly affirmed that "man is the measure of all things". This means that all created things here on earth are for him to domesticate, that he is superior to all of them and that they can only have meaning in relation to him. The intellect, which is the distinctive attribute of man, is at the elementary condition and has to be developed through the process of education, if man must really rise above all things. Consequently, the level of development of the human society depends on the level of development of men who live in it and rule over it.

Henri Lopés is an educated writer who values education and appreciates its importance in the development of man and the society. Already in his *Tribaliques* (a collection of eight short stories which express, in a humorous style, the failures of the first ten years of post-independence Congo Brazzaville and Africa), the novelist highlights the importance of education in the development of the human personality. The admirable Mba is given to us as an example of the new generation girls which Henri Lopés wants to see in Africa. While other girls would waste their time thinking of trifles, of dance-parties, of costly dresses and other luxuries, Mba applies herself seriously to her studies in school. She ends up as a huge success, an intellectually emancipated lady, who takes up the task of giving education to the adult female illiterates of her community. This is to arm them for the fight against male chauvinism in the society and to contribute positively to the development of the society in which they live.

In his first novel, *La Nouvelle Romance*, the personage of Mba is recreated in Wali, the central character. Here we are told that Wali is one of the rare Congolese girls to reach the fifth year of their secondary school education, that her parents and social practice force her to disrupt her education and get married to Bienvenu N'kama – an intellectually weak young man, but a good footballer. Although Bienvenu N'kama belongs to the young generation of post-independence Congolese, he does not value education for women and refuses to accept the saying that to educate women is to educate a nation. His opinion on marriage and education of women is, in the eyes of modernists, as disappointing as it is unprogressive:

> Je veux une femme à moi, qui m'appartienne entièrement et qui reste à la maison pour s'en occuper, me préparer à manger et accueillir mes amis, comme je le désire, à toute heure de la journée.[10]

> (I want a wife who belongs to me entirely, who stays in the house to take care of it, prepare my food and receive my friends as I want, at every hour of the day).

He also believes that:

> Les femmes n'ont pas besoin d'aller trop longtemps à l'école, ça leur ôte leur féminité."

> (Women do not need to go to school for too long a time, it removes their womanhood from them).

There is no wonder then that once married to Wali, Beinvenu N'kama would treat his wife as a slave who should have no identity of her own and who must no longer aspire to have more education. He beats her up when he chooses, especially when he comes back from his numerous escapades with other women, drunk and possessive. Neither Wali's parents, nor even the entire society would help the young wife out of her sufferings; they would rather tell her to resign herself to it as the lot of women in the society.

However, Wali's opportunity to appreciate the need for further education as a means of declaring her liberty and asserting the rights of women in the African society comes when she gets in contact with women in Belgium and sees that they have all the rights which her own society has made the exclusive preserve of men. While in Belgium where her husband is serving as a member of his country's diplomatic mission, in spite of the fact that he is not qualified for the job, Wali rekindles her desire for further education and makes friends with the Impanis family, to mitigate her sufferings. She now begins to make plans to leave her brutal and unfaithful husband who is recalled from Belgium because of his involvement in a sex scandal and a drug affair.

Wali refuses to go back to Congo with Bienvenu N'kama; rather she leaves for Paris, thanks to her old friend, Awa who lives in Paris. In France, Wali takes up a job as housemaid and attends evening lectures until she has her "Baccalaureate" certificate. Wali's story ends with her letter to Elise in Brazzaville, telling her that she (Wali) would come home to start a revolution which would "transform her society" and make it develop by accepting modern values, where the education of the entire citizenry is a necessary prerequisite for progress.

In *Sans Tam-Tam*, Henri Lopès pursues the concept of development which must come through massive education. But, whereas in *La Nouvelle Romance* the accent is on the education of women, here the novelist's purview is on the side of the rural populace which he believes is disadvantaged. Gatsé, the central character and narrator, lends weight and credibility to his story when he says:

> Je parle de l'expérience d'un obscur Congolais,
> enseignant de la brousse, et je pense à la vie
> publique, à l'Afrique.[12]

> (I am talking from the experience of humble Congo-
> lese, a teacher in the bush, and I am thinking of
> public life, of Africa).

Gatsé, a teacher by profession and a one-time top government functionary is offered the prestigious and highly financially rewarding post of Cultural Attaché in his country's embassy in Paris. But since his rather punitive posting as a teacher in the bush, he has come to love the countryside and to appreciate its problems. He decides not to accept the offer of diplomatic appointment in Paris because he now believes that his best contribution to his people is the education of the youths in the rural areas of his country, youths who will be mobilised to hasten social development and guarantee a prosperous future for all in the society - town dwellers and rural communities. At one time Gatsé strongly affirms that intellectual development is the surest weapon in building the future and that the classroom is the teacher's forge for revolutionary activities:

> C'est là que je peux faire l'investissement le plus sur pour une révolution future.[13]

> (It is there [the classroom] that I can make the surest investment for future revolution).

At yet another time, he is afraid that the reading public would accuse him of idealism and admits that he has an unshakable trust in education as a most effective means of cultivating the human being and, by so doing, promoting the development of the society:

> Je fais trop confiance à l'éducation pour transformer les hommes.[14]

> (I have too much confidence in education for transforming men).

One should see in Gatsé the *alter ego* of Henri Lopés, the revolutionary who uses the epistolary technique to stress the importance of education, of intellectual power as the right of every citizen, rich or poor, male or female, young or old, and as an indispensable tool in the necessary task of conquering ignorance, misery, raising political awareness and morality, cultivating the right attitudes and values which will make for positive development of modern African states, and bring happiness to everyone in the developed society.

Although Henri Lopés tells us that knowledge opens the door to development and happiness, he also warns that knowledge is a potential power which can be useless unless it is used to further the cause of humanity. That is why he handles with love and admiration such characters as Gatsé of *Sans Tam-Tam*, Maître Epayo and Mobata of *Tribaliques*, Wali of *La Nouvelle Romance* and Captain Yabaka of *Le Pleurer-Rire*. They work for constructive change and positive development of the society. They can be grouped among those who, according to Antonio Gransci's categorisation of intellectuals, identify themselves with the objectives, aspirations and ideals of the new generation and with the oppressed social and ethnic group.[15] On the other hand, the novelist treats with disdainful irony and outright satire those other intellectuals who misapply their knowledge and their education for purely selfish reasons and thus obstruct development; they are sycophants and opportunists who would always identify themselves with dictators and other oppressive forces in the society. Kalala of *Tribaliques,* Koussi – the corrupt college principal who would give young female students to politicians in exchange for political favours, Zikisso of *La Nouvelle romance*, and Aziz Sonika in *Le Pleurer-Rire* are typical of such intellectuals considered as treacherous by the oppressed masses and inimical to positive development of the society.

DEVELOPMENT OF BASIC AMENITIES

In all the works of Henri Lopés, the novelist's concept of development is people-oriented. When he expresses anguish and disappointment over the inability of post-independence African leaders to provide for their people the necessary basic structural and infrastructural amenities to enhance the living standards of the masses, one should see beyond mere criticism and expression of disappointment and capture the writer's call for development, which constitutes the intrinsic value of the expression of disillusionment.

Henri Lopés does not consider as real development that which is limited to town dwellers and whose construction can only be effected by foreign nationals and experts, as is seen in *Le Pleurer-Rire* and *Sans Tam-Tam*. He decries the developmental gap between the urban areas of his country and the rural communities. In fact, much of *Sans Tam-Tam* is devoted to the comparison between the structural and infrastructural development of post-independence urban and rural communities. He is unhappy that rural life in post-independence Congo has not really changed much from what it was during the colonial period. This phenomenon is indeed not restricted to Congo which is the novelist's immediate fictional landscape; it is the common feature of all Africa. A very recent write-up by a columnist in *Nigeria Patriot* validates our observation. It says, among other things:

> It is evident today, the rural communities have been cut off from the urban areas because their roads have become impassable. Most, if not all our communities, are smarting from their rustic eerie darkness. The people of our hinterland are hungry for development, and desirous of the opening up of their villages to beat back the forays of want, deprivation, poverty, primitivity, superstition. Generally, they long for better living conditions and the benefit of science and technology.[16]

Nothing can summarise better Henri Lopés' concept of development in *Sans Tam-Tam* than this statement of a concerned Nigerian intellectual who may not have read Lopés' *Sans Tam-Tam*, but whose independent observation of rural neglect in his own country is identical to those of Henri Lopés. A country cannot call itself developed if its rural populations are living in abject poverty, squalor and ignorance, especially if they are cut off from the benefits of modern science and technology. This primitive neglect of rural development is what Henri Lopés is revolting against in his novel; it is what explains his devastating irony and sarcasm against post-independence leaders in *Sans Tam-Tam* and against Tonton Hannibal-Ideloy Bwakamabé Na Sakkadé in *Le Pleurer-Rire*.

Although the problem of development, seen from the perspective of the rural communities, runs through all the works of Henri Lopés, it is indeed in *Sans Tam-Tam* that the novelist gives it a disturbing dramatisation. Here, the few available schools are left to rot: no equipment, teachers are not provided liveable accommodation, books are hardly ever seen in the bookshops; potable water is non-existent and people have to manage with either rain-water or water collected from dirty streams, and this adversely affects health. There is no rural electrification and as a result life at nightfall is drab; Gatsé even tells us that absence of light in the night prevents him from doing any useful intellectual work. We cannot help sympathising with him when he tells us, rather comically:

> Je suis. avec la pratique. devenu expert à me raser
> sans lumière. au juge. en me coupant un peu.[17]

> (With practice, I have become an expert in shaving
> without light and, of course. cutting myself a little).

Gatsé is also asking for change and development when, in a flashback, he calls to memory the health hazards and afflictions, which he had to endure during his childhood. Images of such unhealthy conditions are recalled by such words as "jiggers" "anophcles", "scabies", "fungoid growths", "lice", "tapeworms", "measles", "chicken-pox", "whooping-cough", "mumps".[18] If such afflictions still exist in his post-independence Congo, then there is no progress, and a revolution which goes beyond revolutionary slogans thrown about by leaders and their praise-singers must be embarked upon to usher in the real development of man and society.

Also in *Sans Tam-Tam*, the novelist deplores the absence of telephone services in the rural areas of his community, the snail-speed with which letters posted in rural communities travel to the urban areas, the death-traps called roads which make communication between town and village very difficult; he equally raises, albeit indirectly, the problem of rural industries which could stem rural migration to towns and mitigate acute unemployment. His concept of development is thus built on sound socio-economic adjustment programmes which would take balanced care of the living conditions of every community, whether such community is urban or rural; for both city-dwellers and village dwellers, the novelist wants to see built such amenities which are characteristic of developed countries of the world, particularly European countries – tarred roads, grocery shops, doctors, post offices, drinking water and cement houses.

POLITICAL MORALITY

The theme of political morality in post-independence Africa is not new in African literature. Such novelists as Chinua Achebe, Ayi Kwei Armah, Ahmadou Kourouma, Alioum Fantouré, Mongo Beti and Camara Laye of *Dramouss*, have raised it in their works. However, what appears to have dominated Francophone African perspective is the violent nature of politics associated with the one-party system of government. This is so because a good number of Francophone African countries adopted the one-party system (parti unique) after independence perhaps to give the impression that government belongs to the people, and perhaps also as a mark of rebellion against France, the former colonial master. But events have shown that abuse of the system has led to the dictatorship of the party and its president, and generated the feeling that independence is a new form of colonisation by a handful of African elites.

Maître, a principal character in Henri Lopés's *Le Pleurer-Rire*, presents post-independence politics as follows:

> D'abord, la politique depuis l'indépendance, je n'y comprends rien. Un marais rempli de crocodiles et dans lequel aucun de ceux qui s'y aventuraient ne pouvait rester honnête.[19]

> (First of all, politics since independence. I don't understand it. A swamp filled with crocodiles and in which none of those who ventured in it could remain honest.)

If post-independence politics is comparable to a swamp filled with crocodiles, and if no one who gets into it can be honest, then it is dangerous and needs to be reformed. If Gatsé in *Sans Tam-Tam* refuses the diplomatic post proposed to him and prefers to be a school teacher in a rural area, it is because he is aware of the fact that post-independence politics is dangerous, exploitative and misdirected. For him, and for Lopés, there is need for a revolution which can only come through education and re-education of the people, who must be mobilised to create the right political awareness and system to move the country forward.

In *La Nouvelle Romance* and *Le Pleurer-Rire,* Henri Lopés comes down heavily against the prevailing political morality in his country and in Africa in general. Bienvenu, the principal character in *La Nouvelle Romance* has little or no education, yet he succeeds in getting appointment as cultural attache in his country's embassy in Belgium and in Washington, even when he is known to be involved in sex scandals and drug traffic. When Olga expresses her surprise that Bienvenu N'kama could get a political appointment as a diplomat, the latter replies:

> Ouais, mais ça c'est la politique africaine ... pour la faire y a pas besoin de connaître ce qui se passe dans le reste du monde ....[20]

> (Ah! but that is African politics .... To do it one doesn't need to know what is happening in the rest of the world).

In *Sans Tam-Tam,* Gatsé also laughs at post-independence African politics when he rightly observes that his country needs to "cultivate the virtues of modesty and lucidity" and move away from the disquietening era where typists ask to be made ambassadors and ward-maids to be made directors of cardiology departments of hospitals.[21] If Bienvenu N'kama, a man of mediocre intelligence and moral ineptitude, can occupy a high national position, it is because he comes from the same ethnic group as the president; Tonton in *Le Pleurer-Rire* surrounds himself with people of his own ethnic group, makes his brother-in-law minister of agriculture, and reshuffles his cabinet four times so as to eliminate all those he sees as potential rivals. Henri Lopés makes a mockery of these practices and sees them as the wrong political morality, which impedes development. His concept of development is that which is devoid of incessant coups and countercoups prevalent in *Le Pleurer-Rire,* that which respects fundamental human rights, that which is democratic, participatory and where appointments to public offices are based on merit. For the novelist, that is the only guarantee for progress and development of the society.

CONCLUSION

We have argued all along that Henri Lopés is a good African novelist. He draws his inspiration from his immediate environment, which is his country - Congo Brazzaville, but the social contradictions raised in his works can be applied to all post-independence Africa whose progress is badly slowed down, if not fatally impaired by bad leadership. The new African human condition, which is unenviable, is a result of insensitivity, planlessness, violence, coups and countercoups and dictatorships, forced on the society by the ruling elites. The novels of Henri Lopés are replete with this dysfunctional structure of post-independence Africa and the novelist himself forces his time and his people to challenge this order that has been badly established.

Critics have been quick to point out that Henri Lopés expresses anger and disillusionment over the fact that post-independence Congo in particular, and Africa in general have disappointed the expectations of the people at independence. Others see the novelist as a committed writer, "écrivain engagé", who uses his works to fight against social ills. All these critical assessments are correct, but they do not go too far in the sense that the fight itself is given more importance than the goal, which the novelist wants to attain by engaging in the fight. For me, the end which is more important and which in fact dictates the means to be used has been sidelined by critics and, should be more emphasised. I have tried, through a sort of pilgrimage into the novels of Henri Lopés, to show that when the novelist uses irony, satire and sarcasm in casting a critical gaze on post-independence African society, his expression of disillusionment is not the goal he wants to achieve. What is top in his mind, what fuels his creative imagination is the desire for change-for-better-development. A re-reading of all his works cannot fail to reveal to literary critics that development is the quintessential message of Henri Lopés. This development in all its positive and progressive connotations must seek to transform the African and his post-independence society.

Notes

1. J. P. Sartre. *Situation II*. Paris: Gallimard, 1948, p.12.

2. Henri Lopés. *Tribaliques*. Yaounde: Cle, 1971.

3. ———— *La Nouvelle Romance*. Yaounde: Cle, 1976.

4. ———— *Sans Tam-Tam*. Yaounde: Cle, 1977.

5. ———— *Le Pleurer-Rire*. Paris: Présence Africaine, 1982

6. ———— *Sans Tam-Tam*, p.24.

7. ———— *La Nouvelle Romance*, p.15.

8. ———— *Sans Tam-Tam*, p.10.

9. Cheikh Hamidou Kane, *L'Aventure ambigue*. Paris; Julliard, 1961.

10. Henri Lopés. *La Nouvelle Romance*, p.16.

11. *Ibid.* p.16.

12. Henri Lopés. *Sans Tam-Tam*, p.51.

13. *Op. cit;* p.61.

14. I*bid. p.*79.

15. Cf. *Presence Africaine*, No. 143, 1987, p.114.

16. Okey, D. Ebele U. "Reversing the retardation in Ebonyi State", *Nigerian Patriot*, Wednesday 22 - Tuesday 28, 1998: p.14.

17. Henri Lopes. *Sans Tam-Tam*, p.55.

18. *Ibid.* p.29.

19. Henri Lopés. *Le Pleurer-Rire*, p.30.

20. ———— *La Nouvelle Romance*, p.126.

21. ———— *Sans Tam-Tam*, p.74.

10

THE ANTI-HERO IN SONY LABOU TANSI'S NOVELS

Mattiu Nnoruka

We come to the world to
sow: woe betide him who
sows his ruin or his dishonour.[1]

Sony Labou Tansi

INTRODUCTION

Born to Congolese parents at Kimwanza on June 5, 1947, Sony Labou Tansi died prematurely in Brazzaville on June 14, 1995 after a protracted illness. He was 48. Founder-Director of a theatre troupe, Rocado Zulu, Sony Labou Tansi was not only a playwright, poet and novelist, he was also a politician. His Rocado Zulu afforded him an ample opportunity to tour the world in order to sensitise, through his plays, public opinion on social injustices, repressions and other ills prevailing in his native Congo and elsewhere in Africa. His political party (MCDDI), on the other hand, earned him a seat in the Congolese National Assembly where, unfortunately, he naively believed that pressing political and national issues would be discussed and settled once and for all.[2]

At his death, the Congolese author left behind a considerable number of literary works of various genres: novels, poems, plays, and so on.[3] On these productions, critics are unanimous in their verdict: Sony Labou Tansi distances himself from older writers by inaugurating a new dimension in African literature written in French. By this new development his works constitute a landmark in that literature. He himself gives an insight to his stance when he warns in one of his novels that "the world is no longer round, never will it be any longer"[4]. His peculiar use of the French language, almost comparable to that of Ahmadou Kourouma, is well known and has been studied by certain critics.[5] However, if his subversion of the French language with a view to giving his narration a local colour, is one of the characteristics of the new African novel written in French as evidenced in his works, another salient feature and by far the most important in his novels is what Daniel-Henri Pageaux (1985) calls "the revision of the notion of character"[6] and which we name, for the purposes of this write-up " the anti-hero" in Sony Labou Tansi's novels.

Our chosen topic will be limited to the author's first three novels out of the six already mentioned, namely: *La vie et demie, L'Etat honteux* and *L'Anté-peuple*. The last three do not necessarily tally with the objective of our study. *Le commencement de la douleur*, announced shortly after the author's demise, is yet to be published. *Les yeux du volcan*, inundated with incongruous and episodic actors has, meanwhile, an abstract or silent observer as the main character. This unseen personality could be mother Africa, the world in general or the masses who are watching and waiting for an imaginary revolution.[7] *Les Sept Solitudes de Lorsa Lopez* features a chief character of different category, therefore it is not applicable to our study.

Having thus far situated our work, we add that the whole exercise will consist of three major sections sub-headed as follows: hero/anti-hero: definition and features; Sony Labou Tansi's anti-heroes: analysis, and an overview of the ideological relevance of the author's art of characterisation and the conclusion.

HERO/ANTI-HERO: DEFINITION AND FEATURES

Derived from the Greek word "heros", the term "hero" designates in Greco-Latin mythology a demi-god, a person with supernatural powers. Later and up to date, the term became synonymous with the principal figure around whom the story is built in a work of fiction. For example, there is Ulysses in *Odyssey* by Homer or Aenas in *Aeneid* by Virgil, the Greek and Roman authors respectively. These individuals are characterised by their extraordinary bravery or courage, their quest for honour and their determination, in spite of all odds, to concretise the aspirations of their people whose fate is necessarily considered to be in their hands as leaders.

In his analysis of Georges Lukacs' *La théorie du roman*, [8] Lucien Goldmann (1963), who observes a correspondence between the evolution of the novel and the history of bourgeois society in Europe, brings out three fundamental types of novels with three different principal characters as heroes:

> Novel of abstract idealism with demoniacal or problematic hero imbued with very narrow conscience in front of a complex world; psychological novel with a passive hero whose soul is too broad to fit into the world; educative novel with a hero whose conscious renouncement to the world is neither resignation nor desperation.[9]

In a similar line of action, Sunday Anozie (1970), examining the novels of West African authors[10], underlines three types of heroes: a hero of "traditional determination" characterised by his allegiance or fidelity to tradition[11]; a hero of "intro-active determination", otherwise known as a problematic individual[12] and a hero of extro-active determination who is detribalised, as well as a champion of socio-political justice with the traits of ideological messianism.[13]

Unfortunately, neither the heroes studied by Georges Lukacs nor those of Sunday Anozie could fit into our focus. Reflecting two given social and political periods (the bourgeois society on one hand and the colonial and corrupt post-independence Africa on the other hand), these principal characters are subjected to the whims and caprices of the powers that be which, meanwhile, they combat with little or no success. The socio-political context in which Sony Labou Tansi situates the principal figures of his novels is indeed that of post-independence Africa and precisely that period characterised by military intervention in governance and comedy of power tussle among top military officers. As we shall see, the Congolese novelist has no sympathy for the men in the khaki uniform. Those of them who figure as chief characters in his works of fiction are not traditional heroes but anti-heroes. They are the opposite of what the novelist designate as Chief:

> the chief is not he who commands, it is not even he who is right. The chief is he who invents others' generosity; in the same way he takes part in the crucial matters of his time. The Chief is he who teaches and practices self sacrifice.[14]

The dictionary definition of anti-hero goes further. The *Chambers Dictionary* sees him as a "principal character who lacks noble qualities and whose experiences are without tragic dignity".[15]

SONY LABOU TANSI'S ANTI-HEROES

Military intrusion into politics has provided Sony Labou Tansi with a strategic element of characterisation promoting the thematic and aesthetic components of plot structures. The novelist is not a stranger in military circles where he was once used and then dumped.[16] He is, therefore, an insider and the first striking feature associated with the portrait of his principal characters is certainly the absence of a worthy curriculum vitae or civil status. Many of them are of doubtful origin and of dubious character.

The Providential Guide, the main character in the author's first novel, *La Vie et demie,* is not only a criminal but also an impersonator; he is an ex-livestock robber. To escape police arrest, he changes his name from Cypriano Ramoussa to Obramoussando Mbi before fleeing to the northern part of the country where he joins the army and quickly makes his way to the top. From Obramoussando, he alters his name once again to Loanga and then Yambo and becomes the founder and the First Secretary of the only political party in power. Through an unspecified constitutional intrigue, he rises to the position of president, then life president of the party, a feat that confers on him the official and resounding title of The Providential Guide Marc-François Matéla-Péné or Providential Guide for short; he is later crowned His Majesty Cézama the First. This is the man who initiated a dynasty of military dictators, alias Guides, who rule, for several generations, a new independent, fictitious African country called Katamalanasie located in the continent's equatorial region. His sole qualification is his ability to hold and manipulate the gun.

The Providential Guide's civilian successors are no better. Guide Henri-au Coeur-Tendre, Guide Jean Oscar-Coeur-de-Père, Guide Jean-sans Coeur, Empératrice Victoriana-au-Coeur sacré, and so on, all have emerged from nowhere to assume power through coups, contercoups and assassinations. Patara, alias Guide Jean-Coeur-de-Pierre of incestuous origin, in spite of his so-called military and religious education, is better remembered for rewriting the history of Katamalanasie. Indeed, he not only changes his country's name to Kawangotara but proceeds also to procreate about a thousand kids - all male - following his much publicised and simultaneous marriages with fifty virgins. These are the virgins who are selected from the most beautiful in the country and with whom, for forty years, he makes love during a televised programme titled, "The Week of the Virgins or The Guide and production."[1][7]

Other Guides emanating from these unprecedented marriages are to push further their father's work of disfiguring the country through a secession bid, through balkanisation and fractricidal wars resulting in the total elimination of principal actors. This is followed by the complete destruction of the capital cities of the two countries which is compared, in the text, to the destruction of the biblical Sodom and Gomorrah.

The curriculum vitae of the military dictator, Col. Martillimi Lopez, the principal character in the author's second novel, *L'Etat honteux*, is completely nil. Lopez is of peasant origin, living secluded, at his age, with his mother to whom he later gives the official title of Maman Nationale while he arrogates to himself the title of the Father of the Nation. Until his installation as Head of State, Lopez has never been to Oufa, the capital seat of government and the circumstances leading to his military take-over are not clear. At times, he affirms that he ousted his predecessor for reasons bordering on mismanagement, embezzlement and unnecessary government spending. At other times, he says he was elected with 99.9 per cent of votes during an undisclosed election. These are his antecedents.

Unlike the other principal characters of the first two novels who are military by profession, the central figure, Nitu Dadou, alias Mr Director in *L'Anté-peuple*, is a "bloody" civilian of humble origin; his parents are peasants. A promising young man, a talented footballer and a national hero in that sport, Dadou is also an intellectual, a graduate of Lovanium University. Considered as apparently virtuous and honest in a country where nothing goes for nothing, he is appointed to the enviable position of the Deputy Provost of the Girls' College of Education at Lemba-Nord near Kinshasa. But as Mariama Bâ (1979) once said, "Blood carries with it the virtues and humble birth always shows in a person's behaviour".[18] This is particularly true of Dadou as we shall see later.

From the study of the curriculum vitae of the principal characters, let us examine briefly the significance of the official titles with which Sony Labou Tansi "decorates" his chief actors.

In his article, "Le roman africain dans tous ses états", Jacques Chevrier (1985) lists these titles as they appear in contemporary Francophone African literature. If the critic refers to them as "symbols of power, new ogre whose incarnations assume very often the aspect of blood-thirsty buffoons",[19] we, on our part, see them as portraying the urgent desires of their carriers to mask their veritable identities and to psychologically boost their ego or prestige before their powerless and subdued compatriots whose existence is no better than that of zombies. But some intransigent members of the opposition are not dupe. Jean Canon, one of the rebel sons of Guide Jean-Coeur-de-Pierre (*La Vie et demie*), tells his supporters that a good leader does not need titles. One of his brothers, Jean Coriance, rejecting the title of Father of the Nation, warns that "nation-building is the responsibility of all and not the illusions of two or three individuals".[20]

But beyond the scramble for official titles, the Congolese novelist draws his readers' attention to a fundamental malaise peculiar to his principal characters, a kind of mental disorder, which depicts them as clowns and more importantly as anti-heroes. While some are temporarily mad, others are clinically out of their senses.

The Providential Guide (*La Vie et demie*) is certainly not normal when he rushes out of the town hotel naked after his failed sex affair with Chaidana, shouting for help, "not out of fear, says the narrator, but out of near madness".[21] Colonel Martillimi Lopez (*L'Etat honteux*) embarrasses his entourage and his hosts alike in the streets of Paris during one of his pleasure trips when he decides to walk from his hotel to the airport. At the airport itself, he breaks all diplomatic protocol before the journalists waiting to interview him. To crown it all, he pushes aside his official pilot, prefering to fly the plane himself.

Nitu Dadou *(L'Anté-peuple),* described as a human wreck and idiot, after his fall from grace, resorts to drinking and ends up assassinating, in his state of madness, the First Secretary of the anti-masses government, Mr. Martin Nzoma Mouyabas. Commenting on his own act, Dadou believes that he has become mad for good.

Among the chief characters found clinically to be insane are Guide Genri-au-Coeur-Tendre and Guide Jean-Oscar-Coeur-de-Père *(La Vie et demie).* The first is discovered naked (by his guards) and speaking in a strange language. He is then rushed to a psychiatric hospital where he is finally assassinated. The second is responsible for his own death. "Burn me alive",[22] he orders, but when no killer shows up, he commits suicide by burning himself at the stake, clad in red, a colour which, according to onlookers, "is that of the madmen".[23] His last words are revealing: "Dear brothers and sisters, I am dying in order to save you from me. Therein (he beats his chest) yes, therein, I have noticed, it is no longer completely human".[24]

"No longer completely human" is a confessional statement which is also applicable to almost all Sony Labou Tansi's major characters and which informs the author's principal literary themes such as: arbitrariness in decision-making processes, real or imaginary coup plotting, arbitrary arrest and detention, repression, torture, summary execution, cannibalism, horror, sadism, sexmania, waste of public funds, among others.

The Providential Guide *(La vie et demie)* butchers to death Marbian Abendoti, alias Martial, a pro-democracy activist and pastor of a local church, and orders that his corpse be reduced to pudding for lunch. Members of Martial's family (except Chaidana), Dr. Tchitchialia, Kassar Pueblo, the Guide's personal medicine-man, all have their lives cut short by the Providential Guide himself with his famous table knife and fork. The Guide's sadism and repression against members of the opposition reach a climax with the burning down of a town hotel belonging to one Mr Bilancourt. Hundreds of innocent citizens pay the price of the Providential Guide's insanity. The reigns of his successors are equally repressive. Under Guide Henri-au-Coeur-Tendre and Guide Jean-Oscar-Coeur-de Père, people are forbidden to pronounce certain words or to use or wear certain colours. Defaulters are either shot at sight or forced to chew and swallow such documents, books and clothes of theirs containing the offending words or bearing the wrong colours. Guide Jean-Oscar-Coeur-de-Père, in particular, would have the initials J.C.P. marked on the foreheads of his subjects.

Under Colonel Martillimi Lopez (*L'Etat honteux*) "human life is worth nothing",[25] according to the narrator and it is the Colonel's sadism which retains our attention. When Lopez does not spit on the faces of his interlocutors, when he does not slap them or have them caned for one flimsy reason or the other, he orders their summary execution or he resorts to what the narrator calls slow death by sectioning the genital organs of the detainees.[26] His secret agents, taking a cue from him, are on the rampage. An unnamed coup plotter from the Rhaz tribe, has his testicles crushed during his interrogation, among many others.

There are other factors militating against Sony Labou Tansi's principal characters as heroes and which earn them, consequently, the term of anti-heroes. In his study of one of the novels of a French writer and philosopher, Jean-Paul Sartre, Baa Mensa (1998) remarks that "(the) Sartrian hero can only deserve this title if he transcends his individualistic morals, his personal salvation in order to attain group moral and collective salvation".[27] The observation applies also to Sony Labou Tansi's heroes most of whom, if not all, are prisoners of their quest for individualistic values and personal aggrandisement. When they are not leading a presidential lifestyle, summed up by the narrator in three Vs and one F - Villas, Voitures, Vins, Femmes[28] - (villas, limousines, wine, women), they are engaged in unnecessary waste of public funds and building of prestigious projects. Colonel Martillimi Lopez's pleasure trips to Europe, the preparations for his aborted marriage, the window dressing of his capital city during the Papal visit, the construction of his personal grave and a cathedral at his birth place have all impoverished the state treasury at the expense of beneficial projects to the masses. Lopez admits having castles and bank accounts in Europe like his predecessors during a press conference. He clearly sees nothing wrong in his act.

If Lopez and the Providential Guide (*La Vie et demie*) squander millions of the local money for propaganda purposes and for their personal security, the Guide's successors are remembered for their dream projects executed through rampant and reckless imposition of taxes, levies and forced labour. Under Guide Henri-au-Coeur-Tendre, who was assassinated following his madness, attempts are certainly made towards the integration of the Pygmies through projects spearheaded by a Minister of Pygmy origin, Sir Amanazavou. But the new strong man, Guide Jean Oscar-Coeur-de-Père, never hesitates to remind his subjects that "a chief is made to be pleased by his people" and that "power flows from the barrel of the gun". To prove that, he undertakes the construction of control posts throughout his territory where people are regularly searched in order to unmask opposition members whose identity mark is a cross, tattooed on the right thigh. This exercise, according to the narrator, gulped 14 billion units of the local currency. Others include 92 billion for the construction of the Village of Immortals, 48 billion for the Palace of the Dead, 12 billion for the maternity where his son is born, 22 billion for writing, in letters of gold, the articles of his so-called constitution.[29] The list is endless; the reaction of pro-democracy activists is immediate and uncompromising. "Instead of solving the ugly problems of development," they lament, "the Guide is simply busy creating and structuring problems".[30] The protest never deters his successor, Guide Jean-Coeur-de-Pierre for whom, in his dream, blue colour is God's colour, from constructing a scientific laboratory where he spends lavishly in order to produce blue plants, blue rats in readiness for producing blue men and women. There is also his Mirror Palace with 3000 bedrooms built at the cost of four times the national budget. A part of the palace houses the famous fifty virgins.

Apart from the misappropriation of public funds, Sony Labou Tansi's heroes are surrounded by sycophants and praise-singers pretending to be their advisers. They are as blood thirsty and materialistic as their masters and are ready to hold to their enviable positions at all cost. Mr Rognong, a secondary character of European origin who organises torture sessions for imaginary coup plotters in order to rid the State of undesirable elements, sums up this observation in *L'Etat honteux*. "My masters want good result and in the police there is no good result without a good imagination, no good result if one is kind-hearted. Moreover, who does not like beautiful girls, good wine, good cars and good life."[31]

Nitu Dadou (*L'Anté-peuple*), the intellectual and member of the Zairian elite of post-independence Africa, is of a different calibre but shares a common denominator – that of the anti-hero – with other characters identified earlier. Dadou does not possess absolute power in his place of work; he has no access to the state coffers and, therefore, is unable to engage himself in the wasteful spending of state funds. However, he takes special delight in his official title, Mr Director, as already pointed out and always insists on being addressed as such by his interlocutors.

Ironically, the two occasions during which the reader sees Dadou in his establishment are revealing. In one of such occasions, a Reverend Father-teacher complains to Dadou of having been openly insulted while performing his duty by one of the students. Dadou as a Director has three options in cases like this, according to the narrator. These are suspension, withdrawal of bursary award and the demand of a public apology. Rather than take some of these options, he procrastinates and ends up eventually by opting for none of the choices. The second occasion sees Dadou in his boss's office being asked to show cause why he should not be thrown out of the establishment:

> You smell alcohol from head to toe, observes the Director General, and your college is paying the price of your laisser-aller. Absenteeism, indiscipline and debauchery have become the order of the day. There is need for a Deputy-Provost of Girls' College of Education to behave like a man: in any case, if you do not change, if you do not remedy the situation, I shall be forced to terminate your appointment.[32]

Dadou welcomes the ultimatum with an inexplicable smile which embarrasses and infuriates his interlocutor, a smile symbolising, in the final analysis, Dadou's indifference to the crucial issues, expressed often in his eternal and rhetorical question, "what does it matter?" It is not surprising, therefore, when critics[33] liken Dadou's nonchalant and lackadaisical attitude to that of Meursault, the principal character in Albert Camus' *L'Etranger*. Incarnations of absurdity, the two heroes are hostages of their individualistic values in a society which requires absolute conformism to its norms. "You behave as if you were from the planet moon",[34] Yaealdara tells Dadou. There, however, ends the comparison between the heroes of the two writers. There is more, however, to Labou Tansi's portrait of Dadou.

Introduced initially as a purist, Dadou, who condemns everything around him – the system, his compatriots, men and women denounced as rotten (moche) or rottenness (mocherie) itself – in his vertiginous fall, is more rotten than all others. He is nicknamed Mr "Moche" not because of his frequent use of the term but because he deserves the description. In his interview with Bernard Magnier, Sony Labou Tansi reminds his readers that "the rotten man (i.e Moche) is he who abandons his position as a man."[35]

Nitu Dadou is an embodiment of failure; his records as a father and husband are not commendable. In fact, he is responsible for his wife's suicide and the death of his two children whom he calls "devils". His sense of friendship leaves much to be desired. He is undecided most of the time and vacillates when confronted with vital matters. He is incapable of love and is answerable for Yavelde's suicide. He certainly loves Yavelde but refused to openly admit the fact, preferring rather to drown the thought in alcohol. His membership of the revolutionary squad is purely accidental but he ends up by participating in an act he has hitherto hated – bloodshed – and his remorse for the deed throws more light on his wavering and unstable nature.

Sony Labou Tansi's main characters lack generally the much-desired "noble qualities" associated with heroes; their portraits are uninspiring and their adventures are short of "tragic dignity". Having said that, let us examine, in our conclusion, the ideological implication of such an artistic characterisation.

CONCLUSION

A literary work is first and foremost fiction. Nevertheless, the writer does not create in a vacuum. He is rather inspired, very often by the happenings around him. These he appreciates at times objectively and at other times subjectively. The novel remains a privileged medium in this exercise because it is considered, among other literary genres, as a mirror of the society.

African history, before and after independence, is replete with untold hardships and man's inhumanity to man. Since the mid-sixties, the continent has groaned under an unprecedented weight of military dictatorship. Sony Labou Tansi is not indifferent to the new development. His chosen texts are, without doubt, satirical paintings of post-independence Africa under military rule. For the Congolese author, Africa is still trapped, after jumping out of the frying pan into fire.

The novelist is surely silent over the exact names of the countries involved in his works. But the historic names of certain Heads of States caricatured and portrayed as anti-heroes are evident: Idi Amin Dada of Uganda, late Mobutu Sese Seko of former Zaire, late Jean Bedel Bokassa of Central African Republic, among others. All of them took over power through the barrel of the gun and under the official titles we have enumerated and with the consequences already underlined. Between the Providential Guide, alias, His Majesty Cézama the First (*La Vie et demie*) and Jean Bedel Bokassa, alias, His Majesty Bokassa the First, in particular, there are correspondences. A close look shows a striking identity in their biographies: a humble birth, a modest beginning in the army, a phenomenal rise to the top, a coup d'état, the establishment of the one-party system, the rush for official titles. They are also accused of sexmania and cannibalism.

Meanwhile, the personal grave and the Cathedral built by Colonel Martillimi Lopez (*L'Etat honteux*) at his place of birth reminds one of the famous Basilica constructed by the late President of Ivory Coast, Felix Houphouet Boigny, at Yamoussoukro, his native village. As for Nitu Dadou (*L'Anté-peuple*), he symbolises any intellectual of contemporary Africa who abdicates his official and private responsibilities.

Finally, the military opportunists, who, in turns, confiscate the mantle of power by force of arms are, in the eyes of the Congolese novelist, anti-heroes and anti-masses and the end products, which are economic inertia, underdevelopment and dehumanisation, are disastrous for the continent. Human rights and democracy are regarded as ideological slogans suitable only for developed countries. African countries that have gone through or are still under military dictatorship are many years behind, culturally, socially, economically and politically retarded. These are the legacies bequeathed to Africa by men in uniform whose profession is, in any case, to kill and not to save life.

Reading Sony Labou Tansi's novels means cruising through a complex tissue of contradictions and random elimination of human lives. The texts depict societies under perpetual siege, societies of unfulfilled promises and aspirations, a world in stagnation governed by apparently healthy and yet sick individuals who, under normal circumstances, would have been consigned to Freudian psychanalytic clinics. These human inadequacies are reflected in the structure of the novels. With the exception of *L'Anté-peuple* numbered i-xvii, the other two novels have no such indications in lieu of chapters. Particularly in *L'Etat honteux*, actions are not pursued to their logical conclusions and, as for narration, grammatical rules and regulations are thrown overboard. It is extremely difficult to identify the narrator who, here, "has lost his divine omniscience".[36]

Sony Labou Tansi once said that "he does not write French but in French".[37] This statement coming from him should not be taken at its face value. Like the biblical Paul, the Congolese writer is all things to all men. In almost all his works – novels, plays or poems – his military characters (whether principal or secondary) do not speak French but in French. The novelist, as we have seen, is undoubtedly anti-military and he demonstrates this hatred by creating military anti-heroes and their likes.

Notes

1. Sony Labou Tansi. *Les Sept Solitudes de Lorsa Lopez*. Paris: Seuil, 1985, p.3.

2. Matiu Nnoruka. "In Memoriam: Adieu Sony". *Présence Africaine*, No 153. 1996: p.259.

3. Literary works include:

Novels
La Vie et demie. Paris: Seuil, 1979
L'Etat honteux. *Ibid.*, 1981.
L'Anté-peuple. *Ibid.*, 1983.
Les Sept solitudes de Lorsa Lopez. *Ibid.*, 1985.
Les Yeux du volcan. *Ibid.*, 1985.
Le Commencement de la douleur (à paraître).

Plays
Conscience de tracteur. Dakar: NEA-Clé, 1979.
La Parenthèse de sang, suivi de *Je soussigné cardiaque*. Paris: Hatier, 1981.
Antoine m'a vendu son destin, Equateur, No.1, 1986.
Moi veuve de l'Empire, L'Avant-Scène Théâtre, No. 815, 1987.
Qui a mangé me d'Avoine Beghota? Promotion théâtre, 1980.

4. Sony Labou Tansi. *La Vie et demie*. *Op.cit.*, p.10.

5. See in particular Jacques Chevrier, Daniel-Henri Pageaux, Nicolas Marin-Granel. "Le roman africain dans tous ses états", "Entre le renouveau et la modernité", "Le crier-écrire" respectively. *Notre Librairie*1985: pp.31-56.

6 Daniel-Henri Pageaux. *Op.cit.*, p.33.

7 Sony Labou Tansi. *Les Yeux du volcan*. *Op.cit.* (back page, author's comments).

8. Georges Lukacs. *La Théorie du roman*. Paris: Gonthier, 1963.

9. Lucien Goldmann. "Introduction aux premiers écrits de Georges Lukacs" in *Théorie du roman*. Paris: Aubier-Montaigne, 1963.

10. Sunday Anozie. *Sociologie du roman Africain*. Paris: Aubier Montaigne, 1970.

11. *Idem* p.24 (our translation).

12. *Idem* p.41.

13. *Idem* p.57.

14. Sony Labou Tansi. *Les Yeux du volcan*. *Op.cit.*, p.179.

15. E.M. Kirkpatrick et al. *Chambers 20th Century Dictionary*. Suffolk: W.& W. Chambers, 1983, p.51.

16. Mattiu Nnoruka. "In memoriam, Adieu Sony". *Op.cit.*, p.259.

17. Sony Labou Tansi. *La Vie et demie*. *Op.cit.*, p.148.

18. Mariama Bâ. *Une si longue lettre*. Dakar: N.E.A., 1979, p.42.

19. Jacques Chevrier. "*Le roman africain dans tous ses états*". *Op.cit.*, p.38.

20. Sony Labou Tansi. *La Vie et demie*. *Op.cit.*, pp.175-176.

21. *Idem* p.63.

22. *Idem* p.140.

23. *Idem* p.141.

24 *Idem* p.142.

25 Sony Labou Tansi. *L'Etat honteux*. *Op.cit.*, p.117.

26 *Idem* p.151 & p.114.

27 Ba Mensa "*Les mains salles* de Jean-Paul Sartre: une étude thématique", *Ilorin Journal of Language and Literature*, No. 3, 1988: p.64.

28. Sony Labou Tansi. *La Vie et demie*. Op.cit., p.36.

29. *Idem* p.132.

30. *Idem*

31. Sony Labou Tansi. *L'Etat honteux*. *Op.cit.*, p.119.

32. Sony Labou Tansi. *L'Anté-peuple*. *Op.cit.*, p.45.

33. Jean-Norbert Vignonde. "Sony Labou Tansi: *L'Anté-peuple*". *Notre Librairie*, No.79, Avril-Juin, 1985: p.7.

34. Sony Labou Tansi. *L'Anté-peuple*. *Op.cit.*, p.69.

35. Bernard Magnier. "Je ne suis pas à développer mais à prendre ou à laisser: Entretien avec Sony Labou Tansi". *Notre Librairie*, No. 79, Avril-Juin, 1985: p.7.

36. Nicolas Martin-Granel. *Op.cit.*, p.52.

37. Michel Tetu. *La Francophonie, Histoire problématique et perspectives*. Paris: Hachette, 1988, p.297.

Bibliography

Anozie, Sunday: *Sociologie du roman Africain*. Paris: Aubier, 1970.

Bâ, Mariama. *Une si longue lettre*. Dakar: N.E.A., 1979.

Chevrier, Jacques. "Le roman africain dans tous ses états". *Notre Librairie*, No. 78, 1985.

Goldmann, Lucien. "Introductions aux premiers écrits de Georges Lukacs", *Théorie du roman*. Paris: Gonthier, 1963.

——————— *La Création culturelle dans la société moderne*. Paris: Denoel/Gonthier, 1971.

Granel, Martin Nicolas. "Le Crier-Ecrire", *Notre Librairie*, **No.** **78**, Paris, 1985.

Kiarkpatrick et al. *Chambers, 20th Century Dictionary*. Suffolk: W.& W. Chambers, 1983.

Lagarde, André & Laurent Michard. *20e Siècle: Les Grands Auteurs*. Paris: Bordas.

Lukacs, Georges. *La Théorie du roman*. Paris: Gonthier, 1963.

Magnier, Bernard. "Je ne suis pas à développer mais à prendre ou à laisser: Entretien avec Sony Labou Tansi", *Notre Librairie*, No. 79, 1985.

Mensa, Ba. *Les mains salles* de Jean-Paul Sartre: Une étude thématique", *Ilorin Journal of Language and Literature*, 1998.

Midiohouan, Guy Ossito. *L'idéologie dans la littérature négro-Africaine d'expression française*. Paris: L'Harmattan, 1996.

Nnoruka, Mattiu. "In memoriam: Adieu Sony", *Présence Africaine*, 1996.

Pageaux, Daniel-Henri: "Entre le renouveau et la modernité, vers de nouveaux modèles?" *Notre Librairie*, 1985.

Tansi, Sony Labou: *La Vie et demie*. Paris: Seuil, 1979.
　　　　　L'Etat honteux. Paris: Seuil,1981.
　　　　　L'Anté-peuple. Paris: Seuil, 1983.

Tétu, Michel. *La Francophonie, Histoire problématique et perspectives*. Paris: Hachette, 1988.

Vignonde, Jean-Norbert. "Sony Labou Tansi: L'Anté-peuple, *Notre Librairie*, No. 79, 1985.

11

POLITICAL, RELIGIOUS AND MORAL CHAOS IN CONTEMPORARY AFRICA: *GUELWAAR* OR SEMBÈNE OUSMANE'S INDICTMENT

Affin O. Laditan

INTRODUCTION

Like many who consider Sembène Ousmane as Zola's disciple, we also hail the naturalistic realism of this writer who does not shy away from his responsibility as the spokesman of those who cannot speak, or who have no means of expressing their views. Considering men as the originators of all social ills, Sembène, in all his previous and most recent works, denounces the shameless solidarity binding men and by virtue of which low instincts, inadequacies and all kinds of injustices are perpetrated. Of all the pre-independence writers whose works focus on colonisation, Sembène Ousmane is probably the only one who has easily shifted his sight from the colonial master to the post-independence African situation. As a perspicacious observer who abhors passivity, he uses both film and literature to engage in an all-out fight against those whose acts and actions are detrimental to the common man. Sembène Ousmane summarises his conception of *Guelwaar*, one example of his film and novel, thus:

> Where the film gives privilege to the representation
> and to that which is spectacular, the writer, sentences
> after sentences, trims, cuts his relief. Every experienced
> man enjoys reading him. [1]

Indeed, writing *Guelwaar* could not but add to the author's credit as one of the most skilful creators of fiction and defenders of the masses. The focus of this chapter is on the denunciation of the political, religious and moral chaos in contemporary Africa as highlighted in the novel.

THE AUTHOR AND HIS IDEOLOGY

Before discussing *Guelwaar*, it may be necessary to have an overview of the author's previous works and this, we think, will give us a foretaste of his ideology. First, it is important to note that Sembène Ousmane remains a prolific writer when most of his peers have disappeared or have simply stopped writing. In all his previous works, Sembène Ousmane is the mouthpiece of a certain class. On each occasion, he goes beyond the level of a simple witness to present a series of scathing indictments against the authors of the dehumanisation of mankind.

In *Le docker noir*, the inhuman situation to which migrant workers are subjected justifies the theme of revolt outlined in the mode of denunciation of racial discrimination, exploitation and all the abominations inflicted on the black folk.

Ô, pays, mon beau peuple depicts the aspiration of the people seeking for their liberation through a fascinating character, Oumar Faye. Beyond this character that all alone epitomises an unstoppable force, this novel is also about the denunciation of religious fatalism and defeatism. It is the rejection of the social order that paralyses the people.

In *Les Bouts de bois de Dieu* where the main character can be said to be the masses, we witness the transformation of the people from ignorance to a consciousness of the existence of their historic power to oppose threats, corruption and violence. It is also worthy of note that a male African writer sets a good example by portraying the female folk as able and ready to struggle alongside the so-called stronger sex.

"La Noire de..." in the collection of stories, *Voltaïque* is inspired by an incident titled : "At Antibes, a nostalgic black Lady cuts her own throat". It is indeed a reflection of the mishaps and vicissitudes that led an enslaved young Senegalese woman to commit suicide in her white master's home in France.

L'harmattan is conceived not only as an historical document, but also as an epoch-making memoirs. *L'harmattan* thus demonstrates not only the mechanism of subversion in the midst of a liberation struggle, but also the manipulation of men by the oppressive colonial and neo-colonial powers.

In *Le mandat*, Sembène Ousmane makes a U-turn and attacks his people (the Africans). This novel can also be seen as an indictment of the savage bureaucratic bottlenecks that characterise the independence era and which give privilege to the power of money to the detriment of human dignity . A certain Dieng falls victim of the sordid aspects of this new administration with its nepotism, corruption and restrictive clauses.

With *Xala,* Sembène Ousmane lays the blame on the class of the nouveaux riches through the disgrace of Abdou Kader Bèye who cannot consummate his marriage. His material downfall symbolises the inconsistency and the short-lived successes of the new bourgeoisie in the days following independence.

In *Le dernier de l'empire*, the Senegalese government is exposed. (There are obvious references to the political reality of the moment). Sembène Ousmane compares the government to a committee of mandarins who would have loved to be transformed in order to look like the colonial master if it were possible. They are indifferent to their people's misery. Sembène Ousmane's outspoken nature and sarcastic tone tally with the degree of denunciation of unscrupulous ambition and nepotism characteristic of the political system.

In *Niiwan*, social and political changes as the consequences of societal transformation remain the most important theme. One of the most unwelcome happenings in a conservative society is the repudiation of a husband by his wife. This peculiar action by a woman translates Sembène's attitude to the womenfolk. Here, tradition and the rituals are abandoned in favour of more purposeful and more realistic deeds. Here, too, the removal of the gap between castes and clans is underscored. We can begin to understand why Sembène Ousmane is regarded as one of the forerunners of the new literary tendencies that started gaining ground after independence.

Sembène Ousmane is also referred to as a social pathologist. The reason for this could be found in the totality of his films and literary works. He is one of the artists who expose Africa's new problems namely, unemployment, prostitution, ignorance, bureaucracy, nepotism, enrichment through embezzlement, repression, police brutality and the disintegration of social values. Sembène Ousmane is not fooled by the gains of independence; he has continued to denounce the problems in order to inform on one hand and to mobilise public opinion against these social ills on the other hand.

This specific trend in Sembène's literary work is highlighted in *Guelwaar* in which so many misdeeds are pointed out explicitly or implicitly, followed by suggestions of ways to eradicate them. This pattern is just like that of a pathologist who detects the germ responsible for an infection and who recommends the required drugs to be administered.

EXPOSITION OF POLITICAL DECADENCE

Of all Sembène's works, *Guelwaar*, touches the greatest number of themes. What attracts more attention, however, is their usage as a means of indicting the government, the people and the religious organisations. In most of the author's works, the characters and their actions dictate the major themes.

In *Guelwaar*, we have one of the most beautiful and extraordinary pamphlets on the political chaos in contemporary Africa. As a person, Guelwaar is a symbolic character, the mouthpiece of the upright people in a corrupt Africa. His integrity, courage and verbal aggression bring on him the anger of the enemies of progress. Following a planned uprising, he dies, but his corpse disappears in the morning on the day of burial. This disappearance is a visible pretext used by Sembène Ousmane to show how a whole population is enslaved to international aid in form of food, which is accompanied by lots of propaganda and blackmail. If many do not see anything wrong in it, Guelwaar and his likes, deriving strength from their scruples and dignity, equate international aid to begging. In their candid opinion, the so-called assistance enslaves all those who receive it and degrades them to the level of beggars and deprives them not only of their will and initiative but also of their independence as a nation.

There is a noticeable difference between a certain Dieng of *Le Mandat*, the undisputed husband who explains to his wives their status in the most conservative way,

> When you are a good wife, you wait for your husband's order. [2]

and a dejected Guelwaar who is at his wit's end following his wife's tirade. As opposed to Dieng or Moustapha in "Ses trois jours", he becomes sober as a result of the insult which knocks some sense into him. It is after his wife has shut him up that he realises he is not in the best position to teach others and to ask them to reject the *food of dishonour*. Women are no more men's scapegoats. As women, they gear men up and make them feel their impact. In *Guelwaar*, Sembène presents them as intelligent, bold and charismatic women. Indeed, these attributes could be found in the women who reject the so-called assistance that they see as mere alms. Angèle who is the wife of Guignane, the oldest man in the community, is the instigator of the rejection. Even though her jealousy vis-à-vis her younger rival, Honorine, has to do with her tempestuous utterances, it is her political view that retains attention. Replying to her husband who is trying to prove his innocence, she says:

> No! No! ... You are not the one who went crying to the white men's country to tell them: "Our wives and children have nothing to eat." No! ... No! ... You are not the one, Antoine. But your likes did, Antoine. The government people". [3]

After accusing her husband of begging because the latter comes back home with his share of the provisions distributed, she also attacks the government. For a woman without education, this level of consciousness and awareness must be praised. But in a usual village life where gossips are the order of the day and the laudable social habits begin to change, any respectable person in the image of Angèle could react as she did, refusing the food of dishonour.

> My children and I, we are not living on alms.[4]

And to her husband, she shouts:

> What you are doing amounts to begging.[5]

This clearly proves that not all women are responsible for their husbands' misdeeds, as it is usually believed, and that some are rather proud of their poor husbands because they are worthy men. This brings into memory the good old days when men's worth was not quantified in their possessions, but by the amount of honesty and dignity they had. Angèle's political clear-sightedness shows that political awareness is no more the exclusive preserve of men or the educated, but the business of all good observers of the societal changes and the realities associated with them. In that light, the peak of her sermon to her husband is more revealing:

> "Never did our parents wait for anybody, moreover for the white men to provide food for them and their children. Without the white men, you and your likes in government would die of hunger. And you talk of independence. Independence is legitimate for a family man who feeds his family. If he cannot do that, he is not independent. Human wrecks, no dignity."[6] (p.60)

Angèle's sarcasm is also a sharp criticism of the government, which depends on international aid thus making room for foreign domination and neo-colonialism. It is obvious that Sembène Ousmane is telling us through this woman what political scientists summarise thus: "No political independence without economic independence". The eye-opening role played by some women in *Guelwaar* reveals Sembène Ousmane's feminist penchant. Angèle and Marie are the most vocal women who command respect. Each of their interventions is purposeful and result-oriented as they are not talking for nothing. It is only after Marie's tirade on prostitution against Guelwaar that the latter begins to reckon with the fact that the government is to be blamed. This important role of women in men's political revival is not mere fiction. In as much as we know the author by his choice of words, we would want to postulate without any iota of doubt that *Guelwaar* is partly an essay on the full restoration of women to their rightful place in the family. The head of the family fails if the woman is a bad adviser and it is also through her that man can regain dignity if she stands for honour. Here as in *Les bouts de bois de Dieu*, the family is portrayed as the nucleus of the society and the politician as the product and reflection of the society:

> " Angèle's utterances, repeated and amplified by other women hurt the Guelwaaryi elders' pride. "[7] (.62)

Beyond the utterances opportunely put in some women's mouth, we have here an accusatory literary creation targeted at the ruling class. This work is the rejection of international parasitism, the rejection of the constant call for assistance in the name of any natural disaster whatsoever. Like the cantankerous and obstinate hero, who later opposes the humiliating and dehumanising food aids, (thanks to his wife), we can perceive that the author is working to rehabilitate the dignity of a continent that has, for long, lagged behind the western countries. Women are the first to claim this dignity and we can assert that the author is here telling us that women still remain the pride of this continent and that they have been playing some important roles in the background for the development of the continent. Unlike Maryse Condé's heroines, Veronica or Marie Hélène, who are the befitting illustrations of Sartre's concept of insincerity, Angèle does not keep quiet and she refuses to be her husband's accomplice. Her voice that makes an impact on her audience was no more the voice of a lonely woman in her fight against polygamy and her husband's insincerity, but it was the voice of all the women bound by solidarity in their quest for change:

> " On the radio, they keep on telling us every now and then that women should be liberated... Those who say that are ignorant. I, I am going to tell you those who should be liberated: They are the men; they should be liberated from their male chauvinistic mentality. They should be liberated from one another. They should be liberated from their claims as masters. They should be liberated from their begging habits and their subordination to white men ."[8] (p.61)

This cannot but be one of the most scathing diatribes against the African man, his thoughts and conservative habits. Here again is a question raised about the political and economic independence which no African nation could boast of. The idea of " subordination to the white men " is a naked allusion to this fact. A deeper reflection would take us to the conclusion that the writer is denouncing a certain complacency, a certain collusion between white and black leaders.

Guelwaar is also the denunciation of four decades of systematic looting of the resources of the continent. Amadou Fall is the prototype of the shameless politician, an inveterate careerist, the sacred cow who derives power from his double title of MP and Mayor. He is very expensive to the tax-payers with:

> His five luxurious cars, his office and the bedrooms of
> his three wives which were all air-conditioned. [9]

This indecent luxury enjoyed by the civil servant, as well as the broken-down and "decaying" luxurious cars and agricultural equipment in front of what used to be the regional headquarters of the agricultural co-operative, are evidence of waste. If the author refers to the defunct co-operative as a ruin (p.24), this is to show us the seriousness of the tragedy in a society where vices are acclaimed instead of being condemned. Thefts and embezzlement of public funds have become heroic actions.

Guelwaar is also the denunciation of the repressive attitude of the ruling class against the opposition. The refusal to tolerate criticism, the autocratic disposition and lack of tolerance of the local authorities are violently expressed in form of threats and aggression that lead to Guelwaar's death. Violence and assassination, tools in the hands of autocratic governments, are used to muzzle the people, especially those who are politically and intellectually clear-sighted and who could easily point out the government's shortcomings. They are easily tagged both as the enemies of the nation and the regime and they are ruthlessly dealt with. Even though Perr Alioune alias Guelwaar is not an intellectual, his integrity and leading role in the refusal of food aid is a serious threat to the local authorities. This is perceptible in Amadou Fall's utterances when he invites one of his gorillas to deal with Guelwaar:

> Keep him shut once and for all. [10]

This green light to assassinate is an open misuse of the state power to get rid of those whose criticism could correct the wrongdoings of government. About the real political state of things, Pierre Nda says:

> African leaders are power drunk. because of their unlimited and uncontrolled power, they inevitably fall into despotism .[11]

This situation is used against the backdrop of the persisting politics of deceit, which indicts the governments of the African countries. In *Guelwaar*, the MP and Mayor does not hesitate to brandish the spectre of his power. He cares no hoot about who suffers. That is what he seems to be saying when he threatens Gora, the policeman:

> Mr DPO. in the province. the MP and Mayor has enormous power.[12]

These utterances are real confessions, speaking the mind of the power-drunk politicians.

SHAME, MORAL DECAY AND MAN'S ABDICATION OF HIS ROLE

We find in *Guelwaar* an inventory of themes that the critical mind cannot ignore. One of the most striking themes is man's abdication when faced with the responsibility of caring for the members of his family. Once more, it is a woman whose husband ran away who denounces this shameful act. The runaway man has already spent fourteen years away from his family. His son, who binds his mother's hands and legs and forces his younger sister to make love with men to get money, is the epitome of delinquency. If such an atmosphere prevails in a home deserted by man, it is obvious that the author is drawing our attention to the consequences of man's abdication of his responsibilities towards his family.

Guelwaar is also a woman's revolt against tradition, the shame of an era in some conservative African communities. " Oumy was given " by her father as a wife to the impotent and aged octogenarian, Meyssa Ciss in settlement of a very huge debt. This is just to recall the shameless practice of arranged or forced marriages contracted without the consent of the woman involved. Once "given out", Oumy becomes Ciss's property. This is the reason why Mor Ciss plays the husband's role in place of his " weak " brother. This episode throws more light on women's state of nothingness in any conservative African community where such practices exist. One must give credit to Sembène Ousmane for his literary ingenuity, which enables him to transform the woman, who is considered to be an object, into a woman of will. Oumy's revolt and refusal to sacrifice the rest of her youth to satisfy the pleasure of a man who couldn't have been her husband is an eye-opener to all enslaved women. By refusing to portray herself as Mor Ciss's wife at his death, she does not only snatch and proclaim her freedom, she also refuses to be treated as a mere item or property that could be inherited (p. 113). As for the children she is abandoning without regrets, they could be likened to children of circumstance to whom she was forced against her will to give birth. Her comment on the matter

> The children?.... I leave them to their father. I am going forever.[13]

is a confirmation of this assertion. It also would not be an overstatement to say that most women do not like polygamy. In their opposition to the frivolous reasons given by men to justify their involvement in polygamy, Angèle and their likes are more realistic. If in *Xala*, Oumi Ndoye manifests her opposition quietly and Aja Awa Astou plays the ideal wife, here, it is not the case with Angèle who violently bursts out in anger when her husband justifies his status of polygamist as an act of God:

> God. God. is he the one that had a private word with you. telling you to take a second wife. God has nothing to do in that.[14]

That constant and progressive woman's development is perceptible in Sembène Ousmane's works. Angèle is the pinnacle of this metamorphosis. In fact, she incarnates the revolutionary type who gets rid of the handcuffs of fatalism and begins to criticise the system. She also criticises the bogus reasons on which men hang to justify polygamy. We have here the revolt of a jealous woman (it is natural to be jealous) who cannot hide the feelings of a betrayed woman. To her husband in quest of indulgence, Angèle opposes vulgarity, going out of the accepted norms of speech expected of a woman of her calibre:

> When you get a hard-on with Honorine, you think
> Christian. With me, you are a wet rag.[15]

In *Guelwaar*, Sembène's wink in the direction of the female folk catches attention. Truly, if men always usually use the pretext of the fading beauty of their ageing wives to justify a new marriage, the author deems it right to invite women to maintain their marital vows and preserve their bodies. Speaking through Dame Véronique, a mother of eight, whose first son is twenty-five years old while she herself could be mistaken for a thirty-five years old lady, we get the hint:

> A woman should maintain her body and nurture her
> femininity .[16]

But Sembène Ousmane qualifies this position when he shows that he does not approve of skin bleaching, a common practice among our women:

> Oumy was practising xessal, (the bleaching of the skin)
> her face and neck were like an overripe pumpkin. The
> phalanxe joints and the folds in the skin were black.[17]

This description which almost turns into derision is indeed not exaggerated. Maintaining one's femininity should have a limit, the author seems to tell us.

Writing more on female liberty as touching moral issues, two characters, Sophie, Guelwaar's daughter and her friend, Hélène who live in Dakar, symbolise licentiousness and debauchery. They are free young women who give themselves up to prostitution not only to earn a living, but also to ensure the survival of their kin and to maintain their social status. Through Hélène, Sofie's friend, Sembène Ousmane seems to reveal to us the reasons why some young ladies give in to prostitution:

> My parents, they are alive. I have four sisters, three brothers, male and female cousins... I went to Dakar to look for employment. After three, six months, a year! Nothing. I became a registered prostitute with a professional card.[18]

Sembène Ousmane's merit lies in is his ability to create fictitious situations where the African woman can express herself. Sophie and Hélène incarnate a certain degree of advanced freedom according to western norms; they smoke cigarettes and drink beer without any unusual feelings. Their presentation in this novel could be controversial especially if one considers their role in their respective families and prostitution as a means of earning their living. First of all, it is obvious that these women can do with their bodies what men cannot do with their hands. The support that they offer to their families is indisputably a demonstration of their kind-heartedness. This is what we learn through Hélène:

> I send money to my family...None of my family members begs. My elder brother is studying medicine... I must help him. I paid for my father's pilgrimage to Yamoussoukro on the occasion of the consecration of Notre-Dame-de-la-Paix... Sophie also paid for her father's pilgrimage to Jerusalem in the Holy Land.[19]

If Hélène could defend herself by showing off and enumerating all her good deeds to her family, (thanks to prostitution), what seems more critical and worthy of consideration is the judgement of Sophie's brother, a well educated man who lives in Paris. He reasons thus:

> Nobody would like to know that his sister, daughter or mother is a prostitute. But we should not hurry to condemn these girls who involve themselves in the oldest job in the world. Priest, we should have the social

> courage to see how people survive these days. There
> is no virtue in misery and poverty .[20]

For Barthélémy through whom the writer conveys these pertinent thoughts, the society is to be blamed, not these girls and women who are mere victims of prevailing circumstances. This view could also be said to be the younger generation's opinion about prostitution as opposed to the feelings of the older generation that sees it as a terrible reproach, an indelible shame. On hearing that her daughter has become a prostitute, Sophie's mother becomes very distressed. Her reaction as described by the author in the following lines is the typical demonstration of hatred for the prostitute in the African set-up:

Since her mother knew that Sophie was a prostitute in Dakar, she had stopped communicating with her. Though she was mourning, on sighting Sophie, she said:

> you are soiling my room. [21]

The prostitute's relations lose their dignity completely and Sophie's mother is distressed at the idea that her daughter has become a "communal field every monkey could plough at will".[22]

By so doing, Sophie has brought shame not only on the family but also on the whole lineage.

> You have made of me a prostitute's mother.[23]

Shame is one of the main themes in *Guelwaar*. Caused by prostitution, it is also the psychological and moral torture affecting the prostitutes' families. Between abundance and dishonour on one hand and poverty in dignity on the other hand, Sophie's mother makes the difficult choice of deprivation rather than eating and wearing that which is bought by her daughter through prostitution.

After burning all the clothes that Sophie has sent to her from Dakar, she does not hesitate to confront her husband with the honest truth:

> You prefer that your daughter prostitutes herself to
> feed you, to send you on pilgrimage in Jerusalem and
> Rome? Where is dignity? It is you men that spoil this
> country.[24]

Even though this truth is too blunt, Guelwaar has no other choice than to accept it, thereby accepting his fall to the level of a prostitute and those who live on begging and prostitution. If Sembène speaks through a woman, a symbolic and meaningful act, he exposes the loss of parental authority and man's abdication vis-à-vis his duties towards the members of his family. Besides, one could easily read between the lines that Sembène Ousmane is more committed to restoring the already tarnished African woman's image than some previous sexist writers on African women.

FANATICISM AS A RESULT OF IGNORANCE AND INTOLERANCE IN RELIGIOUS MATTERS

Guelwaar is the indictment of the Islamic and Christian religions, and also of their total silence and extreme conservatism. The neutrality of the church and its mission, which are seen to be above the temporal, forbid her to intervene in political life. This makes it look as if God was insensitive to the sufferings some men are enduring under their fellow human beings. On this conservatism, the author makes his own comments through Barthélémy:

> The African Church should be accommodating, she
> should have a pastoral consciousness and preach
> against defeatism. [25] p.135.

Guelwaar is also the critical and boiling moment of dialogue between two religions. It is the denunciation of the intolerance of both the Christians and the Muslims over the resting-place of an innocent dead body. It is also the exposition of people's ignorance about the two religions. One of the most striking examples is Amadou Fall who, though presumably well read by virtue of his position of a Mayor, does not know the origin of both Christianity and Islam. To the critical mind, both religions are agents of destabilisation here rather than being the source of unity and peace among disciples.

> Unlike the majority of his fellow Senegalese artists
> who subscribe to Islam's claim to indigenous antiquity

in Senegal, Sembène Ousmane presents Islam as one
of the forces -the other being Euro-Christianity-
responsible for what Soyinka, (1976:99) refers to as
Africa's enforced cultural Exocentricity.[26]

The ideas and practices considered as Senegalese by these artists
and by the whole society at large are now being re-examined by
more critical minds, Sembène is one of such minds. The insidious
and violent way in which the Arab-Islamic thought came to take
root in Senegal is not different from the way in which the Euro-
Christian ideas and colonisation made inroads into Senegal in
particular and Africa in general. In *Guelwaar*, Amadou Fall is the
representative of those who are ignorant of this fact. As an MP
and Mayor, he symbolises the educated political class in Senegal.
His ignorance is definitely that of his class. Speaking through a
disgusted Barthélémy (p.142) in the face of such ignorance, the
author's enlightenment of his readers on the origin of both religions
should not be seen as a mere utterance. The war between the two
religions is basically the direct consequence of ignorance. One
illustration of this show of ignorance is the invitation by one of the
Muslim characters to kill all the *yeferis* (unbelievers) because,
according to him, killing an unbeliever is an act of piety. (p.129).

CONCLUSION

Sembène Ousmane's ideology and humanism are the real forces
behind his literary success. Committed to progress, development
and justice in Africa, regardless of race, origin or identity, religion
or sex, Sembène remains profoundly respectful of those elements
of African culture and tradition that have shaped his upbringing
and which are not in conflict with his political ideology. It is in that
light that we should see that his denunciation of socio-political
inadequacies does not degenerate into a sweeping condemnation
of tradition and religion. Such a denunciation comes as a result of
a critical and objective evaluation of specific individual or communal
behaviour and practices.

Muslims and Christians in *Guelwaar* are mostly ignorant of the
sacred contents of the holy books. They are carried away by

emotion and by a herd instinct. As for Christianity, Sembène seems to be blaming it for its spirit of fatalism and its inherent message of inertia and passivity. The Islamic religion also has its own fair share of criticism due to the tendency of its followers to be violent. Both religions are shown to be powerless in the face of the practical problems of hunger, poverty, dishonesty and political manipulation. As for the law, it is only on the side of the politicians.

This novel is above all a long denunciation of wrongdoings and social ills, it is also an eloquent plea for the necessary transfer of power and leadership from a class of corrupt people to a new generation of more honest leaders. As said earlier on, the woman is fully restored through the role Sembène gives to her in *Guelwaar*, regardless of her debasement and her descent into prostitution which are blamed on man.

The chaos that cuts across the entire society as described in *Guelwaar* is more or less the summary of Sembène Ousmane's previous works. Indeed, *Guelwaar*, as earlier indicated, reads like a dissertation on religion, tradition and socio-political life in Senegal in particular and Africa in general. *Guelwaar* confirms Sembène's belief in man as the only force capable of solving such practical human problems as are portrayed in the novel.

Notes and References

1. Sembène Ousmane. *Guelwaar*. Paris: Présence Africaine, 1996, p.9.
2. Sembène Ousmane. *Le mandat*. Paris: Présence Africaine, 1966, p.119.
3. *Guelwaar*, p.60.
4. *Ibid.*, p.59.
5. *Ibid.*, p.60.
6. *Ibid.*, p.60
7. *Ibid.*, p.62.
8. *Ibid.*, P.61.

9. *Ibid.*, p.33.

10. *Ibid.*, P.141.

11. Nda Pierre. "Les régimes africains et la lutte des jeunes: De la dictature à la démocratie dans le roman négro-africain d'expression française" In *RENEF: REVUE NIGERIANE D'ETUDES FRANCAISES.* Vol. 1, No. 2, 1994: pp.53-76

12. *Guelwaar,* p.35.

13. *Ibid.*, p.113

14. *Ibid.*, p.57.

15. *Ibid.*, p.58.

16. *Ibid.*, p.42.

17. *Ibid.*, p.87

18. *Ibid.*, p. 68.

19. *Ibid.*, p. 69.

20. *Ibid.*, p.134.

21. *Ibid.*, p.78.

22. *Ibid.*, p. 78.

23. *Ibid.*, p.107.

24. *Ibid.*, p.106.

25. *Ibid.*, p.135

26. Mbye B. Cham. "Islam in Senegalese literature and film" in Kenneth W. Harrow (ed.) *Faces of Islam in African Literature.* London: Heinemann Educational Books, Inc. New Series Books, 1991, pp.163-186.

Bibliography

1. Gurnah, Abdulrazak (eds.). *Essays on African Writing: A Reevaluation,* Oxford: Heinemann Educational, 1993.

2. Macward Christiane et al. *Dictionnaire littéraire des femmes de langue francaise,* Paris: Editions Karthala, 1996.

3. Makward, Idriss. "Women, Tradition, and Religion in Sembène Ousmane's Work" in Kenneth W. Harrow (ed.) *Faces of Islam in African Literature (Studies in African Literature).* London: Heinemann Educational Books, Inc. New Series Books, 1991)

4. Nda, Paul. *Pouvoir, lutte de classe, Idéolgie et milieu intellectuel Africain.* Paris: Présence Africaine, 1987.

5. Nda Piere. "Les régimes Africains et la lutte des jeunes: De la dictature à la démocratie dans le roman négro-Africain d'expression française", *RENEF: REVUE NIGERIANE D'ETUDES FRANCAISES.* Vol. 1, No. 2, 1994: pp. 53-76.

6. Sembène Ousmane. *O, pays mon beau peuple.* Paris: Le livre Contemporain, 1957.

7. —————— *Les bouts de bois de Dieu.* Paris: Le livre Contemporain, 1960.

8. —————— *Voltaïque.* Paris: Présence Africaine, 1962.

9. —————— *L'harmattan.* Paris: Présence Africaine, 1965.

10. —————— *Le mandat.* Paris: Présence Africaine, 1966.

11. —————— *Le docker noir.* Paris: Présence Africaine, 1973.

12. —————— *Xala.* Paris: Présence Africaine, 1973.

13. - —————— *Le dernier de l'empire.* Paris: L'Harmattan, 1981.

14. —————— *Niiwan.* Paris: Présence Africaine, 1987.

15. —————— *Guelwaar.* Paris: Présence Africaine, 1996.

12

I WRITE THE WAY I LIKE: AHMADOU KOUROUMA'S LANGUAGE OF REVOLT

Yetunde Osunfisan

INTRODUCTION

Although there exists in some African countries a veritable, thriving school of literature in autochthonous languages[1], the phenomenon known as African literature remains largely a foreign affair in the sense that most of the writers, from black Africa especially, write in a European language – English, French and Portuguese. This is due in part to their colonial past and the type of education they received, usually in western-style schools and often in European or American countries.

Language, according to the experts, is a product of the society and it is capable of expressing that thing or notion which exists in the society that fashioned it.[2] Therefore, a writer writing about and for his people in a *strange* language will have problems of expression. This is a fact that applies to every writer irrespective of race or colour. For instance, how does one explain *snow* to a black man who has never left his country? And more to the point, how would an African writer explain in a white man's language that phenomenon which is fundamentally African, non-existent within the white man's culture? For instance, in Yorubaland[3] we speak of *agbo 'lé* and *oriki*. The approximate term that the English language has found for these words are *compound* and *panegyric* respectively. Whereas a compound could be just an empty large space within or outside a dwelling, an *agbo 'lé* is a stretch or circle of houses all inter-linked and sharing basic facilities. Each house is accessible to every other occupant, all occupants being members of a single extended family of descendants of a sole individual spanning several generations! That is why the word is also often used to denote a family or a group of persons related by blood.

Also, the dictionary[4] defines *panegyric* as "a speech or piece of writing praising somebody or something" but, *oríkì* is definitely more than that. It is an oral poem, a praise song fashioned out of the exploits and valorous actions of a person's or family's ancestors: humility, trading, singing, war-mongering and so on. It is a distinguished form of oral poetry that enjoins one to live up to the positive reputation of one's antecedents. Obviously, "compound" and "panegyric" do not translate *agbo 'lé* and *oríkì* because they fall woefully short of the actual meanings.

We have digressed, but intentionally. The digression is necessary to better situate the subject of this essay: the peculiar way in which Ahmadou Kourouma manipulates the French language to suit his own particular purposes. It is our intention to demonstrate in this article that such manipulative usage or ab-usages[5] are *en connaissance de cause* that is, deliberate. They reveal the revolt that issues from deep frustration about a situation or thing, in this instance, a situation of "writing black in white".

Revolt can take various forms. For instance, the revolt could:

i.   tolerate the situation or thing and steam in expressed or inexpressible anger.
ii. Reject it outright and substitute it with another, *in extremis,* as a contra-reaction to it.
iii. Reject the situation and every other conceivable alternative(s).

The mini-skirt of the sixties could be said to be in category (iii) of the above examples, because it was a reaction *in extremis* to the high-neck knee-length, drab, shapeless Elizabethan gowns of the preceding decade.

African writers, when faced with the dilemma of "writing black in white", generally do not revolt in the sense that either their feelings of frustration do not go deep enough to warrant a reaction or it goes just deep enough to give rise to a mild or timid one. This reaction is usually expressed in one of three ways, at the level of language viz.:

 i. spicing with African (exotic?) words
 ii. creating new words or extending the semantic scope of already existing ones to suit the African world view[6].
 iii. Use of devices or oral literature, particularly, proverbs and repetition of verbal sequences.

Perhaps because of the complete assimilation practised by the French colonial masters, Francophone African writers feel, much more than their Anglophone brethren, the need to manifest their culture and fingerprint their writing. According to Gassama[7]:

> .... the first school established in Africa were not for the training of (Black) future civil servants for an independent continent; they were targeted towards the complete assimilation of natives. ... Autochthonous culture was right from the start made to feel inferior if not completely despised, even in its most humanistic manifestations.
>
> The schools were meant to form an élite corps capable of understanding and acquiring western table and civilization; to expose the young African to western values while assisting him, surreptitiously and with obstinacy, **to despise black cultural values and even be ashamed of them.** (Emphasis mine).

It is not surprising, therefore, that the first black writer to expand, break and remodel his working language to accommodate the African frame of mind and thought pattern is a Francophone. The writer in question goes about this business in such an unrepentant and unapologetic manner that it became obvious to a sensitive reader that Ahmadou Kourouma is not only making a statement but reacting in the boldest manner possible, to a situation he believes can be helped, can be improved upon. His is not just a reaction, it is a revolt, a challenge thrown at purists of the French language. To those who want to throw a "How dare you?" at him, he responds, tongue-in cheek: "I do not write French, I write in French". "But what is he talking about?". Well, you may not understand since you are not Malinké.

 Now, what does this counter-reaction translate into in linguistic or in literary terms? In what way does Ahmadou Kourouma's writing differ from that of other African writers? What does he do that others are not doing or have not done before?

In this article, we shall be examining the novels of Ahmadou Kourouma, *Les soleils des indépendances*[8] and *Monnè, outrages et défis*[9] in order to bring to light what constitutes the writer's linguistic revolt.

BORIBANA[10] AS FOREGROUNDING

In terms of historical situation and facts contained therein, *Monnè, outrages et défis* (henceforth *Monnè*) is older than and should have preceded *Les soleils des indépendances* (henceforth *Les soleils*). The context of the former is the colonial era, while the latter is a post-independence statement of deception. *Monnè* therefore, serves as the ante-chamber to and preparation ground for the events and corresponding language of *Les soleils*. For instance, the sun that heralded independence and stuck to it like an accursed burr was born in the colonial era, an era which, in Kourouma's Ivory Coast, was particularly disgraceful and tragic. Traditional rulers shamelessly compromised their positions and collaborated willy-nilly with the army of occupation, at the expense of their people. It was fatal: Fama, the central character of *Les soleils*, merely continued the outrage where Djigui, the hero(?) of *Monnè* left off. We recall that when Djigui was buried, his people prayed for the repose of his soul but they were careful not to bid him adieu. Somehow, they knew that it was not yet farewell to *monnew*[11]. The protagonist of *Les soleils*, Fama, the disgraced and disgraceful prince of Horodougou, proved their hunch right.

What we are saying in essence is that Ahmadou Kourouma, like his Malinké ancestors of the two novels, realised that he has been subjected to a kind of literary outrage and abuse; but unlike them, he challenged the situation, for one notices in his writing not only vast creative capabilities but also and, perhaps of greater importance to him, a commitment to the realisation of a particular dream: paving the way for a literature that will be authentically black, no longer a by-product of western literature.

So, what did he do? We shall discuss his contribution under three headings, all components of style: the word, exaggeration and comparison.

WORD OUTRAGE

As mentioned earlier, various African writers sprinkle their works with words from their native languages. This is done either for expediency (where there is no equivalent in the working language) or simply for aesthetic reasons. Occasionally, an autochthonous word is used to save time and space and to avoid the ethnographic explanation. Not so for Ahmadou Kourouma. According to a critic:[12]

> Unlike other African writers, Ahmadou Kourouma does not have recourse to the traditional and abundantly utilised devices of expression such as local slang, pidgin, petit-nègre, exotic words.

He simply creates one that suits his purpose or he expands the rigid semantic framework of an existing word to accommodate the multifarious hues of his mind. Kourouma voluntarily admits that he translates Malinké into French to recover and to restitute unto the language that which it often loses in translation[13]. In the following table, we bring you a sample of such creations and recreations. It is a six-column table, column one contains all the sample words whether complete neologisms or neologisms of sense while the second column, status, states if the word exists in French or not (Y = Yes, it does; N = No, it does not). The latter will be based on the presence or absence of the said word in a standard French dictionary like *Le Petit Larousse* and *Le Robert*. Then comes the column for meaning; the dictionary meaning is given where the word exists and where it does not, a literal one is substituted. The fourth column gives the meaning of author's usage while the following one states what a native speaker's option for the same idea would have been. All words are given in order of appearance in the novels, with page numbers, under the column tagged reference.

Table 1. Word Creations and Recreations: Sample

No	WORD EXPRESSION	STATUS	LITERAL MEANING DICTIONARY TRANSLATION	AUTHOR'S MEANING	NATIVE SPEAKER'S OPTION	REFERENCES SOLEILS	MONNÈ
1	Finir	Y	To end, terminate	To die	Mourir, décéder	7,108. 161,205	
2.	Courber (une prière)	Y	To bend down	To pray the Muslim way	Prier		12, 16, 89, 127
3.	Coucher (quelqu'un)	Y	To make someone to lie down. e.g. a baby	To sleep with: to make love to	Coucher avec. faire l'amour à	10, 79, 89	
4.	Se casser	Y	To fragment. break or disperse oneself	To bend down from the waist	Se courber, se plier	11, 17, 66	
5.	Tuer (un sacrifice)	Y	To kill a sacrifice	To offer a sacrifice	Faire/offrir/im moler un sacrifice	22, 23, 92, 114, 121, etc.	
6.	Avoir (un ventre)	Y	To have a big belly	To be pregnant	Être enceinte	41, 52, 186	

Table 1 contd.

No.	French	Y/N	English meaning			Page
7.	Avoir (un bon ventre)	Y	To have a good belly	To be fertile	Être féconde	135
8.	Fainéantiser	N	To be lazy/ slothful, indolent			97
9.	Vaurienniser	N	To render useless, worthless			97
10.	Misérer	N	To make poor			110, 12
11.	Se sortir	Y	To come out (of a situation, a predicament)	To remember	Se remémorer	117
12.	Négifier	N	To make to become negro		None	119
13.	Asseoir(un deuil)	N	To establish (a mourning period)	To sit through a mourning period	None	138
14.	Nuiter	N	To spend the night	To spend the night	Passer la nuit	67, 98
15.	Dévulver	N	Devulvate?	Vulva	None	135

One would notice from the preceding table that all words chosen are verbs. This is because they constitute a very interesting class of the novelist's usage, apart from nouns, some of which we will also discuss in the course of this paper. Also, about half of these verbs already exist in French, but Kourouma has extended their semantic scope. Others he created from existing radicals and suffixes. Take for instance *finir*. It can be used both transitively or intransitively but it always applies to inanimate things.[14] A work could finish. So also a season. A person also, at least in Kourouma's idiom. But a Frenchman would not use *finir* in the sense of *mourir* (to die) for a human being. The same thing could be said of *courber* (to bend) which he uses in the context of "to bend a prayer". *Nuiter, fainéantiser, misérer, vaurienniser, négrifier* are all new words because they do not appear in any standard French dictionary. They have all been created from the nominal radicals *fainéantise, misère, vaurien et nègre*, to which the suffix -*er* has been added to make them predicates. Thus, *nuiter* is analysable as:

nuit + er ——→ nuiter

that is,

night + do ——→ do night

In other words, "spend the night" while *fainéantiser* is analysable as:

fainéantise + er

indolence + do (make) ——→ make indolent or render indolent.

Kourouma equally makes good use of affixal versatility with nouns and suffixes. For example, to the verbs *saluer* and *prier* ("to greet" and "to pray", respectively) he adds the suffix -*eur* (he who does something):

salue + eur ——→ salueur[15] (he who greets)

prie + eur ——→ prieur[16] (he who prays)

Salueur is not attested in the French language. *Prieur* is, but it does not mean "he who prays"; it refers to a superior in a convent[17].

Dévulver is in a class by itself. This verb is coined from the root noun *vulve*, that is *vulva*. When *-er* is added, it becomes *vulver* where *-er* means "do" or "make" (as in above analysis) or *put into*. It must be said that *vulver* is a hypothetical verb. With an *-er* suffix and a *de*-prefix, *vulve* becomes *dévulver* where *dé-*[18] is "to remove" (as in *déshabiller*: to undress and *déchausser*: to remove one's shoes). Therefore, *dévulver* would mean to "remove from the vulva" or "to terminate the sexual act". One sees how picturesque Kourouma's coinages are and how much they appeal to the reader's imagination: the Muslim says his prayers in various bending positions, therefore, he "bends his prayers". For an animal to become a sacrifice, it has to be killed and its blood shed, therefore, you "kill a sacrifice". Except for the performance of essential bodily functions, a widow is obliged in the Malinké/Muslim tradition, to sit through the 40-day mourning period, therefore, she "sits the mourning period".

This writer is not unaware of the shock often occasioned by some of the collocational classes that he subjects his unsuspecting or uninitiated readers to. In the case of "asseoir[19] un deuil" for example, the verb asseoir (to sit) in the context means "to establish", "to make firm". He who is neither initiated nor Malinké would wonder why on earth any sane person would make mourning a permanent fixture of his life! In any case, Ahmadou Kourouma has said what he wants to say in exactly the way he wants to say it. Not for him approximations that would fall woefully short of the actual or intended meaning.

Such is also the intention for the usage of past participles as substantives while the French language allows only their usage as modifiers. For example, French admits sentences like:

1. *Un homme vidé*: an emptied man, i.e., a man emptied of the essence of manhood.
2. *Un homme assis*: A seated man, i.e., a man sitting down.
3. *Un homme décédé*: A dead man..

where *homme* (man) could be replaced by *femme* (woman) or any other acceptable noun. But Kourouma deliberately leaves out the noun being qualified, keeps the qualifier, thereby imbuing it with a noun-quality, hence,

1.   un vidé: an emptied
2.   un assis: A seated
3.   un décédé: A dead

where the person or thing is implied in the context. This usage is peculiar, to say the least, and would shock a native speaker of French. This is perhaps what a critic[20] was referring to when he said:

> Even when Ahmadou Kourouma's neologisms are elevated to an unbearable level, the writer, by surrounding them with a puzzling kind of nimbus of words and images, often succeeds in unlocking to the reader the door to the enigma.[20]

Take the case of *un vidé*. The writer had foregrounded the idea by describing the character in question in very uncharitable terms – a disgraced and disgraceful prince reduced to begging, husband of a sterile woman — before introducing the ab-usage of *un vidé*.

Kourouma's creative capabilities do not end here. We recall having mentioned that he expands the framework of his writing language to master and contain the frustration an African writer often feels when the inadequacies of his working tool becomes evident and unacceptable to him[21]. According to a critic:

> ... it is not easy for a Black writer to be contented with a foreign language alone to express certain situations and realities peculiar to Africa. It is equally not easy for him to content himself with local parlance when he has chosen to communicate his message in a foreign language.[21]

Larson identified some of the devices in the writing of black African writers and he explains them as being "elements borrowed more or less directly from African oral literature"[22]: repetition of verbal sequences, proverbs, circumlocutions and exaggerations. This last device, that is, exaggeration, is the subject of the next section.

EXAGGERATION AS CHALLENGE

As a figure of speech, an exaggeration often strikes a reader's imagination so vividly that he is forced to reconsider a situation or experience in its finer details and from perspectives other than those from which he has or would have considered it.

People exaggerate for different reasons. It could be to present an issue as being much more important than it is and thus deserving more attention, as in the case of the little boy who called the fire department when his toy car caught fire. He told the officer on duty that their house was on fire. A person may also exaggerate to get out of a tight situation: a tanker driver, caught in contravention of a traffic rule urgently told the policeman that his tanker load of acid could explode if not discharged before a certain hour. The ignorant law officer hastily released him. An exaggeration could also serve as tension-relief to relax an atmosphere, that is, as a comic relief. The popular Nigerian comedian, Baba Sala's "wrist *clock*" is a good example.

We remark that from the foregoing, there seems to be not much difference between a lie and an exaggeration in the sense that both are not true representations of the issue or situation. They are both deliberate choices. However, as a literary device, a writer exaggerates just the way he understates or uses any other imagery and for the same purpose: in his search for expressiveness and emphasis; he utilises it as an instrument to better describe his subject matter and emphasises that which is vital in his estimation. Then because the usage is for literary effect, it generally does not hurt anyone except perhaps in the case of a caricature where an alert reader easily discerns the real character behind the camouflage.

With Ahmadou Kourouma, however, the art of exaggeration has gone to new heights. He does it in such a way that a sensitive reader feels he is being dared to contradict the writer, particularly if the reader is familiar with the elements being described and other African writers handling of the same issue or subject matter.

Apart from simple outrageous description of a person, place or thing, this writer also has another peculiar way of exaggerating: description in superlatives, particularly the usage of expressions like *the most, the only*. We consider this a form of exaggeration because for anybody to be able to make such sweeping statements, he must have the kind of information that are usually unavailable. Let us take, for instance, the following sentence:

> People of Soba started the construction of the sky-
> bound wall which foundation should extend from Soba
> to the sea, a wall high and profound, infinite. **The
> most titanic construction in blackdom.** *Monnè* p.33.

In the first instance it is impossible to construct an infinite wall. Then, *titanic* is already a superlative. *Most* lifts the modifier *titanic* to a higher realm of superiority. But we also know that "the land of the black man" (blackdom) is such a wide expanse that no one can claim to know it all and be in a position to make such a comparison. There could be "more profound" and "more titanic" constructions in Négritie.

So, what are the hallmarks of exaggeration à la Kourouma? And what are its ends? It is often a mark of contempt. For example, when Djigui, the central character of *Monnè* went in search of Samory, the latter was surprised to see him and he asked Djigui how he was able to find him "in this vast Mandingue", Djigui responded:

> I found the flight path of the vultures and the procession
> of the hyenas. Everything was converging towards you,
> Almamy. *Monnè* p.26.

This response in addition to the physical description of the Almamy preceding it, paints this character as contemptible in the sense that not only does he have "the piercing gaze of a bird of prey[12], he is actually a bird of prey himself, a jackal, a merciless exploiter of the misfortunes of others around whom creatures of his ilk were gathering. Of course, we know that it is impossible for a human being, walking, to follow a bird's flight path nor would he dare walk behind a column of hyenas.

This figure of speech also serves as a kind of alarm in Kourouma's repertoire. For instance, in describing how awful the situation of Soba had become after a long period of exploitation (physical, material and spiritual) by the occupying French forces, he wrote:

> The land of the Madingues was drained, ...they knew
> this for a fact because in the evenings hyenas could
> hardly growl and the migrating birds which could not

> avoid flying over our area did so keeping very close to
> the clouds and hurrying as fast as possible out of our
> desolate country. *Monnè* p.28.

Here, the exaggeration of the circumstances underscores the hopelessness of the situation: even animals felt the desolation, suffered as a result of it and avoided it like the plague.

Ahmadou Kourouma has said a lot about the syncretism of the Malinkés which he often describes with some kind of wryness tinged with indulgence. He describes the religion of his people as "a syncretic blend of Malinké fetishism and Islam" and, tongue-in-cheek, qualifies a character as being "the greatest wizard and the most devout Muslim"[23]. A double jeopardy of sorts. It is however plain that this writer does not subscribe to this "neo-tarzanism"[24]. One of the ways in which he shows his disapproval is by painting a caricature of the practice. For example, while Djigui, the king of Soba was offering sacrifices to appease the gods of the land and the spirits of the ancestors so that they will grant his dynasty peace and perpetuity — the same prayers they offered in the mosque — the author intervenes with the following description of the "positive signs that the sacrifices have been accepted":

> The happy omen was confirmed by the cries and flights
> of the vultures and the brutal change in the sound of
> the Wind. *Monnè* p.32.

Anyone familiar with omens would not agree with the writer's categorisation of vultures in flight as a good augur because wherever there are vultures, there is certainly decay around or in the offing. But to attribute an alternation in atmospheric conditions to a sacrifice is carrying the joke a little bit too far. The quotation above is perhaps Kourouma's way of saying "if you mix the unmixable, you will get the impossible", hence the exaggerated dimensions.

The dimension of a situation or person is also sometimes exaggerated to underscore or emphasise such a thing or situation. Take for instance the case of neighbours paying homage to a deceased during his funeral. One of them stood up and recalled that:

> One night, he (the dead man) brought him an
> underwear and a wrapper: his wife's (the neighbour's
> wife, that is) which the wind had blown under the
> deceased's bed. *Soleils*, p.16.

Was someone guiding the wind? Why and how did the clothes land under the man's bed? Apart from emphasis, this passage also implies, from its context, that most of the things people say in such circumstances are not true; people often tell larger than life stories when they pay homage to someone, especially a dead person.

Let us take another example. A few skyscrapers in the midst of several bungalows look out of place and call attention to their uniqueness:

> The tops of the skyscrapers provoked further clouds
> which gathered at and puffed-up a part of the sky.
> *Soleils* p.18.

In other words, the skyscrapers are too tall for comfort, hence the provocation. The clouds were feeling threatened, afraid the tops could, as it were, puncture them. Kourouma's revolt is comparable to independence which he describes as "having multiple tails". What are the other tails? We shall discuss one of them in the next section.

COMPARISON AS TRUTH

The French language recognises three categories of comparison: of inferiority, of equality and of superiority. Here, we are going to limit our samples to the comparison of equality. Of what importance can this be: We note that other African writers also use comparison for aesthetic purposes. The elements compared are generally objects that are familiar to the African, ones with which he can identify, making the comparison clearer and weightier.

Comparisons are also statements of truth, that is, declaration of that which is, in an individual's or language's repertoire, equal in value to another thing. And values differ from one culture to the other. To the white man, snow is white and it is the basis for comparison of whiteness or purity. Whiteness to the Nigerian is symbolised by cotton or the cattle egret. In other words, cotton is white. It is equally true that snow is white. And to a Peul, it is also true that milk is white.

However, Kourouma's truth are off the beaten path; they often go beyond the ones we are familiar with. This does not, however, diminish the truth-quality. On the contrary, it heightens the effect on the reader: for those who are familiar with the objects in comparison, an additional truth is learnt. For example:

> As clear as a full moon on the savannah during the harmattan. *Monnè* p.29.

or

> As clear as the palm of the frog. *Monnè* p.56.

Thus, a full moon is always clear; on the savannah, with the virtual absence of vegetation, it is clearer and during harmattan, it is clearer still. Thus also, the palm of the frog is clear, particularly in contradistinction to the rest of the body. For those who are not familiar with the objects being compared, a new lesson is learnt, an additional information gained, an imagination fired as the reader tries to picture in his mind a full moon over a wide grassy expanse. Consider also:

> ... as familiar as the beads on the buttocks of the favorite wife.

or

> ... as well known as surats (Quranic verses).

As a Yoruba adage goes "Only the comparable is to be compared: the groundnut pod is akin to an *èlírí*'s [25] coffin". The beads on the buttocks of the favourite wife is well known, for obvious reasons. The surats are also well known, because they are committed to memory. Truth and familiarity differ from environment to environment , from culture to culture; one man's bread is another man's poison. We are not saying that Kourouma is the first novelist to use images from his native land but that he is the only one who has chosen to use that and only that which is Malinké. For example, a black man, is familiar with polygamy and the fact of favourite wives but may not be with the idea of women wearing beads elsewhere on their bodies apart from their necks. Obviously, it is won on the buttocks amongst Kourouma's people.

When a writer chooses or prefers one manner or tool of expression over another, he is making a political statement. It is what Jacques Chevrier calls "the politics of literature"[26]. This choice is similar to that which a writer makes when he chooses a particular language or register as his means of expression (pidgin, creole, slang, etc.). He is, according to a critic, adopting a political position; to use the language of the masses is to state in clear terms that he is in total support of this group against every kind of dictatorship.

We are saying that Kourouma's choice of images from the Malinké culture and land is a political choice emanating from a deep-rooted angst against the experience of linguistic colonisation by the French. He seems to be saying "If they could, so can I". So:

It is as sterile as harmattan dust	*Soleils* p.27
... as prosperous as an anthill	*Soleils* p.101
... as white as the feathers of the	
cattle egret	*Soleils* p.113.

We draw attention to the fact that, the harmattan dust, the anthill and the egret are familiar objects to the man of the savannah, the environment of the Malinké.

But in what ways do all the foregoing constitute a reaction, nay, a revolt?

A FRENCH FASHIONED IN GOOD CLAY

We have in passing drawn attention to the colonial master's objectives of teaching French to young Africans in their colonies. A regional governor in one of such colonies was addressing the pupils of a school and he had this to say:

> You must all speak French, my young friends and you cannot know our language except you use it regularly, know how to express all the nuances of its thought pattern by the apt word. *To speak French is to have it in your blood,* never to forget it no matter the condition you are in, to use it for oneself and also *to impose it on others,* to learn it not only as duty but also for its taste, to love it as a second maternal language and to let your hopes and recollections sustain it.[27] (Emphasis ours).

This is the kind of brainwashing and propaganda that people like Ahmadou Kourouma has been subjected to, concurrently with the systematic dehumanisation of their own cultures and tongues. It was an imposition, so thoroughly effective that even as adults, several Francophone writers still feel that writing well is "not to forget grammar lessons of their school days and to heed the advice of the critics" even when critics were more or less pressure groups and extension of school monitoring.[28] Deliberate linguistic constraint is a kind of repression and it could not last, hence the various kinds of the French language registers noticed in the writings of Francophone writers. According to a critic:[29]

> One cannot understand the originality of black literature of French expression without understanding the way in which African writers have had to, in about three quarters of a century, adjust to a language that is strange to them... The colonial school taught them how to write well but black writers obviously did not feel comfortable with this ceremonial French. So, they invented ways and means of indigenising the language...while feeling obliged to apologize for this effrontery before the French audience, their ultimate judge. Today, the new generation writer has overcome this defamation and is inaugurating unreservedly, a literary language of which he is the sole judge.

Going through this commentary by a Frenchman, one understands why Kourouma decided to go the whole hog. We recall that his effrontery was responsible for his being found unpublishable in French. It was not until a Canadian publisher took the risk of putting him in print that French publishing houses followed suit. He simply used what was familiar to him and refused to make excuses, unlike his predecessors who wore themselves out trying to please a foreign audience. Pleasing the foreign audience was a real concern to other Francophone writers, hence, their French was *soigné*. This was necessary because:

> [the writer] was assessed by publishers who often wonder about the worthwhileness of publishing a black writer: "Will it pay?", "Will the white public understand it?" "Who will be its most competent critic?"[30]

If Kourouma had concerned himself with any of the above worries and had tried to satisfy the preferences of a foreign public, albeit more lucrative, *Les Soleils* and *Monnè* would have lost their appeal, all those things that add up to the salt and pepper of Kourouma's writing. His novels demonstrate, in unambiguous terms, a refusal to be intimidated particularly by "What will the critics say?" "How would they receive it?" The so-called critics had no such considerations on their own part. So, if you don't know the savannah or the characteristics of an anthill, too bad. And if the comprehension of his négriture is difficult, well go and learn Malinké. After all, he *learnt* French.

The ambiance or duplicity noticed in his usage reflects the duplicity of his people, therefore, his own. For example, the Malinké are Muslims and know their quranic verses very well, at least this is implied in some of his comparisons. But he also states that the Malinké religion is a combination of ancestral practices and Islam. It is not charitable to say such a thing about one's people — writers of Negritude would not have; they see only the good in Africa and Africans — but it is the truth. This "revolt" against his people is at the root of his deliberate antipathy and exaggeration. These are the calculations of someone who has decided to call a spade a spade and not a farming implement. He is entrenched in his culture, has a symbiotic relationship with it and has decided, like the French, that he will *maintain and perpetuate its values.*

We have already noted that if it was not for foregrounding, some of Kourouma's usage would have remained hermetic. They are like codes open to the initiated-Malinké and African, and not to the stranger, white and foreign. Notice that Kourouma does not have a glossary of difficult terms or expressions. The white man would need to make an extra effort to understand, and that would mean that he is reading for serious business, to widen his horizon and not as a frivolous exercise, for want of something else to do or for need of someone to bash.

Of course, Kourouma is denouncing the negative outfalls of colonialism and independence but in as aggressive a way as the colonial linguistic imposition had been underhand because the latter is the worst kind of slavery. His is a liberating decision.

Kourouma's style is that of a bicultural person but he succeeded in super-imposing the Malinké culture on the French— even though he writes *in French* — somehow wrestling the weaker one to the ground.

CONCLUSION

Having succeeded in dispensing with ceremonial French and imposing on the African literary environment his own brand of *négriture*, other Negro-African writers may want to borrow a couple of leaves from Kourouma and launch out on their own. Of course, they should continue to write for their immediate public but they must write in a way that this public will understand and identify with.

After almost four decades of independence (?), let African writers stand up and be counted with Kourouma.

Notes and References

1. In Nigeria, literary texts in autochthonous languages abound particularly in the three major languages; Yoruba, Igbo, and Hausa. Examples of Yoruba texts are:

Prose

a. D. Fagunwa (1949): *Igbo Olodumare*, London: Thomas Nelson.
b. I. Delano (1955): *Aiye d'Aiye Oyinbo*, London: Thomas Nelson
c. A. Awoniyi (1973): *Aiyekooto*, Ibadan, Onibonoje.

Poetry

a. Adeboye Babalola (1973): *Orin Ode Fun Aseye*, Ibadan: Macmillan.
b. Wande Abimbola (1978): *Ijinle Ohun Enu Ifa*, London: OUP.
c. Olatunde Olatunji (1982): *Ewi Adebayo Faleti* I, Ibadan: Heinemann.

Drama

   a. Adebayo Faleti (1972):*Basorun Gaa,* Ibadan: Onibonoje
   b. Owolabi (1978): *Lisabi Agbongbo-Akala,* Ibadan: OUP.
   c. Oyetunde Awoyele (1983): *Alagba Jeremaya,* Ibadan: OUP.

2. Ferdinand de Saussure (1972): *Cours de linguistique générale* (édition critique par Tuillo de Mauro), Paris: Payot.

3. The Yorubas are found in the western part of Nigeria, mainly in Ekiti, Kogi, Kwara, Lagos, Ogun, Ondo, Osun and Oyo States.

4. *Longman's Dictionary of Contemporary English*, ELBS Edition, 1979, p. 784.

5. Ab-usage: usage that goes contrary to the norm.

6. Sembène Ousmane is a past-master in this aspect: ministrion, gouvenementelet, auto-cadeau-mariage, etc.

7. Makhily Gassama (1978): *Kuma: Interrogation sur la littérature nègre de la langue française,* Dakar: NEA p. 67.

8. Ahmadou Kourouma (1970): *Les soleils des indépendance,* Paris: Seuil.

9. Ahamadou Kourouma (1990): *Monnè, outrages et défis,* Paris: Seuil. All references are to the original French editions and the translations are ours.

10. Boribana: we shall no longer retreat. See *ibid.* p.228.

11.Monnew (singular) monnè (plural). Outrage, injury, wrong, insult, defiance, challenge, contempt, scorn, abuse, humiliation, rage, etc. See *ibid.* p.9.

12. Makhily Gassama (1995): *La langue d'Ahmadou Kourouma ou le français sous le soleil d'Afrique,* Paris: ACC/Karthala, p. 68.

13. *Afrique littéraire et artistique*, No 10 quoted in *ibid.* p.43.

14. *Le Nouveau Petit Robert,* Montreal: Editions Dicorobert Incorporated, 1993, p. 927.

15. Ahmadou Kourouma: *Soleils* pp. 120, 109, 110, 113, etc.

16. Ahmadou Kourouma: *ibid.*, pp. 120, 121, 146.

17. *Le Nouveau Petit Robert:* p. 1778.

18. The prefix *de* in French means approximately the same thing with the English *de*, that is *breach, discontinuance or stoppage*. Hence *dévulver* would mean, hypothetically, the discontinuance of vulvation" See *ibid.* pp. 1760, 537.

19. Asseoir quelque chose: to seat, to set, to fix, to establish, to lay the foundation of, to pitch etc. See Casseil's *New French-English-French Dictionary,* London: Casseil, 1977, p. 54.

20. Makhily Gassama (1995): *op. cit.* p.46.

21. Makhily Gassama (1978): *op. cit.* p. *227.*

22. Charles Larson (1974): *Panorama du Roman Africain,* Paris: Editions Internationales, p.7.

23. Ahmadou Kourouma, *Les soleils...*

24. Wole Soyinka's term for syncretism. From a popular comic strip/film character, Tarzan, a man-beast.

25. *Èlírí:* a specie of rat the size of a thumb.

26. Jacques Chevrier (1989) "Roman Africain: le temps du doute et des incertitudes", *Jeune Afrique*, No 1469.

27. Jean-Claude Blanchère (1993): *Négriture: Les écrivains de l'Afrique Noire et la langue française.* Paris: L'Harmattan. P. 26.

28. *ibid.* p. 51.

29. *ibid.* p.26.

30. Jean-Pierre Makouta-Mboukou quoted by J-C Blanchère: *op. cit.* p.52.

13

WOMEN AS AXE-MEN OF WOMANISM IN THE WORKS OF SELECTED FRANCOPHONE FEMALE NOVELISTS OF WEST AFRICA

Yemi Mojola

> "We are the ones responsible for all these bad widowhood practices. We are the ones discriminating against our daughters ... The power is with us to change our families and then the society".[1]
>
> Priscilla Kuye

INTRODUCTION

African women, it cannot be doubted, have been victims of male subjugation and ill-treatment, indeed violence throughout the ages. According to Ezeigbo,

> Gender oppression is ... a scourge that has its source in religion, tradition and politics. These aspects of society have been structured and solidified by patriarchy to marginalise and silence women who constitute a half of the human population.[2]

However, while the stranglehold of patriarchy and tradition, in the main, deprives African women of social, economic and political self-realisation *inter alia*, they themselves have to face the stark reality, the bitter truth, that they are often their own worst enemies. In Mariama Bâ's *Une si longue lettre*, Daba, first child and eldest daughter of the protagonist, Ramatoulaye, commenting on the marriage of Binetou (who used to be her classmate and best friend) to her father, the late Modou, sets the tone for the theme of this paper: "Comment une femme peut-elle saper le bonheur d'une autre femme?"[3]. We intend to discuss the portrayal of women who undermine the happiness of other women in the works of some Francophone female novelists of West Africa. These fictional characters reflect life and blood women who contribute in no small measure to the checkmating of womanism.

What is womanism? According to Kolawole,

> To Africans, womanism is the totality of feminine self-expression, self-retrieval, and self-assertion in positive cultural ways ... ... Walker's attempt to ground Black feminist or womanist consciousness is a part of the growth of awareness that seeks a unique identity for African women's separate consciousness.[4]

The concept is thus grounded in a particular context, the black African context, both within and outside Africa and it affects the quality of life of the black woman in all spheres: physical, mental and psychological. But African women themselves, by acts of commission and omission, impede the full actualisation of womanism. We shall discuss these obstructionist tendencies as reflected fictionally under three headings: harmful traditional practices, socio-cultural, traditional and religious practices and personal character traits.

HARMFUL TRADITIONAL PRACTICES

In the front rank among the harmful traditional practices is female genital mutilation (FGM), that is, excision/infibulation, which is perceived as a form of violence against women. "It is a human rights problem because 99% of the victims are forced into having the operation without prior knowledge of what it involves."[5] The practitioners of FGM are women: the operation runs counter to the interest of the victims in every way. It can engender genital infections, leading to infertility, incontinence, severe problems at childbirth and ... death. Even if no obvious physical disorder occurs, it provokes a psychological trauma: lack of sexual response.

In Aminata Maïga Ka's short story, *La Voie du salut*, excision is performed on a baby girl of about three months. The frightened mother rushes the baby, bleeding profusely to the hospital. Baba Kounta, the doctor, on seeing the dying baby explodes:

> - Comment avez-vous osé exciser ce bébé et à cet âge? ...
> La jeune mère éclata en sanglots.
> - Docteur, c'est la tradition!
> - Une tradition qui va tuer votre enfant! Car votre
> bébé n'en a plus pour longtemps! Mutiler une chair si
> tendre! Quelle aberration![6]

> (- How did you dare to excise this baby and at this age?
> The young mother burst into tears.
> - Doctor, it is the tradition.
> - A tradition which is going to kill your child! For
> your baby doesn't have long to live! Mutilate such a
> tender flesh! What an aberration!)

The baby girl, "victime de la ténébreuse tradition" (victim of the sinister tradition), soon gives up the ghost.

Although Awa Thiam's *Parole aux négresses* is not fiction, its pertinence cannot be overlooked in this study. P.K., one of the women interviewed, recounts that she was excised at the age of twelve. Taken to the excision hut by her two favourite aunts, she was left with the 'surgeon', an old woman, who was assisted by some younger women. It was a nightmarish experience for the innocent girl:

> Je ressentis un déchirement psychosomatique continu.
> La règle voulait qu'à mon âge l'on ne pleurait pas en
> cette circonstance. Je faillis à cette règle. Cris et larmes
> de douleur furent ma première réaction ... Jamais je
> n'avais autant souffert.[7]

> (I felt a continuous psychosomatic laceration.
> According to the rule, at my age, one must not weep

> in this instance. I fell short of this rule.
> Cries and tears of pain were my first reactions... I had
> never suffered so much.)

Yet women inflict this excruciating pain on girls and young women in the name of a nebulous tradition instituted by men within a patriarchal system! The tragedy is that women within the culture where FGM is practised, have generally been so conditioned to accept the authority of tradition even when it errs flagrantly, that they continue to inflict injury on the female gender. Sheer ignorance as to the harmful effects of FGM and perhaps, for the "surgical team", the benefits accruing from the profession, shut the women's eyes to the suffering of the victims.

Infibulation can have more severe and long-lasting complications than excision. Its purpose is egregious to the enlightened woman and man: to ensure that the woman remains a virgin until she gets married. While morality in itself is desirable, women should not impose it on younger women through a barbaric operation. And what about the young men? Why are they permitted to take any sexual liberties before marriage simply on the basis of gender? This double standard, perpetuated by women, is anti-womanist. Ideally, mothers and fathers should inculcate sound morals into their children, male and female, by example.

SOCIO-CULTURAL, TRADITIONAL AND RELIGIOUS PRACTICES

Although in the traditional and Islamic African setting, male members take the final decision as to who will marry their children, women play a major role in the actual organisation of the marriage ceremony. The payment of a dowry to the parents of a bride to-be by the suitor can constitute a veritable source of wealth. The more the physical and mental endowments of the woman, the higher the demands of her family. The female child becomes a chattel to be disposed of to the highest bidder. In Patrick Merand's opinion.

> La dot joue ce rôle ingrat: elle représente la contrepartie
> monétaire d'un travail domestique. Le "nouvel
> employeur" verse une prime pour avoir le droit

d'emmener avec lui une femme qui travaillera
dorénavant pour lui, toujours gratuitement.[8]

(Dowry plays this ungrateful role: it represents the
monetary counterpart of domestic work. The "new
employer" pays a premium to take away with him a
wife who will henceforth work for him, always free of
charge.)

Married women experience this slave labour situation, yet they
actively support the system for selfish reasons.

In *La Voie du salut*, Rokhaya, the female protagonist, invites
her late husband's self-proclaimed sister and two of her friends for
consultation on the demand of the hand of her daughter, Rabiatou,
a magistrate, in marriage:

> - Rabiatou est une bonne fille. Une fille intelligente.
> Elle fait partie de l'élite de notre societé, dit Adja
> Aïssatou.
> - Pour ces raisons, elle coûtera cher, très cher,
> renchérit Adja Seynabou.[9]
>
> (- Rabiatou is a good girl. An intelligent girl. She is
> part of our society's elite, said Adja Aïssatou.
> - For these reasons, she will be expensive, very
> expensive, Adja Seynabou further added.)

On being informed that her suitor is a teacher, they reject him
categorically because, in their view, teachers are always in debt
from the 1st of January to the 31st of December:

> En tout cas, Rabiatou, par sa beauté et son intelligence,
> peut prétendre à un meilleur parti: ministre,
> ambassadeur, député, homme d'affaires. Voilà des gens
> intéressants qui déverseront sur nous toutes des
> sommes fabuleuses! Un pareil prétendant pourra
> t'emmener à La Mecque, te construire une maison ...
> Mais un instituteur, tcham! conclut Adja Aïssatou.[10]
>
> (In any case, Rabiatou, by her beauty and intelligence,
> can lay claim to a better match: a minister, an
> ambassador, a deputy, a business man. Those are

> attractive people who will pour fabulous amounts on
> us all! Such a suitor can take you to Mecca, build a
> house for you... But a teacher, tcham! concluded Adja
> Aïssatou.)

The insatiable desire to gain as much as possible from the dowry paid on daughters takes a most dehumanising turn in Calixthe Beyala's *C'est le soleil qui m'a brûlée*. Ada, the aunt who brings up Ateba, the main character, watches over Ateba's virginity very closely in order to receive a considerable dowry on her subsequently. One day, Ateba goes out to keep a date without informing her aunt. On her return, not only is she thoroughly battered, she is taken by Ada to an old woman, who in accordance with tradition, inserts an egg into her vagina to ascertain her virginity. Women subjecting another woman to a most devastating humiliation and depersonalisation in the name of tradition! In *Le Prix d'une vie* by Simone Kaya, the step-mother of Clémence, the protagonist, attacks her physically to prevent her from returning to France to marry an African from another country. Her hatred comes from the thought of the huge material loss the family would sustain since, if she were to marry a wealthy powerful man from their country, the family would acquire wealth and position.

Women have so internalised their role as custodians of a patriarchal tradition demeaning to womanhood that they would go to any extent to save the "honour" of the family in case a bride is not a virgin. In *La Voie du salut*, Rokhaya, on her wedding night, has on a white percale wrapper. Very early the following morning, her aunt, Aïssé Diallo, publicly holds up the blood-stained wrapper, proof of Rokhaya's virginity. And the large crowd is beside itself with joy. The whole scene soon becomes a festival. As Médina, a teenager withdrawn from school and forced to marry her cousin whom she has never met, affirms in *Parole aux Négresses*, if she, Médina, had not been a virgin on her wedding night, her aunts perhaps would have resorted to the deceit of spilling a chicken's blood on the bride's wrapper.

Polygamy, or more accurately, polygyny,

> is the epitome of female denigration, exploitation and
> domination in West Africa. If 'home' represents the

> place where one is most at ease, the polygynous home
> is not home but hell for the co-wives and their children
> as tensions reign supreme, fuelled by envy, distrust,
> intrigues and all sorts of destructive passions.[11]

In spite of this hell on earth, polygyny continues to thrive because there are always women ready to be second, third, *ad infinitum* wives for all sorts of reasons: enjoying the material comforts an already married man can provide, the feeling of importance as the favourite wife since the latest addition to the collection is always pampered, helplessness in the face of parental pressure, tradition and religious injunctions.

In *Juletane* by Myriam Warner-Vieyra, (a Guadeloupian resident in Dakar since the sixties), Ndèye, the semi-literate, immoral third wife of Mamadou, completely monopolises their husband and even boasts about his sexual prowess to the hearing of her co-wives. Awa, the first wife, is reduced to the role of cook and childbearer while Juletane, the young West Indian second wife, is considered a mad woman. Ndèye has no occupation but in spite of the family's financial difficulties, she always stocks beer, her favourite drink, and whisky for Mamadou and wears the most expensive boubous and jewelry. In Beyala's *Maman a un amant*, Soumana becomes Abdou's second wife even in Paris and her importance derives only from her childbearing capacity since M'am, the first wife, is barren. In *Un chant écarlate*, Ouleymatou, an empty-headed semi-literate, deliberately seduces Ousmane, already married to Mireille, a French lady, who stretches herself to save her marriage. As Ousmane's second wife, Ouleymatou, with the full support of Ousmane's mother, monopolises him.

The above examples show clearly that women are often threats to and even destroyers of other women's happiness and stability. Sonia Lee observes:

> Pour les femmes - écrivains, la polygamie nuit à
> l'épanouissement du couple ... Et même si elles sont
> conscientes que le mariage monogame n'est pas une
> garantie de bonheur, il reste à leurs yeux une marque
> de respect pour la femme, partenaire à part entière
> dans le mariage.[12]

> (For female writers, polygamy is injurious to the development of the couple... And even if they are aware that the monogamous marriage is not a guarantee of happiness, it still remains for them a mark of respect for the woman, a full-fledged partner in the marriage.)

Indeed, any woman who gets married to a married man or encourages the advances of a married man impedes the total emancipation of womanhood from the grips of phallocratic authority. Women who catch others in this betrayal with their men react in diverse ways: Aïssatou in *Une si longue lettre*, without hesitation, makes a clean break from her husband, Mawdo, and resolutely reorders her life for the better. Her childhood friend, Ramatoulaye, on the other hand, adapts herself to the situation and refuses to divorce Modou. But after Modou's passing, her determined rejection of Daouda Dieng, her first suitor, speaks volumes for what women can do to curtail and subsequently put an end to polygyny. She rejects Dieng in spite of the emotional and material benefits that would have accrued to her and her children on the grounds that she does not love him and that she cannot come between him and his family.

Another area in which women actively work against the interests of other women is at the demise of a husband. Rather than support his widow, his sisters could, for example, openly inflict on her the disgrace and humiliation of not doing her hair as required by Senegalese tradition, if she had not tolerated their excesses. As the narrator in *Une si longue lettre* succinctly puts it, 'C'est le moment redouté de toute Sénégalaise' (It is the moment most dreaded by every Senegalese woman). To avoid the public disgrace, a wife sacrifices her possessions, even her individuality and dignity to gain the favour of her in-laws, especially the female in-laws. When a wife insists on maintaining her self-respect, older women, mothers and mothers-in-law, would often do everything possible to ensure that she conforms to the destiny which tradition imposes on her.

A further example of exploitation of widows by in-laws with sisters-in-law acting as front for the late husband's family, is what Ramatoulaye in the same novel describes as "la phase la plus déroutante"(the most baffling period) of the third day ceremony of the funeral. Traditionally, by way of assistance, sympathisers gave millet, rice, cattle, milk, flour and sugar to the widows. With modernity, monetary assistance has become the norm. Every gift is carefully recorded for payment in identical circumstances. However, in the case of in-laws, whatever money they offer to the widows must be doubled by the latter and given to the in-laws on the spot. Thus it is that Modou's sisters exploit his widows by contributing, in a public display of opulence, the sum of one hundred thousand francs from the paternal side and an equal amount from the maternal side. Each widow, of course, doubles the amount for them. Ramatoulaye comments that the in-laws carry off the bundles of currency notes laboriously doubled by them and leave them, the widows, who actually need material aid, "dans un dénuement total" (in total penury).

PERSONAL CHARACTER TRAITS

In this section, we shall discuss some of the character traits portraying women as axe-men of female aspirations to self-fulfilment and self-assertion. Many women prey upon other women: for example, some mothers use their daughters as chattel; some women relish in malicious gossip to the detriment of others. Other women, through their life styles such as prostitution, profligacy and absolute dependence on men emotionally or economically, debase womanhood.

In *Une si longue lettre*, Binetou is withdrawn from school because of pressure from her mother, nicknamed Dame Belle-mère by the narrator-protagonist, in spite of the marginalisation of girls in education. She is literally forced to marry Modou, a man old enough to be her father and who already has twelve children. Binetou prefers to continue her studies but "sa mère est une femme qui veut tellement sortir de sa condition médiocre" (her mother is a woman who desires so much to leave her mediocre condition) that she subsequently succumbs to her pleas. As Daba informs her mother, Ramatoulaye:

> Binetou, navrée, épouse son "vieux". Sa mère a
> tellement pleuré. Elle a supplié sa fille de lui "donner

une fin heureuse, dans une vraie maison" que l'homme
leur a promise. Alors, elle a cédé.[13]

(Binetou, broken-hearted, marries her "old man". Her
mother wept so much. She begged her daughter "to
give her a happy end, in a real house" which the man
promised them. So she gave in.)

Modou bears the expenses for a pilgrimage to Mecca by Dame
Belle-mère and Binetou's father – they acquire the titles of Hadjia
and Alhaji. Modou constructs a three-bedroom apartment behind
his chic SICAP villa for Dame Belle-mère and pampers her with
various gifts. The innocent daughter is sacrificed to the god of
materialism. As the narrator comments with respect to the sharing
of Modou's property after his death, while Dame Belle-mère sobs
incessantly because it was not in their favour, Binetou does not
react. "Que lui importait ce qui se disait. Elle était déjà morte
intérieurement ... depuis ses épousailles avec Modou"[14] (What was
being said meant nothing to her. She was already inwardly dead...
since her marriage to Modou).

In *Le Prix d'une vie*, the mother of Clémence abandoned her
children for no apparent reason as she was in a monogamous union
and her literate husband did not maltreat her even though she was
an illiterate. Clémence was then only four years old. She went to
school only to return in the afternoon to discover that her mother
had permanently left for God knows where with her younger sister.
Her cries of anguish rent the air; her tears were uncontrollable and
the fever, which she developed, left nobody in doubt that it was a
traumatic experience. Ateba, in *C'est le soleil* had a worse
experience. Not only was she eventually abandoned by her mother,
Betty, she was a witness to her prostitution, her countless abortions,
her infanticides. At a tender and impressionable age, an incalculable
damage was done to Ateba's psyche. Moreover, in *Tu t'appelleras
Tanga* also by Beyala, Tanga, the protagonist, underwent FGM on
her mother's insistence so that she could "keep all her men": Tanga's
prostitution is her family's means of survival. Double violence is
thus done to her, engineered by her mother. E. A. Brière points out
this inverted role of mother/daughter, with respect to Beyala's *C'est
le soleil* and *Tu t'appelleras Tanga*:

... c'est Ateba, l'enfant, qui joue le rôle maternel,
nourrissant, lavant, massant sa mère Betty lorsqu'elle
rentre à la maison, éreintée par son travail de
prostituée. Dans *Tu t'appelleras Tanga,* la survie de
la famille dépend du travail des enfants.[15]

(... it is Ateba, the child, who plays the mother's role,
feeding, washing massaging her mother, Betty, when
she returns home, exhausted by her job as prostitute.
In *Tu t'appelleras Tanga,* the survival of the family
depends on the children's work.)

Brière interpretes this abnormal role inversion whereby mothers
"devour" their children as evidence of their being victims of African
post-colonial rapacity themselves.

Women do destroy other women's reputation and peace of mind
through malicious gossip. In *Juletane,* Ndèye has two very close
friends, Binta and Astou. However, whenever any of them is absent,
the other two do not hesitate to make a swipe behind her back. In
Un chant écarlate, Yaye Khady, the mother of the male protagonist,
Ousmane, on being informed that her son had got married to a
white woman, cannot sleep, worried about other women's
backbiting. The irony of it is that she is just as guilty as the other
scandalmongers.

The lifestyles of some women detract from womanism. By
engaging in prostitution, for example, in order to satisfy their
material needs, women reduce themselves to the level of objects.
The male client sees the prostitute as his possession for the period
for which he has paid. The woman is depersonalised. In *C'est le
soleil,* Betty complains to Ateba "... l'homme avec qui je suis sortie
hier soir a un mauvais sang" (... the man I dated yesterday evening
has bad blood), thereby indicating the dehumanising treatment
received from her client. In proper perspective, this self-abasement
is self-inflicted if, as in many cases, a woman prostitutes herself for
material gain. In the same novel, Irène, a young friend of Ateba,
sleeps with any man, white or black, who can satisfy her craving
for material pleasures. She smokes endlessly, "son éternel Coca-
cola entre les jambes". She subsequently becomes pregnant - for

no definite man, of course - and loses her life in trying to abort the foetus. However, it should be pointed out that some women become prostitutes due to circumstances beyond their control such as abject poverty or coercion by delinquent adults. Some women are high society prostitutes who lure married men into marrying them thereby breaking up otherwise settled homes. Such is the case of Soukeyna Fall, a 'drinké' (high society woman), who snatches Rabiatou's husband in *La Voie du salut*. Rabiatou, seven months' pregnant, on being informed that her husband, Racine, whom she went through thick and thin to marry, had taken Soukeyna as a second wife, staggers, then falls, never to regain consciousness.

Women like Yama in Aminata Sow Fall's *Le Revenant* and Arame Dieng in Ka's short story, *Le miroir de la vie*, display their opulence in a sickening manner. Yet they depend absolutely on their husbands for survival. Even at home, they do nothing; they engage in idle gossip, go shopping for the most expensive clothes and jewelry and entertain with unrivalled profligacy for the most frivolous reasons. As Arame Dieng's husband bursts out to her over the participation of their son in a bomb attack, "Au lieu de veiller à l'éducation de tes enfants, tu ne penses qu' à te parer, à te pavaner et à jeter l'argent par les fenêtres"[16] (Instead of watching over your children's education, you only think of adorning yourself, of strutting about and throwing money out of the window). Some other women feel that their existence cannot be sustained without a male presence. Thus Ada, in *C'est le soleil*, constantly bemoans: "Il faut un homme dans cette maison" (We need a man in this house). For Betty, her sister, the same retrograde thinking holds:

> Betty aussi pensait qu' une maison ne pouvait vivre en l'absence de l'autre. Elle soutenait qu' une femme pouvait faire ce qu' elle voulait mais à condition d'avoir un homme sur qui elle pouvait compter. "Un titulaire, selon ses dires".[17]

> (Betty also felt that a house could not cope without the other. She maintained that a woman could do whatever she wanted provided she had a man to rely on. "A permanent occupant", according to her).

Even the adolescent Irène affirms that without a man she is only an illusion. Women who refuse to be self-reliant, women who privilege men retard the emancipation of women.

One of the worst manifestations of anti-womanism is the conscious exploitation of other women out of self-interest and greed, widespread among mothers-in-law, sisters-in-law and co-wives, in particular. In the Senegalese society depicted in *Une si longue lettre* and *Un chant écarlate*, the culture of expecting gifts from the wives of sons and brothers reaches a frightening proportion. In the latter work, Rosalie, a married Senegalese friend of Mireille advises her:

> Aie toujours prête une piécette ou mieux quelque billet pour "libérer" tes visiteurs, s'ils sont de ta belle-famille, surtout ... Je n'insisterai jamais assez sur la nécessité de donner. Ici, donner, plus que partout ailleurs, résoud bien des problèmes.[18]

> (Always have ready a small coin or even better some currency notes to "free" your visitors, especially if they are your in-laws... I will never sufficiently insist on the necessity of giving. Here, more than everywhere else, giving solves many problems.)

Mireille follows her friend's advice to the letter, but her mother-in-law, Yaye Khady, is not satisfied because the average Senegalese mother-in-law expects her son's wife to be at her command, be her servant, her workhorse. "Évoluant dans ses privilèges jamais discutés, la belle-mère ordonne, supervise, exige. Elle s'approprie les meilleures parts du gain de son fils"[19] (Evolving in her unquestioned privileges, the mother-in-law commands, supervises, exacts. She takes the best share of her son's earnings). In an interior monologue, Mireille's mother-in-law ruminates on her expectations which she considers legitimate:

> Elle méritait une prompte relève. Beaucoup de femmes de son âge, à cause de la présence de leur belle-fille, n'avaient plus que le souci de se laisser vivre

agréablement. Elles se mouvaient dans la paresse et l'encens. Leur bru les servait ... L'oisiveté convenait à leur âge ..."[20]

(She deserved an immediate relief. The only worry of many women of her age, due to the presence of their daughters-in-law, was how to lead a pleasant life. They moved about in laziness and burning of incense. Their daughters-in-law served them... Idleness suited their age...)

Yaye Khady ensures the rupture of the love between her son and his wife.

Bâ's affirmation in the same novel that some mothers-in-law actually behave as rivals vis-à-vis their daughters-in-law finds confirmation in Tante Nabou's vengeance against Aïssatou in *Une si longue lettre*. Tante Nabou, still clinging to her privileged origins, believes firmly in the caste system. How can her "only man", Mawdo, with blue blood flowing in his veins, marry a low-caste goldsmith's daughter who will burn everything on her path like in a forge? She carefully plans her revenge; she undertakes a tedious journey into the hinterland of Senegal to request her brother to give her his daughter, her namesake, ostensibly to help her in the home. She sends the young Nabou to school, gets her trained as a midwife and hands her over to her son as a gift from her brother to thank her for the worthy manner in which she brought her up. Mawdo accepts to marry the young Nabou to please his mother, confesses to Ramatoulaye that he does not love her but uses her to satisfy his sexual urge. Nabou, through the machinations of her aunt, becomes a sex object for Mawdo. In the wake of her vengeance, her son's harmonious marriage with the woman he claims to love breaks up. Yet making a home is of central importance to African women.

CONCLUSION

It is obvious from the examples given from the literary texts that women hinder the realisation of female liberation from domination through sheer ignorance (lack of education), selfishness, materialism and conditioning by patriarchal traditional/religious practices and beliefs which make many women accept the fallacy of being inferior to men.

What is the solution? Massive female education, economic independence, determined selfless assistance to other women and female bonding - not against the male gender, but working together for the upliftment of womanhood and society. Sembène Ousmane's *Les Bouts de bois de Dieu* provides an example: during the strike, every woman, including the blind Maïmouna plays a role, a useful role. No woman seeks to destroy, denigrate or weaken other women. This is the ideal example. Working together, embracing education and economic self-reliance, women will eventually attain the much-desired emancipation.

Notes

1. "Traditional Practices Affecting the Health of Women and Children", *The Guardian on Sunday*, Dec. 8, 1996.

2. Ezeigbo, T. A. "Women Empowerment and National Integration: Bâ's *So Long a Letter* and Warner-Vieyra's *Juletane*", in Emenyonu E. N. and C. E. Nnolim (eds.) *Current Trends in Literature and Language Studies in West Africa*. Ibadan: Kraft Books Limited, 1994, p.15.

3. Bâ, M. *Une si longue lettre*. Dakar-Abidjan-Lome: Les Nouvelles Editions Africaines, 1980, p.103.

4. Kolawole, M. E. M. *Womanism and African Consciousness*. Trenton: Africa World Press, Inc., 1997, p.24.

5. Saffiatou K. Singhateh quoted in Toubia, Nahid. *Female Genital Mutilation: A Call for Global Action.* New York: Women Ink., 1993, p.38.

6. Ka, M. A. *La Voie du salut* suivi de *Le Miroir de la vie.* Paris: Présence Africaine, 1985, p. 19.

7. Thiam, A. *Parole aux négresses.* Paris: Denoël, 1978. p.81.

8. Merand, P. *La vie quotidienne en Afrique noire à travers la littérature Africaine.* Paris: L'Harmattan, 1984, p.78.

9. Ka, M. A. *Op. cit.* p.73.

10. *Ibid.* p.74.

11. Mojola, I. "The onus of womanhood: Mariama Bâ and Zaynab Alkali", in Stephanie Newell. *Writing African Women, Gender, Popular Culture and Literature in West Africa.* London and New Jersey: Zed Books, 1997, p.128.

12. Lee, S. *Les romancières du Continent noir. Anthologie.* Paris: Hatier, Collection Monde Noir Poche, 1994. p.

13. Ba, M. *Op. cit.* p. 55.

14. *Ibid.* p.103.

15. Brière, E. A. "Le retour des mères dévorantes". *Notre Librairie,* No. 117, avril-juin, 1994, p.68.

16. Ka, M. A. *Le Miroir de la vie,* p.155.

17. Beyala, C. *C'est le soleil qui m'a brûlée.* Paris: Stock, 1987, p.90.

18. Bâ, M. *Un chant écarlate.* Dakar-Abidjan-Lomé: Les Nouvelles Editions Africaines, 1981, p.148.

18. *Ibid,* p.111.

19. *Loc. cit.*

Bibliography

1. Bâ, M. *Une si longue lettre*. Dakar-Abidjan-Lomé: Les Nouvelles Editions Africaines, 1980.

   ———— *Un chant écarlate*. Dakar-Abidjan-Lomé: Les Nouvelles EditionsAfricaines, 1981.

2. Beyala, C. *C'est le soleil qui m'a brulée*. Paris: Stock, 1987
   ———— *Tu t'appelleras Tanga*. Paris: Stock, 1988
   ———— *Maman a un amant*. Paris: Albin Michel, 1993

3. Brière, E. A. "Le retour des mères dévorantes". *Notre Librairie*, No. 117 avril-juin, 1994; pp.66-71.

4. d'Almeida, I. A. "Femmes? Féministe? Misovire? Les romancières africaines" *Notre Librairie*, No. 117 avril-juin, 1994; pp.48-51.

5. Ezeigbo, T. A. "Women Empowerment and National Integration: Ba's *So Long a Letter* and Warner-Vieyra's *Juletane*" in *Current Trends in Literature and Language Studies in West Africa*. Ibadan: Kraft Books Limited, 1994, pp.7-19.

6. Fall, A. S. *Le Revenant*. Dakar-Abidjan-Lomé: Les Nouvelles Editions Africaines, 1970.

7. Ka, M. A. *La Voie du salut* suivi de *Le Miroir de la vie*, Paris: Présence Africaine, 1985.

8. Kaya, S. *Le Prix d'une vie*. Abidjan: CEDA, 1984.

9. Kolawole, M. E. M. *Womanism and African Consciousness*. Trenton: Africa World Press Inc., 1997.

10. Lee, S. *Les romancières du Continent noir. Anthologie*. Paris: Hatier (Collection Monde Noir Poche), 1994.

11. Mérand, P. *La vie quotidienne en Afrique noire à travers la littérature africaine*. Paris: L'Harmattan, 1984.

12. Mojola, I. "The onus of womanhood: Mariama Bâ and Zaynab Alkali" in *Writing African Women, Gender, Popular Culture and Literature in West Africa*. London: Zed. Books, 1997, pp. 126-136.

—— "La signification de l'amour dans *Le Prix d'une vie* de Simone Kaya", *RENEF*, Vol. 1, No. 05, Août, 1997, pp.77-94.

13. Mokwenye, C. "La polygamie et la révolte de la femme africaine moderne: une lecture d' *Une si longue lettre* de Mariama Bâ", *Peuples Noirs Peuples Africains*, 31, jan.- feb., 1993, pp.86-94.

14. Mouralis, B. "Une parole autre: Aoua Keïta, Mariama Bâ et Awa Thiam", *Notre Librairie*, No. 117 avril-juin, 1994, pp.21-27 (Nouvelles Écritures Féminines).

14. Ndinda, J. "Écriture et discours féminin au Cameroun", *Notre Librairie*, No. 117, avril - juin 1994, pp.6-12.

16. Thiam, A. *Parole aux négresses*. Paris: Denoël/Gonthier, 1978.

17. Toubia, Nahid. *Female Genital Mutilation: A Call for Global Action*. New York: Women Ink, 1993.

18. Warner-Vieyra, M. *Juletane*. Paris: Présence Africaine, 1982.

THEATRE

14

FEMALE CHARACTERISATION IN FRANCOPHONE AFRICAN DRAMA

Gertrude Edem

INTRODUCTION

The African woman has been part of sub-Saharan Francophone African drama since theatre in its written form first took root in French African territories, starting at the École William Ponty in the mid-1930s. It should be noted that the first Francophone African playwrights were graduates of the all-boys École William Ponty which was the first school in Africa to accept the possibility of an African drama and, for whatever reason[1], encourage its students to pursue their interests in the area by providing them with the means and opportunity to do so. However, though the African woman features more and more frequently in Francophone plays, her participation in the plot still remains limited as male playwrights, who continue to dominate this genre, appear to struggle to find a suitable part for her to play. As a matter of fact, her role is often insignificant, rarely having any bearing on the development of the main plot, and leaving her quite dispensable as a character. Female Francophone African playwrights only started contributing to the theatre repertory in the mid-1970s[2] and, to date, only the Camerounian Were-were Liking has shown any interest in using drama as a means of literary expression.

Unlike its Anglophone counterpart, Francophone African theatre has attracted little critical attention and its critics, generally more fascinated by performance, tend to record, analyse, and report on stage production of plays, virtually neglecting the study of theatre as a literary genre. As proponents of feminist criticism and its application in theatre studies (like Ajayi-Soyinka, 1993 and Case, 1990) have pointed out, Theatre departments emphasise theatre history and the training of theatre practitioners, while foreign languages departments (including English and French) even in African universities and colleges, still view classical European plays as the acme of theatre, and list them as preferred works for critical analysis in their courses.

Studies on the portrayal of women in Francophone African theatre are even more scarce. In the last two decades, scholars most of them feminists critics and theorists (such as Lee [1974], Chemain-Degrange [1980], Kembe [1984], Brière [1993], Davies [1986]), in their quest to draw attention to the African woman's "plight" as recorded in literature, have come to pay close attention to various forms of female depiction in the Francophone novel and poetry. However, the few critics who study Francophone African theatre have said astoundingly little about female characterisation. If the African woman happens to be cast as the main protagonist and, as such, needs to be acknowledged by virtue of her importance to the plot, discussions about her are generally sketchy and superficial, virtually ignoring her role, but rather emphasising the flaws in her representation. Also, such discussions are usually couched in more conventional critical approaches, with the woman being considered not as a protagonist, but in relation to a theme or to some ideal that the playwright is trying to put across.

This study attempts to highlight images of the African woman as she is portrayed in the dramatic texts of male sub-Saharan Francophone Africans. However, given the sheer number of the plays involved and the broad nature of the issues discussed, the paper will limit itself to selected dramatic works by a variety of playwrights across the continent, and span the first two decades of political independence in Africa, that is from 1960 to 1979. Also, representations of the African woman in this body of literature are quite varied, a fact that is reflected neither by the paucity of studies on her nor by the narrow reading of the roles attributed to her. For the purposes of analysis, this study will look at female characters as traditional women, political figures and social activists, wives and mothers, as well as women with a variety of occupations.

TRADITIONAL WOMEN

The geo-historical setting of a play does not necessarily determine the mentality of its characters. The African woman from pre-colonial days is usually viewed as traditional and often depicted as naive, enduring, quietly accepting and fulfilling the roles traditionally ascribed to her by society (Lee, 1974; Kembe, 1980, etc.) . However, in some Francophone African plays, the pre-colonial woman is cast in roles where her avant-garde ideas make her stand out as an activist against the backdrop of her rural community's traditional mentality. Women of this latter group will be discussed as political figures or social activists, irrespective of the period in which they are depicted. The focus of this section will be those women who are traditionalists in their outlook, even if they are cast in contemporary times.

Most women in historical plays are of a traditional mentality. They are usually royal women with very strong characters, and they command authority. Some women have accepted political roles in the society. An example is Princess Sogona in Djibril Tamsir Niane's *Sikasso*, which dramatises King Bemba's resistance to the annexation of his kingdom by the French. In the play, Sogona is portrayed as a strong leader among the women who admire and greatly respect her. Her authority is evident throughout the play, as difficult matters involving women are referred to her. When, for example, the local store runs out of salt during the siege of Sikasso by the French and some women are so angry they are about to start a riot, Sogona is brought in. At her appearance, calm seems to be restored. She chides the angry women, but also reassures them by telling them that the siege should be over soon. Being herself the mother of a young baby, Sogona is naturally afraid: she hates the invasion of the kingdom and dreads the superior force of the French army. However, she stills her own fears so as to help the other women deal with theirs and, exhorting the women to bravery, she leads them in singing to cheer on their husbands and sons leaving for a battle from which they will probably never return. Sogona's strength of character is equally obvious in her parting chat with her husband, Prince N'FaFatini, King Bemba's brother and an army general, whom she rebukes for deluding himself about victory over the French troops:

> Ne parle pas de victoire quand tu cours à un combat
> aussi inégal et aussi désepéré. (p. 58)

However, on hearing of her husband's death, Sogona herself loses her lucidity, for she leads the women to the King demanding weapons and a chance to avenge the deaths of their husbands and sons against the same French army. This show of courage wins them the following tribute from King Bemba:

> Je vous reconnais, dignes mères de Sikasso, et votre
> demande gonfle mon coeur d'orgueil ... Si, comme on
> dit, tout homme vaut ce que vaut sa mère, le courage
> dont vous faites preuve en venant jusqu'à moi ne me
> fait plus douter de nos guerriers. (p. 62).

In a crisis situation like this one, women are traditionally stoical; they are expected to show strength, bravery, and endurance. Sogona and the other women live up to those standards and expectations, thus proving themselves to be worthy wives and mothers of Sikasso.

Like Sogona, the women in Cheikh A.Ndao's *L'Exil d'Albouri* are strong and dutiful. In the play, King Albouri too refuses negotiation with the French who want to annex his kingdom but chooses exile over engaging in a war against the superior French army and causing unnecessary loss of lives for his people. In the Wollof tradition, the king's sister is *la Linguère,* that is the king's lieutenant for the women. La Linguère Madjiguene in *L'Exil d'Albouri* fulfils her duty to the point of practically neglecting her own husband and children because she lives in the King's court where she carries out her state functions:

> Mon rôle de Linguère m'a toujours tenue à tes côtés.
> Je transmets tous tes ordres touchant aux femmes du
> Djoloff. (p. 34).

As the king's lieutenant, Linguère Madjiguene accepts without question and defends Albouri's decision to flee his kingdom and

1otherland. The queen mother Yây Diop, on the contrary, isapproves of exile because of the dishonour it would connote. ʿây attempts to protect Albouri's reputation by advising him to tay back in his capital and, if necessary, die there rather than betray is blood and honour by fleeing.

Both Yây Diop and Madjiguene accept and fulfil their :aditional roles faithfully. Anything less would be frowned upon, s is the case with the attitude of Albouri's twenty-year-old wife,)ueen Sêb Fall, who complains about loneliness, the court protocol 1at separates her from her husband, and the tradition that requires er to communicate with the king through his sister La Linguère. :xpressing physical and emotional needs openly is quite ntraditional for a queen. However, Sêb puts her womanly nature nd needs first and foremost, relegating her queenly duties to the ackground:

> Etre noble, avoir des droits au trône du Cayor, être
> belle et séduisante, et ne pas voir mon mari comme je
> l'aurais voulu (...). O, voir mes seins qui bourgeonnent!
> (p. 38).

 êb does not want to waste her youth and beauty, or lose her rivileges by going into exile with King Albouri. She bypasses her ister-in-law and, ignoring protocol, goes directly to seek audience /ith the king who readily accommodates her. Sêb's revolt is short-ved, though: her meeting with Albouri convinces her of his love ɔr her, so she decides to embrace the queen's traditional role, but ows not to let her responsibilities come between her and her usband.

In non-historical plays set in the colonial and post independence ras, the traditional woman is a peasant portrayed as lacking in ignity and courage. If, as is often said, historical plays attempted ɔ assert the dignity of Africa by revitalising its impressive past Ndao, 1970), non-historical plays appear to do just the opposite, specially in their depiction of the traditional African woman. She ; portrayed as subdued, submissive, self-effacing, often treated /ith disdain, and somewhat lost in these times of new concepts ke church, school, and public service, times for which she shows curious mix of scorn and admiration.

A case in point is the female protagonist in Jean-Laforest Afana's *La Coutume qui tue* who is simply referred to as "La Veuve" (The Widow). The play centres on her husband's funeral rights. La Veuve, as the appellation suggests, is role-playing the part of the newly bereaved African woman in a Camerounian tradition. She is portrayed as weak, passive, and confused, understandably so, given her loss. In addition, she has to endure insults, starvation, and beating by just about any man: tradition requires and expects that of a woman in her circumstances. She is also held accountable for her husband's death, and accused of killing him[3]. But through it all, La Veuve remains stoic, neither protesting nor putting up a resistance: she appears lifeless, as if she was just going through the motions in a ritual from which she can't escape.

In Guy Menga's *L'Oracle*, Louvouézo, a traditional woman in colonial times, is also portrayed as totally accepting the role ascribed to her, though it is not clear whether it is by tradition or by her husband. The play discusses Louaka's triumph over her father Biyoki in a struggle involving her schooling, marriage, and bride price. Louvouézo's husband Biyoki had put their daughter Louaka in school against her wish, because he hoped to eventually marry her off for a lot of money. However, six months before Louaka is to obtain her certificate, Biyoki decides to withdraw her from school and marry her off to Mamba, a rich old polygamist who has just returned from the white man's country with trunks full of riches. Louvouézo's initial objections to the marriage fade away when Biyoki discloses how much riches are involved and insists that they should act quickly so as not to miss the opportunity to become rich:

> Cesse de t'entêter ainsi, Louvouézo. Les périodes d'abondance ne se présentent pas fréquemment. Profitons donc de l'occasion qui s'offre car ton nez, comme le mien s'incline de plus en plus vers la dernière demeure : le lendemain est une incertitude pour tout humain, te le sais très bien. (pp. 28-29).

Though Louvouézo sees Biyoki as a lazy, good-for-nothing drunk, she submits to his tyranny as required by tradition, and remains completely loyal to him. So she supports Biyoki in his greed, stops trying to reason with him, and accepts the gifts that Mamba had sent her. She even agrees to persuade her eldest brother to accept Louaka's marriage to old Mamba.

Some traditional women also appear in Guillaume Oyono-Mbia's *Trois prétendants ... un mari*, a play that gives an insight into what Bjornson rightly calls rural Africa's maladjustment to new values imposed by colonisation[4]. Makrita and Bella, Juliette's mother and grandmother, share the same traditional values. Both are docile, subdued and treated with little consideration or respect, and excluded from important family decisions, like choosing a husband for Juliette, the only college student in the village, a venture around which the plot of the play is woven.

Though Makrita and Bella are from two different generations and have, most probably experienced tradition differently, Makrita thinks very much like Bella. By juxtaposing the two women, Oyono-Mbia emphasises the point that little or no evolution has occurred in the women of Mvoutesi over the two generations. Bella submits totally to her husband, Abessolo's control and she takes her cue from him. When Abessolo regrets the "good" old days when wives were not allowed to wear clothes, eat the meat of certain animals, or take part in decision-making, but were just beaten (though he doesn't bother to say why), Bella commiserates with him over his lost privileges: "Qu'est-ce qu'il y a encore dans ce monde d'aujourd'hui, mon pauvre mari? Je vois des femmes manger même des vipères, des sangliers, des ...." (p.15). Her confusion becomes apparent when, moments after this apology for tradition, Bella is overjoyed at the thought that her Juliette will marry a great civil servant from Sangmelina who is a "*real* white man!" (our emphasis).

Makrita appears even more confused. Spanning both tradition and modernity and unable to come to grips with either, she is torn between Abessolo's crude ideas of the old days and what she sees of the new ways which include consulting a woman about things. The problem, however, is that the new ways still leave Makrita a victim, for though her husband, Atangana would like to consult Juliette about her marriage, the consultation does not include her. Makrita has no say in the matter of Juliette's marriage. In fact, when Mbia, the civil servant, comes to ask for Juliette's hand, the playwright's stage directions indicate that all the men move towards the road to meet the newcomer, while the women (including

Makrita) move towards the kitchen. However, whether she is included in the decision or not, Makrita is delighted at the proposed marriage between her daughter and the civil servant who has come like a real suitor, wearing a "terylene suit" and probably carrying wine in his car. Makrita has never seen Mbia, but she believes he is definitely the right husband for a girl like her daughter. Like Bella, Makrita longs for the advantages that come with having a civil servant for a son-in-law. However, Bella oscillates between tradition and modernity, quite oblivious of the fact that Mbia, the "*real* white man," her family's future status symbol, is also the embodiment of modernity and, as such, equally symbolises the end of the traditional values that she appears so eager to cling to. Makrita, for her part, has nothing to cling to.

Whether she is cast in pre-colonial or post-independence Africa, the traditional woman leads her life according to traditional norms which she accepts without questions. She is totally immersed in these norms and accepts whatever social role is handed down with them, particularly through her husband who portrays himself as all-knowing where tradition is concerned. The traditional woman makes no attempt and expresses no desire to view things differently, and trying out new ways of doing things appears completely out of the question, as is evident in Louvouézo's fear of supporting Louaka against Biyoki even though she feels her daughter should stay in school. If the traditional woman agitates and questions, she eventually apologises and explains away her behaviour somehow: Queen Sêb Fall, for example, blames her "capricious" revolt on her youth. So such an agitation does not lead to action, and the status quo remains.

POLITICAL FIGURES AND SOCIAL ACTIVISTS

In sub-Saharan Francophone African theatre, just as in most of Africa during the first two decades of independence, the political arena is reserved for men. King Douga of Koré in Eugène Dervain's

Saran ou la Reine scélérate sums up the general attitude towards female participation in politics as follows: "Une reine ne doit pas savoir ce qui se discute au conseil du prince," (p. 23). And in Guy Menga's *La Marmite de Koka-Mbala*, Bobolo, the chief seer and first councillor of Koka-Mbala, echoes that opinion when he challenges King Bintsamou for inviting his favourite wife, Queen Lemba to a meeting of Koka-Mbala's supreme council:

> Lemba ici, au milieu de cette auguste assemblée? Depuis quand les femmes ont-elles le droit d'assister aux réunions des hommes, qui plus est, traitent des affaires d'État? C'est un affront.

In this study, however, political figures and social activists have been identified. The women involved distinguish themselves by their awareness of the social and/or political problems in their society, their concern for improvement, and the initiatives they take to bring about the desired change. The plays included in the study contain no records of political parties or associations to which women in this category belong or could belong. Nor are there any women's movements or women's demonstrations such as could be found in Eastern Nigeria in the 1950s. The women identified act individually and on their own, except in Bernard Dadié's *Les Voix dans le vent* where four women of various ages deliver an ultimatum to King Nahoubou I in his palace. A number of the female characters in this category are royal women and, as such, are already singled out by their status. However, some of the most influential political figures and social activists in Francophone dramatic texts of the 1960s and 1970s are ordinary everyday women struggling not only to make ends meet for their families, but also to resolve issues that affect their entire communities. Such ideas, activities and involvement in community affairs make these ordinary women stand out as social and political icons.

The legendary Queen Abraha Pokou[5] remains one of the most impressive personalities in African literature. In *Assémien Dehylé*, Bernard Dadié recounts the legend of this queen who sacrificed her baby boy to the river gods in order to secure a safe passage for her people across the river and away from the enemy at their heels. After getting to safety and building a new village, the beneficiaries of Abraha's sacrifice adopt the meaningful word "Baoulé" ("the child is dead") as the name of their clan. Queen Pokou's example of the essence of traditional African leadership is used to give a lesson in altruism to twenty-two-year-old Assémien Déhylé, soon to become King of Sanwi. The legend shows that putting the people's needs before the leader's personal interests is a necessary component of good leadership.

In Charles Nokan's *Abraha Pokou*, Princess Abraha Pokou's altruism expands into a struggle for justice for everyone, including the slaves. Abraha's intervention starts early in the play. When the assembly of lords, shocked to learn that Prince Dakon is in love with a slave and desires to marry her, objects to Dakon's plans, the princess retorts:

> Mon frère fera ce qu'il veut. Les esclaves nourissent les nobles. Les premiers travaillent pendant que les seconds se livrent au vice. Ceux-là valent donc mieux que ceux-ci. La guerre et la famine ont respectivement permis à nos ancêtres de faire des prisonniers et de troquer de l'or ou des ignames contre des personnes. Cela ne nous autorise pas à les humilier. (p. 18).

Obviously, this outburst in the presence of her grandparents is totally unacceptable, and quickly reprimanded: her grandfather scolds, reminding Abraha (who is already a wife and mother!) that children should keep quiet when adults speak, and her grandmother sends her to bed!

The princess is endowed with intuition, foresight, and good judgement. She takes initiative based on her intuition and is often proved to be right. When, for example, her brother plays down her warning against a physical fight for the throne with their cousin Ouaré for fear the latter might poison him, the prince actually gets poisoned by Ouaré during the fight. Much to her husband's dismay, Abraha gives up her royal privileges after her brother's death and leaves the kingdom with her baby boy and a number of free and bonded men and women who share her ideals. She loses her baby in an ambush laid for her fleeing party after a cowardly slave breaks away and reveals her route to her estranged husband. After the party builds a new village and settles down, the people naturally choose and crown Abraha their queen. However, she uses her authority to eliminate the monarchy and replace it with a chieftaincy ystem requiring the chief to be elected. By giving the people the ight to choose their own leaders, Queen Abraha effectively ensures hat they have a say in how they are governed. In the village election hat follows, Abraha, who had already lost one son, openly .ampaigns against her second son, Djissa, because he does not avour the reform. Rather she gives her blessings to the other .andidate, Bassa, the son of a slave. She explains this seemingly .nnatural and certainly novel attitude by saying: "Je tiens moins à a parenté qu'à la camaraderie, qu'à la fraternité dans la lutte." (p. .5).

Like Abraha Pokou, Queen Yangouman seeks justice for her .eople in Raphael Koffi Atta's *Le Trône d'or*. However, (angouman is very much the opposite of Abraha, the peace-loving .ommunication enthusiast. She is warlike, tyrannical, brutal, and .s sanguinary as the Zulu king, Chaka. She brings to mind the .uthless Amazons of Benin, some of whom we see in Jean Pliya's *{ondo, le Requin*. However, in Pliya's play, the Amazons are .oldiers and take their orders from King Gbehanzin, while (angouman is Queen and really the one in charge of the throne of \bron that she shares with her pacific brother, King Adiningra. (angouman's belligerence impresses even the Ashanti King {oimnan-Bonsou, and her pride sparks off the problem that .onstitutes the plot of *Le Trône d'or*.

Abron, a vassal state of the Ashanti kingdom, has a golden throne hat the Ashanti king covets. However, Koimnan-Bonsou chooses .› wait till Queen Yangouman is absent from Abron and distracted .y a military campaign against her own subject states before .emanding Abron's prize golden throne which the weak and pacific \diningra relinquishes without much argument. On her return, (angouman not only condemns her brother's action, but also orders .er craftsmen to make a more stately throne which she refuses to .and over to the Ashantis. Abron is attacked and defeated but, .ejecting the dishonour of being captured and killed by the Ashantis, (angouman kills her brother and then commits suicide.

Queen Lemba, the favourite wife of King Bintsamou in Guy /lenga's *La Marmite de Koka-Mbala*, is one of the few queens .ast in plays about Equatorial Africa, where colonisation was very harsh (Maquette et al, 1970), and where the tradition of African royalty was destroyed very early (Conteh-Morgan, 1994). In this play whose plot is woven around the elders' greed and the resulting generational conflict in Koka-Mbala, Queen Lemba has no apparent authority attached to her status, and does not enjoy the high profile which invariably protected the queen mothers, queens, and princesses of West African kingdoms. However, Lemba works hard to earn King Bintsamou's trust and confidence, and, through her humility and solicitousness, eventually brings the king to feel sufficiently comfortable to talk freely and listen to her, seek her advice and take advantage of her intelligence, foresight, and perseverance. Lemba pleads the cause of the youths, advocates the king's leniency with them, and encourages the king to initiate changes that will benefit the entire community, not just the elderly. In fact, she becomes a very important ally for the king - she gives him an honest assessment of any situation he brings to her, informs him of the people's reaction to his initiatives, and warns him against Bobolo, the first councillor and chief seer's disloyalty and ambition to become king himself. Queen Lemba is invited to a meeting of the supreme council where Bintsamou openly seeks and obtains her advice. Also, she takes advantage of her presence in council to declare herself the representative of the women of Koka-Mbala and make demands on their behalf.

In *La Tragédie du Roi Christophe*, Aimé Césaire links Christophe's wife inextricably to the Haitian ruler by naming her "Madame Christophe" and, thereby, denying her a personal identity and autonomy. In the play which examines the implications of political freedom for a new and inexperienced nation with no allies, Mme Christophe is the king's wife and nothing else. She takes this responsibility quite seriously, but the former slave woman does not let her new status as the queen get to her head:

> ... j'ai été servante, moi la reine, à l'Auberge de la
> Couronne! Une couronne sur ma tête ne me fera pas
> devenir autre qu'une simple femme (p. 58).

Nevertheless, she has foresight and discernment and can see the danger in her husband's "slave-driver attitude" towards the people as he grapples with the problems of governing the new state. Better than the king himself, Mme Christophe seems to understand the need for a new nation to grow and progress at its own pace and in its own manner. She warns her husband against forcing ideas from elsewhere on his people, drawing his attention to the fact that that could put excessive pressure on everyone - men, women, and children alike:

> *Attention!* Christophe à vouloir poser la toîture d'une
> case sur une autre case; elle tombe dedans ou se trouve
> grande! Christophe, ne demande pas trop aux hommes
> et à toi-même, pas trop! (p. 58).

Referring to the real life fig tree in whose shed the Haitian Roi Christophe held his court and passed judgement on people, Mme Christophe accuses her husband of using his power to stifle his people rather than to provide them with the security they need to grow and blossom. She can't exactly serve as a counterpoise to her husband, but she is the only person who dares to speak in his presence, and she speaks boldly and truthfully.

So far, the royal women in this study use their authority to resolve problems, argue cases, or seek redress on behalf of their people. Even Mme Christophe attempts to reconcile King Christophe to his people. But Queen Saran of Koré in Eugène Dervain's *Saran ou la reine scélérate* does nothing of the sort. She rather uses her status to destroy her own people and kingdom, a very unusual occurrence in sub-Saharan Francophone African literature where women usually assume peace-making roles. Married to Douga, king of Koré, nineteen-year-old Saran lives in a palace where the norms and protocol must be strictly observed. The teenage queen resents the norms. Also, though Douga showers her with gifts, she cares little for her husband's generosity, and would rather have the king spend time with her, and show her affection. When Saran ventures to go after him, the king rebuffs her:

> Servantes, vous savez que nul ne doit me déranger
> lorsque je siège avec mes conseillers. (p. 23).

Saran's search for attention leads her to Prince Da Monzon who was sent by his father, the king of Ségou to punish Douga, king of Koré for

Koré for harbouring the griot, Tiécoura Danté who dared to choose Koré over Ségou! The stipulated punishment is the conquest of Koré. Though Saran is as enamoured with Da's youth and bravery as he is in love with her beauty and boldness, their love cannot flourish, because Da must defeat Saran's husband and conquer Koré before he can yield to his feelings for her. However, Koré is strong and has very powerful fetishes, so Da asks for Saran's help, and she agrees to spy on her husband. Thus, a seemingly innocent quest to kill boredom and find attention puts Saran in the middle of a political conflict between Koré and Ségou, and starts a case of betrayal, complex espionage and treason that leaves Koré defeated and several people killed, including Saran herself and King Douga, her husband and victim of her betrayal. Ironically, she is buried next to the husband she had betrayed.

If the royal woman's political actions involve kingdoms and peoples, the activities of the everyday political or social activist are more community oriented, as illustrated in the next set of examples. A number of ordinary women are identified in the plays of Bernard Dadié who rehabilitates the everyday woman by using her to highlight the social issues and injustices in her community, then to initiate and champion changes aimed at resolving the issues and correcting the injustices. In *Min Adja-o (C'est mon héritage)*, the widow, Amah challenges the Agni traditional system of inheritance, which favours the maternal cousins of the deceased. Amah's late husband, Kablan, a defunct civil servant, financier, and farmer in colonial Côte d'Ivoire had made a will leaving his inheritance to his wife and children. After unsuccessful attempts to claim late Kablan's belongings including his wife, Kablan's cousin, Boua, unaware of the existence and the importance of a will, seeks the help of some elders to force Amah to comply with the tradition. But Amah will not discuss with Boua let alone marry him, and she pours away the potion traditionally given to new widows to gauge their fidelity to their deceased husbands. Her actions force the elders to recognise and honour Kablan's will.

Though this is one family's private situation, Amah's refusal to abide by tradition will have widespread impact on the community and usher in a different future for Agni people. In fact, even the elders present think that Boua should not inherit from Kablan:

> Parlons net. Nous connaissons tous l'histoire de ton frère
> ... D'abord fonctionnaire, il s'est fait traitant. Cela l'avait
> conduit loin. En ce moment critique, vous l'aviez
> abandonné. Lorsqu'il plantait, il était seul. Il est mort
> de fatigue, de soucis. Je pense comme lui que, qui veut
> manger d'un plat doit aider à le préparer. (p. 109).

In *Monsieur Thôgô-gnini*, Brouba and Akaboua, her sister-in-law
seek and obtain redress against Mr Thôgô-gnini for the benefit of
the entire community. Being the king's cane bearer, Thôgô-gnini
had taken advantage of his king's weak leadership to set up personal
lucrative commercial deals with some white men who came seeking
trade links with the king. Once he is financially established, Mr
Thôgô-gnini uses the power and glamour resulting from the trade
relationship to intimidate and exploit his compatriots, taking their
produce without paying, having them thrown into jail for claiming
what is due to them, and seducing or trying to seduce every woman
who catches his eye.

Brouba, also called "L Femme" (that is "The Woman", meaning
an embodiment of everything a woman can be) in the scene at Mr
Thôgô-gnini's house, shows up uninvited to ask for her brother,
Paul N'Zekou who had gone to claim money Mr. Thôgô-gnini owed
him for palm oil. For Mr Thôgô-gnini, Brouba's presence is no
doubt an opportunity for a potential affair with yet another beautiful
woman (Brouba's physical attributes are uncharacteristically
emphasised here: sub-Saharan Francophone African playwrights
don't usually dwell on beauty): he is not deterred by the declared
purpose of Brouba's visit. Rather, he makes serious attempts to
seduce Brouba, asking her to feel his heart and note its palpitations
for her. However, Brouba's matter-of-fact attitude and demands
for clear and honest talk soon bring him back to reality, and he has
her thrown out of his house.

Before leaving Mr Thogo-gnini's house, an angry Brouba
accuses her ungracious host of dishonesty, greed, and shady business
tactics that have caused much suffering in the community. She
continues the fight in the tribunal where she appears as a witness

for her brother, N'Zekou who had been thrown into jail on bogus charges. Brouba accuses Mr. Thôgô-gnini of fabricating the charges against her brother, spreading deprivation and despair in the community through his callousness and machinations. She pleads for justice for her brother and all the other victims of Mr Thôgô-gnini. Here, N'Zekou's wife, Akaboua joins Brouba in the fight. Though she had been paid by Mr Thôgô-gnini to testify against her husband, Akaboua rather uses her court appearance to publicly denounce Mr Thôgô-gnini and dissociate herself from him. She pleads for clemency for N'Zekou, calling on the judge to put an end to Mr Thôgô-gnini's madness and bring life and joy back into families. The courage and tenacity of the two sisters-in-law result in profound changes in the community, starting from the judicial system – the judge releases N'Zekou.

Women in *Les Voix dans le vent* also play very important roles that help to move the plot along, and their actions have great impact on people in the unidentified kingdom where the dictator Nahoubou I is king. The play begins with one of the final scenes where an insomniac, power-hungry Nahoubou I is grappling with guilt over some of his atrocious crimes, like killing his mother and brother in order to pave his way to the throne. The rest of the story is then revealed through a series of flashbacks, and the plot unfolds as King Nahoubou remembers some landmark events of his life.

A strong female presence was part of Nahoubou's childhood and early adult life. His mother, Nabli was endowed with good memory, knowledge in matters of tradition, force of character, intelligence and foresight. This contrasts sharply with his father Nahoubou's short memory and limited vision leading to a *laisser-faire* attitude with regards to raising their son. Nabli remembers the seer's warning that Nahoubou, the son, should never hurt any living thing – mammal, reptile or bird. However, her concern that their son is killing lizards, birds, and people's cats and dogs is laughed off by Nahoubou, the father, who sees courage in his son's brutality and callous disregard for other people's property, and rather predicts a lucrative hunting career for his son. Ironically, he is struck and killed by an arrow that his son shoots carelessly into the air.

Nahoubou's nameless wife, his early adulthood companion, has a very strong character also. Like Brouba in the scene at Mr Thôgô-gnini's house, she is referred to as "La Femme" (that is "The Woman"), leading one to view her as the embodiment of womanhood, a sort of women's representative. "The Woman" has to cope with a very serious situation: her husband is a subdued, inoffensive, see-no-evil, hear-no-evil, do-no-evil man unable to provide his family with the basic needs of food and security, let alone leadership. In fact, Nahoubou has gone from the brutal, daring, callous, and head-strong boy he used to be to a totally despondent victim of constant despoilment at the hands of the king's men and who, despite his wife's urging, refuses to fight back. The Woman, like Nahoubou's mother, Nabli, proves to be of superior will-power: she leaves Nahoubou and the life of deprivation he offers, vowing to find herself a real man. Disbelief at his wife's abandonment shocks Nahoubou back to reality. However, his desire to reclaim his manhood again turns into uncontrollable hunger for power that leads him to seek the help of a sorcerer and kill his mother and brother so as to become king.

Now a king, the autocratic and tyrannical Nahoubou I has no woman with whom to share his life, and he is so intoxicated with power that he believes he can have any woman he wants. However, the intelligent, sensitive, and beautiful Losy proves him wrong for, turning her back on the gold, diamonds and the throne Nahoubou offers her, Losy elopes with a penniless fiancé. This further underlines the king's inadequacies as a man and reduces him to playing "catch-up" with women who, from now on, are always one step ahead of him. Humiliated and furious about Losy's rejection, Nahoubou declares war on the village harbouring the fleeing lovers, but his army is defeated in battle after battle, resulting in a tremendous loss of lives. His army's attempt to force a young girl from a neighbouring village to marry Nahoubou also fails, leading to more loss of lives. It is in this crisis situation that four women who have been widowed or rendered childless by Nahoubou's wars march to his palace and put him on notice that there will be no more war in the kingdom. The women's action incite the masses to revolt against Nahoubou, thereby putting an end to his mad reign.

Dona Beatrice in *Béatrice du Congo* is the only one of Dadié's female protagonists that meets with a tragic end. This historical and political play dramatises the familiar theme in African literature of a partnership gone sour between a European state (the imaginary state of Bitanda [referring to Portugal]) and an African people (the kingdom of Kongo). Under the guise of spreading Christianity and enlightenment, the European state actually colonises the African kingdom, steals its artifacts, destroys its sovereignty and proceeds to plunder its resources. The character, Dona Beatrice is based on a real historical, but mystic proto-nationalist figure that was burnt at the stake in 1706. In terms of the traditional African woman and roles attributed to her in society, Beatrice is not the typical, ordinary, everyday woman that Dadié usually picks to carry his message. She is an unwed mother who names Saint John as the father of her child, and is said to be demented because of her lofty anti-Bitandese ideas about the reunification of the Congolese kingdom.

Beatrice clearly stands out as the most politically active of Dadié's female characters. She is an intelligent and courageous organiser, and successfully mobilises the people. She sees through the Bitandese claims of Christian fraternity, but is also keenly aware of the Mani Kongo's greed for money and appetite for power. So, she doesn't only warn the king against his naive trust and blind faith in the Bitandese, she also condemns him for leaving his kingdom and people at the mercy of the Bitandese who destroy the Congolese sovereignty, religions, and customs, while he amasses wealth for himself. Afraid of Beatrice's influence on the people, the Bitandese have her killed, burning her at the stake as a deterrent to others who might think of inciting the masses again.

Whether they are ordinary women or members of the royalty, the female characters described display qualities that are not usually associated with women, when they find themselves in situations of crisis. Queen Abraha is portrayed as a political figure who puts the general interest first, even at great personal cost, and as a leader who not only believes in justice and freedom for all, but also takes the initiative to put her beliefs into practice. Lemba is a confidant, comforter and counsellor to her husband, King Bintsamou, and an effective representative for the women of Koka-Mbala. The former slave woman, Mme Christophe boldly condemns her husband's excesses. Though she has little or no influence on King Christophe, she does what she has to do; the rest is up to the king. Even Queen Saran proves to be a very effective and capable spy.

The ordinary women, such as Amah, Brouba, Dona Beatrice, and Nahoubou's nameless estranged wife, who do not enjoy any status or authority whatsoever, are just as non-conformist as the royal women. Empowering these women is critical because the men in their communities have been bought over or are too weakened by fear to stand up for the people. When the soldier assigned to kill Dona Beatrice asks her why only women preach revolt, she replies:

> Les femmes ont levé l'étendard de la dignité parce que l'amour de l'argent a tué le courage   dans le coeur des hommes, parce que les honneurs ont corrumpu les hommes ... mais nous sommes déterminées à leur apprendre ... A ne plus avoir peur ... (p. 148).

This echoes statements made by the widows and childless women who force Nahoubou off the throne.

> **La Femme la plus âgée:** Devant la passivité des hommes, devant le silence apeuré et obstiné des hommes, nous avons décidé de parler, nous les femmes. (p. 145).

> **Première femme :** Il faut que nos enfants et nos maris rentrent chez eux
> **La Femme la plus âgée :** Que les hommes courbent la tête! Nous, on la relève fièrement...
> **Les femmes :** fièrement...
> **La Femme la plus âgée :** pour te dire que nos enfants n'iront plus à la guerre.
> **La Femme la plus âgée :** Que nos maris
> **Les femmes:** n'iront plus à la guerre. (pp. 147-148)

These women describe a situation common to *Monsieur Thôgô-gnini, Les Voix dans le vent* and *Beatrice du Congo*. Either willingly or through coercion, men in these plays join forces with leaders to oppress the ordinary people, making women's empowerment crucial to the plot. Like the foreign traders, local leaders, both political and economic, use fear as a weapon against the people and pay off the men who agree to collaborate with them to exploit the people and steal from the country. Rehabilitating women, therefore, becomes salutary for the community, the society, the whole nation. In fact, it is presented as the last resort. In all three plays, women act with an eye on the future, hoping that their actions will impact positively on their communities and shape the future for the benefit of all.

Wives and Mothers

Wifehood and motherhood are common features in Francophone African theatre of the 1960s and 1970s. In fact, all the mature women are married and, with the exception of twenty-year-old Queen Sêb Fall and nineteen-year-old Queen Saran, all have children. Sêb desires to have a child with King Albouri, while Saran, being unsure of her feelings for her husband and marriage, does not mention children. Having children is very important to the female characters. Losy tells King Nahoubou I that, for a woman, not having a child would appear like a curse. However, childlessness is not considered an issue in any of the plays included in this study.

Mothers in Pre-Colonial Days

Wives and mothers are usually described as "spiritless" and "stereotyped" in African literature. However, a few of the female characters identified in this study can be described in those terms. As earlier demonstrated, most wives and mothers in Francophone African theatre are hardly the conventional or usual type. The Linguère Madjiguene, for example, leaves her children with her husband and the servants so as to free herself for her state duties as the king's lieutenant (*L'Exil d'Albouri*). Queen Abraha Pokou sacrifices her six-month-old baby boy to the gods of the Caméo River to secure a safe passage for her people (*Assémien Déhylé*). In another representation, Queen Pokou organises the first ever elections in Francophone African theatre, then campaigns against her own son and in favour of the son of a slave who shares her ideals (*Abraha Pokou*).

Motherhood is viewed as a normal part of a woman's life cycle, not as a hindrance to her regular activities. Besides, having children generally makes the woman think about the future and work towards a better and safer tomorrow for everyone, including her children. The depiction of the women discussed in this study clearly illustrates this concern for the common good - the two portrayals of Queen Abraha, the offer of the widows and mothers of Sikasso to join in the battle to defend and preserve their city, Akaboua's request that the judge should bring back life and joy to families in her community, Brouba's struggles for the benefit of the women, children, and old people left cold, hungry, and homeless by Mr Thôgô-gnini, the women's intervention to stop Nahoubou's wars, and Dona Beatrice's mission to reunite the Congolese people and kingdom, all of these actions are for the good of the community.

However, though Yây Diop in *L'Exil d'Albouri* thinks that a mother can guess her child's thoughts, mothers are often not in agreement with their children. Yây Diop herself is surprised that her son, Albouri is walking away from a war against the French and rather opting for exile. Besides, the mother-child relationship appears to be determined more by the woman's expected role in society, rather than by her maternal feelings or the absence of such feelings. The mother is more for the community, as shown by the Linguère Mandjiguene and Queen Pokou, than for the individual child whose needs are usually treated as part of the needs of the community. So when a mother figure is romanticised or idealised, as is the case with Abraha Pokou, it is because she has proven to be selfless, strong, devoted, and loving towards everyone, a mother to the entire community, not just to her birth children.

Mothers in Colonial and Post Colonial Times

However, once the connection with the community is severed and the woman is left to cater only for the needs of her own children and family, she seems to lose focus. This happens in several plays set in colonial and post-colonial times, some of whose characteristics are the beginning of individualism, (even in children) and the loss of the safety net the community had usually provided. Children have also found their voices and are no longer just seen; they are equally heard in discussion with their mothers. In such cases, however, the focus tends to shift from the child's concerns to the father's will, and the mother invariably teams up with the father and becomes hostile towards the child, especially the female child. Madame Suzanne N'Gandou in Sylvain Bemba's *L'Homme qui tua le crocodile*, for example, stands passively by as her husband beats their daughter, Parfaite for daring, in her innocence and ignorance, to fall in love with the son of her father's enemy, but she readily chides Parfaite for wondering why a quarrel between parents should involve the children:

> Comment oses-tu parler ainsi, Parfaite? Les filles d'aujourd'hui n'ont plus un grain de bon sens. (p. 46).

In *L'Oracle*, Guy Menga blames this rather discomforting mother-daughter relationship on the weight of tradition and superstition on mothers. Louvouézo will not let her husband, Biyoki beat Louaka for questioning his decision to withdraw her from school, but her loyalty and sympathies are with him, and she will not take part in her daughter's rebellion:

> **Louaka:** De quel côté es-tu exactement?
> **Louvouézo:** Moi? Mais je ne peux être que du côté de mon mari. Il faut que tu comprennes cela. (p. 43)

Louvouézo is completely disempowered and feels that, as a woman, she is incapable of accomplishing anything without a man's help. Furthermore, she believes that she will be punished if she supports her daughter, a fatalistic attitude that leaves her indifferent to her daughter's needs.

> **Louaka:** Mon cri ne touche pas ton coeur de mère?
> **Louvouézo:** Quel cri? Celui de la rebellion? ... Tu veux aller à l'encontre de la volonté de ton père. C'est offenser les esprits et ta mère ne peux t'appuyer dans une telle action. (p. 43)

Makrita in *Trois prétendants ... un mari* is just as disconnected from Juliette. Makrita, too, badly wants her daughter to marry the highest bidder. The big difference is that she wants the money .not for herself, but for her son, Oyono, so he can pay the bride price on his own future wife. Naturally, Makrita's concerns for her husband and son override any compassion she might have for Juliette.

Mothers generally treat their sons with decency. Mafo in *Un Père aux abois*, for example, knows nothing about school, but she trusts her son, Demanou, and believes whatever he says about his studies at the boarding school he attends. However, Mafo treats her daughter, Lucia, who still lives at home, with much suspicion, wondering if she really goes to school or if she just fools around with boys.

Urban Mothers

Urban mothers are generally portrayed as shallow and thoughtless. In Samuel Nkamgnia's *La Femme prodigue*, for example, Assen is determined to start a fight with her husband, Mr Jules, for no apparent reason. She uses her daughter, Sylvie and son, Claude as pawns in this unexplained vendetta. Colette in Oyono-Mbia's *Notre fille ne se mariera pas!* had lived and studied in France and, though she now lives and works in Cameroun, wants to raise her son like a French child. But she goes after superficial things, like forcing her son to eat camembert cheese which the child finds smelly and awful-tasting. Also, Nathalie's nameless and illiterate mother in Jean Pliya's *La Secrétaire particulière* proves to have been negligent in allowing her minor daughter to have an affair with her married boss, Mr Chadas. However, when she discovers that Nathalie is pregnant and abandoned by Mr Chadas, she quickly assumes her motherly responsibility and stands by her daughter, giving her the support and reassurance she needs.

Unlike the aforementioned urban mothers, Madame Thérèse Balou in *L'Homme qui tua le crocodile* is calm and thoughtful; she talks and acts with much control. Her only child, Jean, is a twenty-two-year old college student with whom she enjoys a unique and ideal relationship based on mutual respect, trust, and a confidence that seems to stem from Jean's upbringing. Thérèse lets Jean make his own decisions, even about his intended marriage to Parfaite, the daughter of her husband's arch enemy, because she trusts him to make the right decisions.

Wifehood

Wives are rarely portrayed as partners in a marriage, but they are not shown as being there just to prop up their husbands and make them look good, while they remain in the shadows. The concept of wifehood and spousal relationship varies greatly from one era to the next, and even from one couple to the next. As already discussed, royal women in historical plays are invariably treated with respect. However, in non-historical plays with a rural setting and in plays set in a post-independence urban environment, conjugal relationship depends largely on the man and woman involved. In Guy Menga's *La Marmite de Koka-Mbala*, for example, Queen Lemba is held in high esteem by her husband, King Bintsamou (though Bobolo, the chief seer and first councillor of the kingdom publicly insults her). However, the story is quite different in Menga's other play, *L'Oracle,* where Biyoki sums up a wife's worth as follows:

> Ma mère, ma grand-mère ont bien vécu. Et elles ont été des épouses modèles ... Elles savaient vous pétrir le manioc, entretenir une propreté absolue dans la case, frire le poisson, cuisiner la viande et préparer des sauces dont l'odeur seule met l'estomac en état de panique gloutonne ... Et c'est, cela une femme. Rien que cela! Une machine à balayer, à cuisiner, à moudre du plaisir et à faire des enfants. (p. 41).

And Abessolo's words in *Trois prétendants ... un mari* seem to complete the picture:

> ... aujourd'hui, vous laissez vos femmes s'habiller! Vous les laissez manger toutes sortesd'animaux tabou! Vous

leur demandez leur opinion sur ceci et cela! ... Que
voulez-vous d'autres? Je vous le dis encore, il faut battre
vos femmes! Oui, battez-les! (p. 10).

Urban Wives

However, educated wives in urban environments tend to get more
respect from their husbands. Thérèse Balou in *L'Homme qui tua
le crocodile* is one of the very rare wives portrayed as being in
partnership with her husband. She and Henri have profound respect
for each other. They form a common front in the conflict with
Théobald N'Gandou, compare notes, and plan strategies for
resisting N'Gandou's insults and attempts at seduction, slander,
lawsuits, and seditiousness. They discuss family matters and resolve
marital problems together. Communication flows quite freely and
smoothly between the two. Collette in *Notre fille ne se mariera
pas* does not communicate so well with her husband, Mr Atangana,
and the two don't seem to have much in common. Collette is quite
superficial and extremely class conscious, she is quite offended,
for instance, to learn that Madame Essomba, the wife of a junior
officer who never studied abroad, buys groceries at *her*
supermarket. Atangana, on the other hand, is very down-to-earth
and cares little for appearances. In spite of these differences,
Collette is treated with respect by her husband. Things are quite
different when the urban wife is an illiterate. She is portrayed
barely discussing with her husband and getting little consideration
from him. Again in *L'Homme qui tua le crocodile*, Suzanne
N'Gandou stays in the kitchen and only comes to the living room
when her husband summons her. When faced with the near crisis
caused by Parfaite's friendship with the Balou boy, Suzanne offers
no opinion or suggestion, but silently supports whatever conduct
her husband dictates to their daughter. Also, Suzanne is either too
docile, afraid, or simply ignorant of her husband's carryings-on
and licentious activities with wives and minor girls whose husbands or
fathers happen to owe him money: she never refers to those things.

Monogamy

Most of the marriages in the plays studied are monogamous. This is true for all settings and periods. However, kings and village heads have many wives, which gives the impression that polygamy has to do with status. In general, only the favourite wife of the king or village head appears in the play; other wives are merely mentioned. However, in *Kondo, le requin* and *Notre fille ne se mariera pas*, a few of the other wives are included, but they play very minor roles that don't affect the plot. In *Kondo, le requin*, for example, Gbehanzin is often in the company of a number of his wives, but the play focuses on the conflict between him and the French: the rapport amongst his wives is not developed. And in *Notre fille ne se mariera pas*, Chief Mbarga's first wife, Cécilia, plays mom to his latest acquisition, the very young, Delphina, who will accompany Mbarga and Cécilia to see their daughter, Charlotte in Yaoundé. Other wives, especially Martha, start an argument with Cécilia out of jealousy, because they cannot go to Yaoundé. Mbarga resolves the problem by instructing Martha to get ready and join the travelling party. Apparently, polygamy is not a serious issue in sub-Saharan Francophone Africa of the period. If it is, dramatists probably prefer not to deal with it.

Women and their Occupations

Occupations here are not necessarily money-making ventures, but rather things that keep the women busy. Royal women in historical plays have a very comfortable lifestyle and have servants waiting on them, and a few of them, like Linguère Madjiguène and Sogona, have political roles as well. Other than that, traditional women are generally depicted as not pursuing a career of any type. Even trading and farming (large or small scale), which are money-making activities commonly undertaken by women in English-speaking African literature, are not at all emphasised here. The few cases of women farmers, like Louvouézo in *L'Oracle* and Makrita in *Trois prétendants ... un mari*, do so at minimal subsistence level. Women are also mentioned in connection with work on plantations in *Monsieur Thôgo-gnini* and *Béatrice du Congo*, but they are not working for their own benefit.

Female characters in plays set in colonial and post-colonial times are more occupation-oriented. Some work in conventional professions like nursing and secretarial duties, a few are public servants and fewer still are lawyers, and a good number of them operate and make a living as sex workers of some sort. Finally, though schooling is a temporary career, this study considers students and recent graduates as a category of young women actively engaged in an occupation, since the play captures them at that particular point in their lives.

Nurses

Nursing is a popular and well respected career for female characters. Louaka in *L'Oracle* and Lucia in Joseph Kengi's *Un Père aux abois* aspire to train as nurses after completing primary school. However, some trained nurses don't seem to understand the importance of the nursing career itself. A case in point is Matalina in Oyono-Mbia's *Jusqu'à nouvel avis ...*, a certified nurse with a diploma from France, who is married to a medical doctor. Months after Matalina and her husband return to Cameroun, she whiles away her time at home, waiting for an opening in a big hospital that has equipment similar to those she had used in France, because such sophisticated equipment would give her an edge over her not-so-qualified Camerounian colleagues. She gives no thought to using her training and skills for patient care.

The other certified nurse is Thérèse Balou in *L'Homme qui tua le crocodile*. Thérèse is conscientious, experienced, and very responsible, quite the opposite of Matalina. Even though she doesn't appear in her job at the hospital, Thérèse does put on her nurse's hat towards the end of the play when her son, Jean is wounded by N'Gandou's henchmen. Acting quite professionally, she administers first aid to Jean, then places a phone call to the hospital, identifying herself as Thérèse in "Chirurgie 1-2-3". She asks for her colleagues by name and tells them what to prepare as they wait for her to bring in her son.

Secretaries

Secretarial work for women is a controversial issue for, as will be discussed later, few women who go by the title of "secretary" are real, bona fide secretaries hired for their qualifications to perform the functions of a secretary. Probably as a result of this, secretaries are not respected or taken seriously. In fact, some unscrupulous bosses and departmental heads are incapable of maintaining a professional relationship with their female secretaries, and want to use them for other purposes, even as sex mates. A case in point is Miss Sambouche in Dadié's *Mhoi-Ceul*, a play set in a government office in post-independence Côte d'Ivoire. Miss Sambouche serves as an errand girl and a buffer between her boss and departmental head, Mhoi-Ceul, and the "undesirable" public that her boss refuses to deal with. However, when her brother is appointed minister, Mhoi-Ceul sees an opportunity to use her to get into the good graces of her brother whom he can then use to protect and further his own career. So he tries to seduce Miss Sambouche, giving her presents, money, furnished accommodations and an official vehicle. Then Miss Sambouche's brother loses the ministerial position and, realising she can no longer be useful to him, Mhoi-Ceul demands the lodgings and vehicle back, but Miss Sambouche refuses to cooperate.

Another example is Virginie in *La Secrétaire particulière*, whose plot also unfolds in a government office in post-independence Africa. A rare graduate from a secretarial school, Virginie is hired by the government and assigned to work in the section where Mr Chadas is departmental head. However, her qualification, efficiency and professionalism do not translate into job security. For, after attempting and failing to seduce Virginie, her boss tries to avenge himself by writing a very negative report on Virginie, hoping to get her fired. His plan is pre-empted by an executive directive that requires all typists and secretaries to write and pass a departmental examination in order to keep their jobs. Virginie scores the highest marks in that examination and gets moved to the Minister's office, out of Chadas' reach.

Public Servants

The public service, like most institutions that stemmed from the colonial master, hardly includes women. In *Notre fille ne se mariera pas* however, Charlotte and Colette work in government offices and, because they graduated from college in France, it can be assumed that they hold important positions. According to Charlotte's father, Chief Mbarga, Charlotte works in a big office in Yaounde and "controls everyone in the big office". Little is known about what Charlotte actually does in the big office. This is normal, since workers in general and civil servants in particular are rarely cast at work: issues to resolve usually have little to do with characters' professional life.

Lawyers

Much more than the public service, the law business is clearly a man's domain. Mr Chadas doesn't believe that a woman can be a lawyer and, in no uncertain terms, tells the young woman lawyer, Denise in *La Secrétaire particulière*, that little girls like her should not be on a man's playground. However, Denise is a trained lawyer with her own law practice. She comes against Mr Chadas in a hit and run case where she is the victim's attorney. Mr Chadas feels so threatened by this "little girl on men's playground" that he loses faith in his own lawyer and opts for an out-of-court settlement with the victim of the accident on condition that Denise is not involved in the discussions.

Denise is quite professional in her dealings: she follows the procedures even when it involves members of her own family. When Mr Chadas pushes down his pregnant mistress, Nathalie causing her to faint, Denise who is Nathalie's cousin, insists on obtaining Nathalie's consent before going after Mr Chadas whom she charges with brutality, corrupting and threatening a minor on his staff. Mr Chadas' only concern is his career, and the scandal, if exposed, will hurt it. So he begs to settle quietly, offering to marry Nathalie and take care of her child. When the Minister shows up, Denise quickly briefs him on the shady activities of his protégé, Mr Chadas.

This way, Denise not only ensures that Mr Chadas is arrested, but she also draws the Minister's attention to the abuse against young girls who have bosses like Mr Chadas, which leads the Minister to promise a full investigation. Finally, Denise helps Nathalie get back on her feet by offering her a job in the law firm.

Students and Graduates

A good number of the female characters are students or graduates. Characters in this group stand out quite distinctly from the other young women who have not been exposed to western education. In *Trois prétendants ... un mari*, Abessolo sums up the situation in this near-desperate declaration: "Les écoles ont tout gâté!" (p. 22). Students and graduates definitely think and act differently; they reason, ask questions, seek and find solutions to problems they come up against, whatever the nature or source of the problem. Abessolo's granddaughter, Juliette uses treachery and dishonesty to get her father, Atangana's blessing on her union with her pauper student boy friend, Oko, thus making her marriage what she had always wanted it to be: a love union with no bride price. Her cunning is sanctioned by Oko who forces Atangana to acknowledge his daughter's wishes by insisting that Juliette should publicly accept to be his wife.

Jusqu'à nouvel avis and *Notre fille ne se mariera pas*, the two plays that, together with *Trois prétendants ... un mari*, form Oyono-Mbia's trilogy on the bride price and marriage, also feature female protagonists who have gone to the white man's school and who, like Juliette, use craftiness to get around the bride price issue. In *Jusqu'à nouvel avis*, Matalina completes her studies in France, but comes back to Cameroun married, thereby putting before her father Abessolo and her many uncles a *fait accompli*. Charlotte in *Notre fille ne se mariera pas* also uses the fait accompli tactic. After studying in France too, Charlotte dutifully returns unmarried to Cameroun to take up an office job in Yaounde. She wants to marry an agricultural engineering student, but her father, Chief Mbarga and her uncles consider her fiancé unsuitable, because they believe he will work with his hands like a common villager. To stay on top of things, Chief Mbarga and his brothers simply decide that Charlotte should not get married till she has worked long enough to pay back what they consider reasonable compensation for money spent on her studies. So, Charlotte marries her student engineer in secret, only to find out that her father has been informed of an agricultural engineer's potential wealth and is now anxious to have her fiancé for a son-in-law.

However, not every school girl or graduate abandons traditional values in favour of the new way of resolving problems which seems invariably to involve dishonesty. Louaka, the primary school student in *L'Oracle*, handles things quite differently. First of all, Louaka distinguishes herself by her goal which is to complete primary school, unlike the other students' or graduates' singular ambition to marry the man of their choice, possibly without a bride price. Louaka is committed to her goal and would like to study further and become a nurse. Contrary to Oyono-Mbia's protagonists who use cunning and craftiness to get their way, Louaka gets to stay in school by successfully combining the knowledge she acquired in the white man's "house of wisdom" with knowledge from her traditional heritage. She refuses to give up, like her mother, Louvouézo recommended, but rather seeks help first from the seer, then from her grandfather who forces the seer to join in a plan to back her up. Louaka's success is three-fold: first of all, she doesn't have to leave school and marry old Mamba; secondly, her grandfather brings her a fiancé who will support her academic and career ambitions: it is her school teacher who turns out to be her cousin[6] and, finally, the grandfather orders that Louaka be married without a bride price, but for a symbolic gift as it used to be in the past.

Sex Workers

The term "sex worker" is used here to refer to a woman who generates income through activities involving the use of her sexuality and body. This includes prostitutes and kept women of all types - mistresses, students, and la "secrétaire particulière" (or private secretary) who does not do much typing. Few female characters are cast as kept women in sub-Saharan Francophone theatre of the period studied.

Prostitutes

Prostitutes of the usual type (cigarette-smoking, heavily made-up, and provocatively dressed women, the likes of Jagua in Cyprian Ekwensi's *Jagua Nana* or Simi in Wole Soyinka's *The Interpreters)* are rare in this body of literature.

One of the few women portrayed as a prostitute in sub-Saharan Francophone African theatre is Ya-Gba in Dadié's *Monsieur Thôgô-gnini*, a play set in 1840. Ya-Gba is not physically described, but details are given about her accessories: she smokes cigarettes, wears make-up, carries a mirror and lipstick in her purse, and wears a wrist watch, all of which point to the fact that she is sophisticated and quite up-to-date in the profession. Ya-Gba knows the importance of time in her trade, so she gets to her appointments on time. In fact, she gets impatient and she consults her watch at ridiculous intervals as she awaits her rendezvous in the bar. But, when Mr Thôgô-gnini shows up with a friend, she quietly leaves the bar, because she also understands discretion. Knowing how important it is to stay young in her trade, Ya-Gba claims to be fifteen, nay ten years old, when she appears before the tribunal as Mr Thôgô-gnini's witness. However, she also swears she is a mother of six children, leaving an air of mystery around herself. Ya-Gba is the perfect companion for the pompous crook, Mr Thôgô-gnini: she satisfies his needs for comfort and reassurance and, in return, she gets "to drink tea from China on the coast of Africa" (p. 51), something only Thôgô-gnini can provide!

Private Secretaries

Though Ya-Gba is cast in a plot set in 1840, the sex worker is usually viewed as a by-product of modernity and, thus, appears more often in plays about colonial and post independence times. The most popular type of sex worker in terms of frequency in plays is the private secretary. As her title implies, she is hired in a government office as a secretary, but usually for her looks and/or her youth, rather than for her qualification or skills in secretarial duties. This is a true reflection of a real life situation so rampant in sub-Saharan Africa that Francophones in the region have coined the special title of "la secrétaire particulière" (the Private Secretary) for the position. In general, she works exclusively for one man, usually an older man who already has one wife or more, and she performs duties that have little or nothing to do with, and go far beyond typing and shorthand. State funds are used to provide the Private Secretary with a glamorous lifestyle that includes an excessive wage, fine clothes, accommodation, parties and, depending on the status of her boss (or should we say partner), an official vehicle.

Quite often the Private Secretary is young and inexperienced; sometimes, even a minor, but she plays along for the glamour and security (albeit false and temporary) that an amorous liaison with the boss offers. Some girls feel trapped and believe they have little choice in a context where sleeping with the boss is a condition for a young woman to get and keep a job. Jean Pliya explores this issue in *La Secrétaire particulière*, a play that dramatises the story of Nathalie who, in spite of her very poor secretarial skills, is hired by Mr Chadas as a private secretary and kept as a mistress though she is a minor. Nathalie discovers soon enough that her boss has eyes for every young woman who comes into his office, and that being his mistress doesn't guarantee her a job. When she fails the departmental examination, she loses her job even though Mr Chadas had repeatedly promised to speak to the Minister on her behalf. Worse still, Nathalie is pregnant and her boss will have nothing to do with her or her baby:

> Nathalie: Tu as tout exigé et obtenu de moi. Et quand
> je t'annonce les conséquences de tes actes, tu changes
> de mine." (p. 76)

But she vows to put up a fight:

> ... j'ai échoué à mon examen et je n'ai plus d'illusion
> sur tes précieuses recommendations. Tu crois me
> brimer sans crainte parce que je suis orpheline de père.
> Mais les faibles aussi savent se défendre quand on les
> pousse au désespoir. (p. 76)

Nathalie demands to know what will become of her and the baby, and refuses to leave Mr Chadas' office. A scuffle ensues, she faints and, in the confusion that follows, Nathalie's mother, her cousin, Denise who is a lawyer, and the Minister are called in. Mr Chadas is arrested: charges against him will include brutality and corrupting a minor on his staff.

Unlike the minor, Nathalie who ends up jobless, pregnant and with a court case, some girls have learned to take care of themselves while taking advantage of the lust, ostentation, and craving for conquest from which some men seem unable to escape. Some of them just show up in offices asking for jobs, but expecting to be propositioned, and they are rarely disappointed. In *Mhoi-Ceul*, for example, Mademoiselle Chérie Beauzieux (Miss Darling Beautiful Eyes) comes to Mhoi-Ceul asking for a woman's job. She puts on a show of naivety that fools this deparmental head and leaves him believing that he is actually making all the moves. He invites her for a swim and hires her on the spot as his own very private secretary. Beauzieux will work at home and be introduced as his niece:

> **Beauzieux:** Du travail à domicile?
> **Mhoi Ceul:** N'avez-vous pas compris? *Je vous garde*
> *pour moi* ... Pour les amis, vous serez ma nièce ou la
> nièce de mon cousin ...
> **Beauzieux:** Ou la cousine de ton cousin.
> **Mhoi Ceul:** Non, il vaut mieux que vous soyez *pour*
> *les amis, ma nièce.* [our emphasis]. (p. 36)

Following this first meeting, Beauzieux gets a backdated job offer, a grossly exaggerated salary, a sumptuously furnished six-room flat, an official car, and a private telephone line. Before long, this very private secretary demands more – money, a villa, vacation in Europe, etc. – things that are far beyond the means of a departmental head. However, as soon as the opportunity offers itself, Beauzieux turns her attention to Centroux Crodurs, Mhoi-Ceul's crafty and dishonest foreign associate, marries him, and leaves the country with him.

In Oyono Mbia's *Notre fille ne se mariera pas*, Charlotte's younger sister, Maria has no typing skills, but is hired as private secretary for the Commissioner of Police because of her sensuous gait. After starting a "career" as the favourite actress/singer of a producer who recently got imprisoned for embezzlement, Maria becomes a private secretary almost overnight, much to Charlotte's consternation.

University Students

Paulette in *Le Train spécial de son excellence* is a sex worker of a new breed that is found in universities and other post-secondary institutions. The difference between these students and the regular prostitute is that the former do not work out of brothels or entertain several clients. They rather deal exclusively with one man (at least, at a time), and the man is usually rich and married. But, seriousness about education is always an important character trait in such students. In this regard, Paulette is unusual because, though her lover, the director of a big foreign company, buys her an apartment and a car to facilitate going to classes, she trades education for the "good life" – movie theatres, night clubs, and champagne. She repeats Year I university three times and fails each time. Her ambition is to go and study in France, because Camerounian schools are not good enough for her. Meanwhile, she wants her lover to spend as much money as possible on material things, so she can maintain a very flashy lifestyle. So she uses her sexuality and smooth talk to get what she wants for herself and for her family. She gives her kid brothers the new 400,000 CFA francs stereo her lover had brought to the village and wonders why he is upset:

> ... Il ne faut quand même pas que mes parents croient
> que tu ne peux pas dépenser 400,000 francs pour me
> faire plaisir! Ils nous observent, tu sais? (p. 51).

As uncharacteristic as the loose morals implied by this practice are, parents do not frown on them, but rather implicitly and sometimes even openly support and encourage their daughters. Maria's father, Chief Mbarga, for example, proudly announces that he will soon marry Maria to the Commissioner of Police who hired her as a private secretary, without asking any of the questions parents usually ask when their daughter finds herself a fiancé. As discussed earlier, Nathalie in *La Secrétaire particulière* dated her boss for months with her mother's knowledge and blessing. Matalina's brother, Mozoé in *Jusqu'à nouvel avis* ..., outlines the attitude of most parents in this conversation:

> **Mozoé:** La dactylographie et la sténographie ne
> s'apprennent pas en quelques jours! Mais Thérésia fait
> de très, très grands progrès : figurez-vous que Sinabé
> lui offre déjà un emploi!
> **Cécilia :** Qui lui offre un emploi?
> **Mozoé:** Sinabé, l'homme qui dirige l'Orchestre des
> Compagnons de la Boisson, plus connu sous le nom
> de "C.D.B." Il a rencontré Thérésia à l'école où elle
> apprend à taper à la machine, et il lui a offert un
> excellent emploi.
> **Nkatéfoé:** Pour qu'elle aille taper à la machine?
> **Mozoé:** Non, bien sûr, Tita Nkatefoé. Pour qu'elle aille
> chanter avec les autres membres de l'orchestre.
> **Abessolo** (*Pratique*) : C'est un grand homme aussi,
> celui-là?
> **Mozoé:** Beaucoup d'argent, Tit'Abessôlô! C'est
> pourquoi j'ai recommandé à Thérésia de veiller à ne
> plus jamais se faire voir en compagnie de quelqu'un
> d'autre! Qui sait? Sinabé va peut-être parler de
> l'épouser. On a toujours intérêt à avoir beaucoup de
> grands hommes dans sa famille!
> **Tous les hommes:** Tu dis la vérité! (p. 29-30p).

This attitude ties in neatly with that of the village chief and Paulette's father, Atangana in Oyono-Mbia's *Le Train spécial de son excellence*. He and Paulette's mother, Matalina, encourage their daughter to date her married lover (referred to as "Son Excellence" (in the play) whom they proudly receive and entertain in their village home, all in the hope that the latter will send Paulette to study in France:

> **Atangana:** ... Le jour où Paulette viendra me montrer son billet d'avion, tu sauras qu'elle n'est pas la fille d'un gueux! Je veux qu'elle aille étudier en Europe! (p. 54)

Analysing the occupations of the African woman in sub-Saharan Francophone African dramatic works is not an easy task, considering the leap from the times when money-making ventures were not part of the traditional woman's environment to these days when the so-called modern woman gives herself, willingly or otherwise, as a sex object to a stranger in the hope that the latter will eventually talk of marriage or send her to study in Europe, and all that happens in between. Nevertheless, a number of occupations have been identified, and the African woman seems to perform the functions of her chosen occupation admirably well, whether the said occupation is salutary and commendable or not.

CONCLUSION

Based on the foregoing discussion, it is obvious that the African woman in sub-Saharan Francophone African theatre is described in a variety of ways, and that her portrayal cannot be uniform, considering the diversity of cultures and traditions that inspire her image. As can be seen from the analysis, examples of the female character have been drawn from different parts of sub-Saharan Francophone Africa, such as the Congo, Senegal, Cameroun, and Côte d'Ivoire. Each country has its own particular characteristics with regards to the role of the woman in the society. Nevertheless, a few of the characteristics are common to women in a number of the plays. One such common characteristic is that the royal African woman acts freely within and outside the confines of the role socially ascribed to her. Another is that the traditional African woman of pre-colonial days is a very active participant in both family and community lives, while the traditional African woman in colonial and post-independence times is disconnected to varying degrees from her family and the community. Finally, the educated woman is slowly moving from a state of confusion resulting from being bombarded by conflicting values from different systems, to one of selective adherence to cultural values she herself has tested and accepted, be they traditional African or imported.

For further research, it would be interesting to look at the African woman's portrayal and role not only in the plays published in the 1980s and 1990s, but also in other samples of plays from the first two decades of independence that could not be included in this study, especially those dealing with the issue of military dictatorships that cropped up in Africa shortly after independence. Also, now that more sub-Saharan Francophone African women are publishing their dramatic works, it would be worthwhile examining the depiction of the African woman from the female playwrights' viewpoint. In terms of thematic analysis, several possibilities come to mind. Among them, analysing the African woman vis à vis her economic and political role, if any, in contemporary Africa and the reaction to her participation in those areas, examining how the woman in position of power relates to her male subordinate(s), as well as drawing a parallel between female playwrights' portrayal of the African woman and the perspective of male dramatic writers who continue to dominate the genre.

Notes

1.a) According to the Ivorien scholar, Bernard Mouralis: "the missions used ... theatre as a means of propaganda and made the African (students) put on patronage plays in French." "L'École William Ponty et la politique culturelle" in *Le Théâtre négro-africain, Actes du Colloque d'Abidjan - 1970*, Paris: Présence Africaine, 1971, p.33.

b) The Ponty School theatre tradition actually started off as a pedagogical activity in the form of a "holiday assignment" aimed at improving the students' French language-writing skills and giving them a better and clear idea of their traditional cultures.

c) Gary Warner gives us a further insight into the motivations of the French colonial authorities through the following excerpt from a speech by the Governor-General at the time the Ponty School was coming into being: "We expect the educated natives to reveal to us some of the secrets or their people's souls, to guide our actions, to help us achieve through intelligent and sympathetic understanding this coming together of races which is one of the levers of our missions" (Warner 1976, cited by Conteh-Morgan 1994).

2. The first recorded play by a female Francophone playwright , i.e. *Obali* by the Gabonese Josephine Kama-Bongo was published in 1974.

3. Eventually, the focus of the accusation is shifted from the widow to a male relative of the deceased, who is forced to drink a potion to prove his innocence: the man dies just before a male nurse shows up and declares that the deceased, who was his friend, had suffered from malaria!

4. Bjorson, Richard: Introduction to *Faces of African Independence: Three Plays by Guillaume Oyono-Mbia and Seydou Badian*. Translated by Clive Wake, Charlottesville, University of Virginia Press, 1988.

5. Though the chronological focus of this paper is the 1960s and the 1970s, we find it necessary to include Bernard Dadié's depiction of Queen Abraha Pokou as per the Baoulé legend in his play *Assémien Déhylé, Roi de Sanwi* created in his William Ponty days in 1936. This will provide a comparative viewpoint to Charles Nokan's representation of the same personage.

6. According to Louaka's grandfather, the custom in this particular ethnic group allows the oldest daughter to marry into her father's family, which could mean marrying her first cousin, like in Louaka's case: her teacher is the son of Biyoki's late brother. (*L'Oracle*. 75-77).

15

THEATRE ON THE AIR: A THEMATIC OVERVIEW OF THE RADIO PLAY IN FRANCOPHONE AFRICAN DRAMA

Tundonu Amosu

INTRODUCTION

It is generally accepted that drama in Francophone Africa had the required ingredients for a lasting tradition. What started as holiday projects by students of the Ecole Normale William Ponty went on to become a full theatre pattern with official backing, in colonial times, at the highest level. At the peak of its popularity, the Ponty theatre was frequented by the colonial high society, which flanked the Governor-General of French West Africa at the annual end-of-year productions by the students. The Ponty tradition paid special attention to plays with a strong anthropological and unwittingly ideological bent, which tended to portray the colonial entreprise as a civilising mission to rid Africa of its bloodthirsty tyrants. This mode of theatre gave Francophone Africa its first notable playwrights: Benard Dadié, Amon d'Aby, Seydou Badian and so on.[1]

When independence arrived in the sixties, the Francophone theatre assumed a different coloration. On the one hand, it continued to reflect the Ponty streak with a large dose of historical plays. On the other hand, the erstwhile tyrants were transformed into heroes of African resistance to colonialism. In the one-party system, which characterised French-speaking African governments, drama could only flourish as an integral part of state propaganda. Indeed, the drama groups, which were under state control, were directed by persons openly loyal to the ruling party. They became national troupes under the full control of propaganda units for command performances essentially devoted to praise-singing sessions for life presidents and providential "Fathers of the Nation"[2]. While it is true that other groups chose to take drama to the people, they were often exposed to official pressure and even harassment, which worsened ultimately their material condition. Such groups went elsewhere outside the country or elected to concentrate on less explosive subjects.

The cultural role of the French mission continued to be very important in the former colonies after 1960. With an entire ministry devoted to Africa in the name of co-operation and cultural agreements, the French Cultural Centre came to be a rallying point for the perpetuation of French influence. It provided an ideal platform for the spread of French ideas and culture among the assimilated elite more at ease with *croissants* and *café* than with the cassava-based diet of the tropics. By virtue of the homogeneous nature of French policy particularly in the area of education, the new generation of African leaders were more or less products of the same cultural conditioning which began in William Ponty and continued in France. Such a comprehensive programme of cultural midwifery naturally produced completely assimilated Africans (*peau noire, masques blancs!*). Consequently, the audio-visual landscape for the average French-speaking African was hardly different from what obtained in metropolitan France. Just as the models of literature were André Breton, André Gide, Jean-Paul Sartre, and so on, the cultural preferences were not different. Besides, it must be said that African literature in French owed much of its development and growth to the very active support of French mentors and publishers who openly launched some writers through the channel of literary prizes. The tradition of literary awards was responsible, in no small measure, for the appearance of names like Léopold Senghor, Abdoulaye Sadji and Ferdinand Oyono. But while this was true in the case of poetry and the novel, the dramatic author could hardly hope for such a break, probably because drama had come to be equated with Ponty, that is, textbook plays.

After independence, the wind of change directed African writing away from consent and later to protest and conflict stemming from disillusionment. It quickly dawned on all that the new African regimes, more ruthless and totalitarian in their one-party ideology, were prompt to brand unco-operative or dissident writers as felons to be exterminated or driven into exile. When the stage was eventually cleared, there was no more talk of highlighting the failures or disappointments of independence. Instead, a new set of writers emerged to support rulers through hastily written scripts while the nascent bourgeoisie sought refuge in French programmes on radio and television. Subsequently, the uniformity of thought and cultural preferences which were the direct results of identical academic programmes produced similar tastes from Dakar through Abidjan to Brazzaville. Thus, when the radio stations, hitherto under the absolute control of the colonial authorities, were transferred to African administrations often complete with technical crew and equipment, they dutifully went on with programmes originated by and designed for Frenchmen. In the absence of local initiatives (the local languages had not received the support of linguists!) and given the intense acculturation, there was indeed no cultural resistance to the commanding French presence on the waves. French news were eagerly awaited along with popular features such as "*Le jeu de mille francs*" by Lucien Jeunesse and "*Les maîtres du mystère*", the thriller series in play form. It was in the sixties and television had not acquired its presence and social relevance as a means of communication and leisure.[3]

FROM THE STAGE TO THE WAVES

It has been pointed out that the Ponty theatre produced great names even if it did not record any masterpiece. The new post-independence stage drama rolled out many good texts on subjects ranging from history in the revisionist mode to contemporary issues of ethics and politics. The historical plays sought above all to rehabilitate the likes of Samory Touré, Ba Bemba and Chaka the Zulu. Officially, there was drama when the historical plays coincided with the ideological enterprise of the new regimes in search of myths capable of forging the various ethnic groups into a nation. For example, in Senegal, *L'Exil d'Albouri* and *La mort du Daniel* tried to revamp the image of the discredited rulers of Cayor. Senghor's *La mort de Chaka* and Nénekhaly Camara's *Amazoulou* were instrumental to the redefinition of the role of the Zulu leader in nation building. However, whereas embarrassment to former colonial masters earned no appreciable repercussion, there was serious danger for the playwright when, after independence, he turned to issues like corruption and politics. It is true that no African ruler could arrest Aimé Césaire, the Caribbean writer, for his views in *La Tragédie du roi Christophe* and, more particularly, *Une Saison au Congo* which made little attempt to respect the Zairean dictator, Mobutu Sese Seko. However, the same was not true of Louis-Marie Pouka-Mbayé's *Nouvelle entrevue d'Outre-tombe ou réhabilitation de Ruben Um N'Yobe*. In 1964, the Camerounian president, Amadou Ahidjo was not inclined to rehabilitate a man who had fought the French and was still a source of pride to his supporters.

In the face of official hounding, many writers were forced to become 'command artists', churning out bits tailored to fit the ideology of the state. It was by no means an easy task because it inevitably led to the demise of craftsmanship. Little wonder then that such texts often never went beyond performance day and their texts now gather dust in official cupboards. At a time when the Anglophone scene was very active with names like Soyinka taking the centre stage, Francophone drama still chafed under the yoke of official ideology. There were indeed attempts but, most of the time, it was an unholy blend of Ponty and vaudeville. At any rate, they tended to be formal occasions presided over by the head of state or some high ranking official who initiated applause which the audience dutifully imitated.[4]

THE AFRICAN RADIO PLAY

The advent of the radio play by Africans was sequel to the realisation, among African cultural policy makers and their French partners, that they could not continue to air only plays by French dramatists. Apart from the accusation of French cultural imperialism so obvious in many other areas such as food and fashion, it was believed that the time had come to think "Africa for Africans", by allowing writers on the continent to come on board.

The idea of an African radio play competition was introduced in 1967 during the meeting of African radio executives in Paris. The colonial experience had deprived Africa of all cultural initiatives with the exception of exotism, drums, folk dances and silly *Banania* stereotypes. Meanwhile, the Anglophones were taking giant strides in Ghana and Nigeria with the dance band theatre [5] and with formal, written theatre. The disparity was indeed becoming very obvious within the context of cultural censorship in the one-party state. The goal of the competiton was therefore to obtain a reasonable amount of material, which could replace the French plays on the air. There was also the vague hope that the continent, which produced Senghor, Oyono and others, certainly had Francophone equivalents of Soyinka as well.

To encourage active participation, the organisers of the radio-play competition promised grand cash prizes and the possibility of being published. A trip to France was also a possibility. With such a package, many writers quickly sharpened their quills to produce the desired texts.

Initial responses to the call for entries were very encouraging and went well beyond the expectations of the initiators of the competition. Jacques Chevrier notes that the *Concours Théâtral Interafricain* received 150 entries in the first edition while the number then moved to 394, then to 576 by the third edition; entries for the 11th edition stood at 3,992.[6] The major problem soon became how to get judges to plough through the manuscripts. Inevitably, a large number of them were dismissed as clumsy attempts to imitate French radio plays. The scenario and style could hardly fit into any known African pattern of life. Besides, most of the authors did not have any firm ideals on theatre. However, there were many excellent texts, which won the admiration of the judges.

The next stage was the short-listing of the plays for eventual production. This made it possible for budding talents with good radio voices to bring the plays to life while experts in sound effects completed the picture. The final selection only took place after all the selected plays had been aired. It was thus possible to reach a reasonable consensus and give credit to worthy writers. In his conclusion, Chevrier explains that the originality of the winning plays lay essentially in their anonymity because they did not reflect any particular ideological leaning and neither were the authors recognised intellectual or political giants. In this sense, the radio play competition offered a wonderful stage for unknown authors often ignored by the French or even official publishers. The authors were able to give free rein to their imagination and feeling and the *Concours Théâtral Interafricain* conceded total freedom in the subject matter and the form. Since the plays were intended for listeners, most writers did not feel hampered by any practical issues of production. In the belief that any sound could be produced, a lot of authors dreamed up scenes with thunder and lightning while troops stormed enemy strongholds, which were defended with cannon fire. Since the notion of production was already left to the organisers, all that was required of the author was his imagination.

A THEMATIC OVERVIEW

The entries showed great originality in the spread of their themes. Naturally, history and tradition as well as the new realities of independence were major issues. The oral tradition mode was infused into some plots while the stark reality of daily life threw up disquietening problems of corruption and immorality. Finally, the question was whether the plays should end comically or in tragedy. Probably on account of the generally pessimistic stance of most authors, there were more tragedies, which often included pathetic scenes. In all, the *Concours théâtral* became an avenue for replenishing the Francophone repertoire and a sort of benchmark in terms of quality of production.

The earliest winners of the *Concours* were Guy Menga's *L'Oracle* and *La marmite de Koka Mbala*, which have become classics in their own right. This was followed by Pierre Dabrié's *Sansou* and Jean Pliya's *Kondo le Requin*. These early winners responded promptly to the call for texts because they were already actively engaged in the 'command performance' system of scripting sketches at very short notice.[7] Guy Menga was a ministry official who had actually authored texts for his country's Ministry of Propaganda. As for Jean Pliya, he was able to cash in on the comic streak flowing in from Ghana and on Togo's concert party styles to launch his historical play, *Kondo le Requin*, a worthy prelude to *La Secrétaire Particulière*, which upbraids sexual harassment by the bosses in the office. The historical play was also recognised in R. Atta-Koffi's *Le trône d'or* which provides justification for the Ashantis' reverence for the golden stool, throne of the Asantehene and symbol of Ashanti unity. The war carried out by Sir Garnet Wolseley (Sagrenti) is thus portrayed as something akin to the destruction of the ancient Benin empire under Oba Ovonramwen Nogbaisi about the same period - 1895/96. In the same way, *L'Europe inculpée* by A. Letembet-Ambily attempts to show the very aggressive incursion of Europe into Africa in order to conclude that Africa is indeed in a position to claim and obtain reparations.

The comic mode began to acquire its reputation of a Camerounian genre with *Notre fille ne se mariera pas* by Guillaume Oyono Mbia. The Camerounian writer clearly blazed the trail in arousing rib-cracking backslapping laughter with his manner of highlighting the ridiculous sides of the marriage question, particularly the choice of suitors and the dowry requirements. His more popular play, *Trois prétendants ... un mari* was already in the works here since, the writer neither changed his subject nor even the mode of approaching it. Although Sylvain Bemba's *L'Enfer, c'est Orpheo* takes us back to mythology with African connotations, other entries by 1970 were now aware of the disappointments of independence which made them to give more relevance to ideology and new ways of developing mind and manpower in Africa.

In 1970, J.P. Obama won the competition with *Assimilados*, a play set against the backdrop of the Portuguese colonial experience in Africa (Angola) and the absurd situation of its *assimilaçao*. Obama produced what can be considered an authentic African drama in a style specifically meant for the radio as is indicated in the introduction. Obama added that he adapted the form of the Yoruba dance drama and applied it to the intrigue in *Assimilados*. In the Angola of the play, there is no systematic discrimination (as in Rhodesia (Zimbabwe) and South Africa) but "un étrange mélange de races admis par la loi de Lisbonne bien que sous le signe de terribles restrictions du régime dit des Assimilados". (p.12)

Obama's play pitches the white Portuguese administrator against Mukoko, the griot on the plantations. Ngola, his wife, abandons her job as maid to become, at night, Ngono, her imaginary sister, who is the administrator's mistress. The fruit of the affair is a mulatto, Ndangho, on whose behalf the mother and Mukoko claim the benefits of "la loi de Lisbonne". The coffee brown evidence is all the Portuguese needs to confer the status of assimilado on the boy. A triumphant Mukoko can then claim victory for his people:

> Reçois donc, courageux fils d'Angola, pour toi et les tiens
> la carte d"Assimilado" pour élever Ndangho, né mulatre,
>
> et pour rendre ses frères noirs aussi riches que le "Blanc".

This rather immoral way of "passing for white" and thus acquiring privileges finds its justification in the desire of Mukoko and all Africans to get even with the white man with the active connivance of Ngola.

In the same year, 1970, another winning text was Baba Moustapha's *Le Commandant Chaka*, the code name of a mysterious rebel against the régime of the dictator and life president, General Dos Santos Bagoza. Chaka turns out to be Chico Samora, the highly educated son of a cement factory hand. The student Chico won the hand of Grace, the daughter of the local chieftain but left his wife and children in Europe in order to spend many years as a guerrilla leader. What is ironical is that the crack captain chosen by Bagoza to catch Chaka is the son Samora left in Europe. Finally, the dictator is killed in a palace revolt which allows for reunion between father, son and the faithful Grace.

Le Commandant Chaka could be considered a transposition of many contemporary African countries where those in power are fighting against well-organised and potent opposition. In 1970, wars of liberation were still raging in Angola, Mozambique and Guinea Bissau but Moustapha already foresaw the disastrous consequences of one-party countries with life presidents.

Another character, who also calls himself Chaka, is the leader of militant Africans in *On joue la comédie* by Senouvo Agbota Zinsou, winner in 1972. Zinsou's play is a mixture of the theatre goer's natural inclination for comedy in Africa and the portrayal of the apartheid situation in South Africa. When Chaka and his men capture two white policemen, they force them to lead the rebels to the local jail where, as fake prisoners, they are able to free other jailed blacks. One of the policemen even shows admiration for such an act of courage because, after being freed by Chaka, he chooses to stay:

> "Vous avez tout sacrifié pour une cause qui doit etre
> celle de tous les hommes épris de justice." (p.73)

Chaka knows fully well that the fight for liberation is not an easy one and admits that revolutions are never really mass movements at the onset:

> "La révolution est toujours l'oeuvre de quelques
> hommes décidés et non de la marmaille. C'est quand
> ça réussit que la marmaille vous suit." (p.83)

Zinsou's play addresses the issues of apartheid in very schematic terms. In the South Africa where "Whites only" is bodly written on public seats, the inequalities are glaring: "il est prouvé scientiquement et historiquement que le gorille est cent fois supérieur au singe" (p.98). 'Gorille' and 'singe' are, of course, white and black workers.

Oral tradition often blends with history in many winning entries. While *Le trône d'or* of Atta-Koffi is a rehabilitation of Ashanti culture, the same holds for Mamadou Seyni Mgendue's *Le procès de Lat Dior*, the Senegalese ruler who resisted French incursions into his territory before he succumbed to their cannons. Oral tradition sources are also highly visible in Sory Konake's *Le grand destin de Soundjata* and Tsino's *Nyia Bariba*.

The story of Soundiata and the Mandingo saga[8] is well known but the originality of Konake was to tell the extraordinary story of the mythical deformed Sogolon who gave birth to a crippled prince. The unhappy boy was mocked for his condition and, one day, decided to order crutches. This is the action which triggers off his destiny because the craftsman eagerly hands him the pair of sticks saying:

> "La canne que tu viens commander était déjà prête du
> vivant de mon père. C'est lui qui l'a forgée." (p.41)

When Soundiata finally walked, he became the great founder of a kingdom which was to last for many centuries.

Oral tradition also serves as the point of departure for the play of Massa Diabaé, which recounts how Ba Bemba, king of Keredougou, adopts patience as a tactic before waging war on Samory. *Une si belle leçon de patience* shows that, against the all-conquering Samory, Ba Bemba chooses to disregard the sneers and only engage battle at the most opportune moment. When he attacks, it is Samory who immediately sues for peace.

Nyia Bariba by Tsino is a folktale of sorcery and a wicked monster. Told in verse, most probably for an informed audience, the play presents a young bride who decides to free herself and the people from the grip of the powerful monster. When a young mother loses three children successively after childbirth, she decides to recover the last one, Bariba, or perish in the belly of the monster. Armed with a talisman given to her by her mother on her wedding day, Nyia (mother of) Bariba overpowers the monster, who is in fact her mother-in-law:

> Quand, triomphante
> La mère de Bariba
> Dorénavant redevenue
> Une heureuse maman
> de trois beaux enfants
> rentre au village
> de ses fils accompagnés
> Sa belle mère avait vécu
> De son enterrement on revenait. (p.64)

Tradition sometimes enters into conflict with modernity as we can see in Sylvain Bemba's *Une eau dormante*. In the foreword, J. P. Tati-Loutard states that the criticism of tradition is not designed to dismiss it but to caution against age-long injustice which finds a ready ally in tradition. Thus, when Sosso, the owner of the only pond in a village forbids Olessa to fish in it unless he paid two-thirds of the catch, he makes an unreasonable amalgam :

> "Ce n'est pas la justice qui fait la tradition, c'est la
> tradition qui fait la justice." (p.10)

Sosso, however, wants to have an affair with Olessa's wife, Bobomela. He succeeds so well that it is impossible for Olessa to digest the fact that he alone cannot change a tradition. He cannot understand why

> "celui qui ne travaille pas gagne beaucoup et pourquoi
> celui qui travaille gagne peu." (p.38)

But when the play ends, it is a triumphant Olessa who leads the youths of the village to drive out Sosso and all the exploiters hiding under the cloak of tradition.

If tradition is such an important source of inspiration, it is perhaps a reflection of the preponderance of Ponty worldviews among many entries. Another explanation may be the very important role given to traditional rulers under French colonial rule which gave them considerable powers in their domains. Tradition in such societies braced up to the changes after independence and actively supported the autocratic structure of one-party rule. For example, the plight of Olessa, forced to slave for Sosso, is a direct reflection of the local tradition which allowed a single man to be the source of something as basic as water. No just law protected the poor from such exploitation and this set the stage for the stark inequalities so characteristic of rural and urban centres in Africa. There was the need to show concern for the continent suffering from bad laws and rulers, which made co-operation quite arduous between the exploiters and the sufferers.

Diama and Alkali Koba illustrate this through recourse to allegorical characters in *Les Hommes du bakchish* in which they portray the sad history of Africa's dealings with exacting and unreasonable "business" partners. After the unholy alliance between slave traders and slave raiders, the author attempts to unmask the new form of 'co-operation' with shark loans which are invariably designed to impoverish the African continent. This same warning is found in *L'Afrique Une* by Mbaye Gana Kébé where the masses are expected to stand for their rights. Of course, it is common knowledge that the same masses are never included in any political process except to echo party orders. The masses, sweating in the sun, are instruments of 'spontaneous' ovation during official ceremonies and Gana Kébé can only mouth the feeble protest of revolutionaries:

> "Le peuple jugera car le seul souverain." (p.16)

Any watcher of African and third world politics knows fully well that nothing is ever farther from the truth.

Earlier on, we pointed out that comedy received an initial boost with the arrival of Guillaume Oyono-Mbia and his hilarious exploitation of the marriage theme. The Camerounian drama has, on account of Oyono-Mbia, found itself permanently classified as comedy, often of a riotous nature. [9] After *Notre fille ne se mariera pas* and *Trois prétendants ... un mari*, Oyono-Mbia apparently handed over the baton to Protais Asseng. In *Trop, c'est trop*, we are at the limit of the imaginable. Bissabey who is hoping that his wife will have a tenth child, thus qualifying her for the title of Mother of the Nation, suddenly discovers that his own body is experiencing changes and sensations compatible with a pregnancy. When the pregnancy is medically confirmed by his friend, Dr Assike, Bissabey now has to contend with the ecstasy of his wife, Bakony, who wants to prepare her man for his impending "pa/ma/ternity"! Bissabey even contemplates abortion but Madame is categorical:

> "Mais l'avortement est un crime. Nous devons toujours respecter la vie. Et puis, dans ton cas, une interruption de grossesse pourrait être fatale." (p.113)

Bakony, therefore, advises her man to settle into his new life because "une grossesse n'est pas une maladie" (p.123) Finally, Bissabey is relieved of his state when he discovers the power of his own auto-suggestion. What is most interesting here is the concentration of dialogue to sustain the comic level with the result that Asseng's play received a large following among radio listeners.

Given the plethora of plays, it is easy to understand the difficulties faced by the panel of judges. However, three texts indicate their preference for plays that are capable of provoking reflection long after the last scene. In Sangu Sonsa's *La dérive ou la chute des points cardinaux*, the action takes place in the isolated convent of Mother Superior Thérèse d'Avila whose small community eagerly awaits the arrival of an intellectual monk fleeing from the world to the monotonous quiet of the convent. But his arrival becomes the cause of a violent quarrel with a white nun who has a lot of respect for the African voodoo against the background of modern Catholicism. This reasoning infuriates Brother Chrysostome to the extent that his railing against the white nun, Monyama, pushes the latter into a fit of rage, which causes her to faint. A distraught Mother Thérèse d'Avila then has to caution Chrysostome who believes that Monyama has abandoned Cartesian logic for foolish voodoo ideas:

> "Comme David, votre chute à vous, Frère Chrysostome, a commencé le jour où, tout entier dans votre rôle de médecin, vous avez contemplé la féminité nue de soeur Monyama." (p.32)

Monyama's mysterious death forces the play to end abruptly as Chrysostome hurriedly leaves the convent in search of a quieter retreat. *La dérive* translates the confusion, which arises in a closed society like a convent where the introduction of a man like Chrysostome suddenly awakens repressed sensations and activates what leads to a tragic end.

The intellectual joust between the main characters in *La dérive* is unlike the preoccupation of the main character in Amadou Koné's *De la chaire au trône*. Here, in the name of tradition, a university lecturer ascends the throne of his people in the knowledge that after twelve years of unrestrained felicity, including unfettered access to all the ravishing maidens of the kingdom whether betrothed or not, he will commit suicide. But, on the eve of the appointed day, the lecturer-prince calls in foreign guards to protect him whereas it was already agreed that:

> "A la dernière heure du dernier jour du dernier mois de la dernière année du règne, cet heureux prince doit mourir." (p. 27)

The prince, an educated man, is not unaware of what tradition demands. As he tells the maiden sharing his bed:

> "En principe, la coutume est intraitable. Cela se déroule toujours comme prévu. Toujours." (p.32)

This being the case, one then wonders why the prince is so desperate to escape from his chosen destiny. In the end, the solution is found within the cossetted walls of the palace when the old custodians of tradition decide to mount pressure on the maiden to murder the prince.

The latter, who overhears the discussion, decides to spare his companion the trouble of committing such a crime and he chooses to die instead. Tradition is thus saved but the main question is raised by a bewildered guard:

> Comment peut-on juger ce type qui était professeur d'université, qui était quand même aisé et qui a voulu une vie fastueuse? (p.60)

Koné, a lecturer himself, showed the limits of madness in the name of tradition which improverishes the masses so as to maintain an aura of affluence in the midst of abject poverty. Even the lecturer who should ordinarily resist such crass materialism now occupies the throne probably with the hope of changing the situation. He fails because, once again, it has been demonstrated that the transformation of tradition can only result from collective effort. In our view, the merit of the play lies in the manner in which even the prince is made to see the futility of resistance since he was unwise enough to have accepted the incredible bargain in the first place.

The final jewel in this collection of radio plays is *L'étudiant de Soweto* by Maoundoé Maïndouba. All along, the South African situation of apartheid had remained in force, producing poignant texts such as those of Peter Abrahams, Bessie Head, Alex La Guma and many others. The lure of apartheid was strong enough to inspire Maïndouba particularly after global condemnation which followed the Soweto massacre when police gunned down striking black students resisting the imposition of Afrikaans, the Boer language, as the language of instruction. The story of So(uth) We(st) To(wnship), the sprawling shanty town outside Johannesburg is also a story of the black student leader, Steve Biko who died in jail from maltreatment.

In 1981, Maindouba's *L'étudiant de Soweto* casts Mudube, president of the Soweto's Students' Union, as a fugitive from justice who finally surrenders to a police inspector in the latter's home in order to save from police torture his parents who were held hostage. Bakuole, father of Mudube is himself a veteran of strikes which cost many lives - Carltonville Coal Mines in 1973; Transvaal, 1974, 150 dead, 1976, 350 dead. In the Soweto massacre, figures were close to 500 dead and 2,000 injured although official bulletins only declared 6 dead, including two "gallant" policemen.

When Mudube surrenders, the inspector Nelson is forced to recognise his humanity and discover that apartheid is indeed a terrible thing. Nelson realises that it is whites like his boss, the police commissioner, who sustain the system for their selfish end. Nelson then decides to leave South Africa and apartheid:

> "Je vais m'installer ailleurs, loin du carnage, commissaire, loin de ce massacre de pauvres innocents." (p.69)

His boss, knowing that Nelson would be a credible witness against the cause of apartheid, especially in the wake of condemnation of the massacre, decides otherwise. Nelson must not be able to live to tell the story:

> Vous connaissez beaucoup trop de choses (p.70)

Nelson is thus killed and carries to the grave the truth of apartheid and its atrocities which are gradually being unearthed in today's post-apartheid South Africa. In the view of the chairman of the panel of judges, Max-Pol Fouchet, "*L'étudiant de Soweto* est une piece engagée, vigoureuse."

The Soweto question was still fresh in the minds of people and South African watchers readily identified Mudube with Biko. The originality of the play is not therefore in the subject matter but in the vivid style of reconstructing the cold mechanism of institutionalised brutality and manipulation of the truth. The listener, in his privileged position, thus sees the magnitude of apartheid's crimes. It is clear that Maïndouba's text reveals a promising author with a lot of talent for sustaining attention over a long period.

CONCLUSION

From the technical point of view, many texts sent in for the *Concours Théâtral Interafricain* were often in the tradition of the French radio play transposed into the African setting. The notion of "spectacle dans un fauteuil" gave free rein to the authors' imagination and enabled them to imagine situations of unlimited extravagance. If the subjects were more or less satisfactorily envisaged, a critical reading of the text showed that stage instructions often forget a few basic principles of drama presentation and this was easily the main flaw in the plays. In order to remedy this, Radio France organised the production itself with liberal changes incorporated into the final text.

Sequel to their performance on the air, a good number of the plays were then rewritten for the stage. Radio France International was able to raise theatre troupes which performed the plays in French cultural centres and schools. In her review of the *Concours Théâtral*, Françoise Ligier traced the careers of the early winners to those of the more recent names like Asseng and Naïndouba. She added that a study carried out in the seventies showed that 80 per cent of Francophone plays were from the repertoire of the *Concours*, thanks, perhaps, to the prospect of wonderful cash prizes including the study trip to France.

By 1992, the *Concours* ceased to be an exclusive African affair with the new name of "RFI Théâtre", which was now open to all Francophone writers. The African response, however, remains very positive and most encouraging. Even the fear that the African entries would be overrun by the new entries, particularly from France and Belgium, has been proved wrong. Africans have continued to hold their commanding positions. Indeed, with the active support of publishing houses such as NEA, Nouvelles Imprimeries du Niger, Multipress Gabon, CEPER of Yaoundé and many more, there is a considerable volume of plays which, from all indications, are not just RFI products but also those that have come from other sources. It is now clear that Francophone drama has reached the age of maturity but we must not forget the fact that its growth has been greatly influenced by the Radio France initiative.

Nowadays, and beyond the general appellation of Francophone drama, there is the incontrovertible fact that more names are appearing at national and international levels. The experiments of Were-were Liking and the initiatives of Sony Labou Tansi[10] in their respective countries can be compared to the popular theatre as a factor of social mobilisation currently in vogue in Mali and Burkina Faso. Whatever its demerits, the *Concours Théâtral* has indeed bequeathed a lasting legacy to Francophone African literature.

There remains however the disturbing fact that the theatre in Francophone Africa is forever seeking relevance and recognition without instead of within. It has already won the battle of relevance within the social context of each country but it would seem that it is still very much concerned with international awards and invitations. An example is recognition by the Theatre Festival in Limoges, which has become some kind of necessary accolade for all. In this way, the techniques are inevitably tributary to French modes of representation, a situation which has its serious disadvantages because, these days, the home audience is less inclined to adapt culturally to French norms.

Notes and References

1. I refer particularly to Jean-Pierre Guingane. "De Ponty à Sony", *Notre Libraire*, 102, Juillet-Août 1990: pp.6-11.

2. The Sily National Théâtre in Sekou Touré's Guinea easily comes to mind just like the Togolese National Theatre under Senouvo Zinsou in the seventies.

3. Françoise Ligier, "Lettre à Monique Blin à l'occasion d'un anniversaire", *Notre Libraire*, Numéro hors série, Sept. 1993: pp.10-13.

4. The case of Bernard Dadié is patent here. From his Ponty background, Bernard Dadié went on to write plays such as *Monsieur Thôgô-Gnini*, *Beatrice du Congo* and *Les voix dans le vent* which invariably benefited from official patronage for their production.

5. See Joel Adedeji. "Trends in the Content and Form of the Opening Glee in Yoruba Drama", *Research in African Literatures*, Vol. 4, 1, 1973: pp.23-47.

6. Jacques Chevrier. *Littérature nègre*. Paris: Armand Colin, 1984. p.166.

7. J.P. Tati-Loutard. "Itinéraire, littérature congolaise", *Notre Libraire*, 92, 3, 1999 recalls that *La marmite de Koka-Mbala* (1967) was written at the request of officials of the Mouvement National de la Révolution. The same holds for Sylvain Bemba's *Une eau dormante*.

8. See L. Kesteloot & B. Dieng. *Les épopées d'Afrique noire*. Paris: KARTHALA, Editions UNESCO, 1997, pp.97-118.

9. "Au Cameroun, le théâtre est une fête de convivialité où il arrive que certains montent sur la scène pour danser." in Jacques Scherer's *Le théâtre en Afrique noire francophone*. Paris: P.U.F., 1992, p.51.

10. See Sony Labou Tansi. "Le théatre d'utilité publique", *Notre Libraire*, Sept.1993, pp.9-13.

Bibliography

Winning Plays (and year) of the *Concours Théâtral* published by Radio France Internationale.

1. G. Menga. *L'Oracle*. 1968.

2. ———— *La marmite de Koka-Mbala*. 1969.

3. P. Dabire. *Sansoa*. 1969.

4. J. Pliya . *Kondo le Requin.* 1969.

5. R. Atta-Koffi. *Le trône d'or.* 1969.

6. M. Berte. *La colère de Baba.* 1969.

7. A. M. Letembet-Ambily. *L'Europe inculpéé.* 1970.

8. P. Ndidi-Penda. *Le fusil.* 1970.

9. M. Malinda. (S. Bemba). *L'enfer, c'est Orfeo.* 1971.

10. J. P. Obama. *Assimilados.* 1972.

11. M. Seyni Mbengue. *Le procès de Lat Dior.* 1972.

12. G. Oyono-Mbia. *Notre fille ne se mariera.* 1973.

13. D.& A. Koba. *Les hommes du bakchich.* 1973.

14. S. Konake. *Le grand destin de Soundjata.* 1973.

15. S. Sonsa. *Le dérive ou la chute des points cardinaux.* 1973.

16. Tsino. *Nyia Bariba.* 1973.

17. M. Gana Kébé. *L'Afrique a parlé.* 1975.

18. M. M. Diabaté. *Une si belle leçon de patience.* 1975.

19. S. A. Zinsou. *On joue la comedie.* 1975.

20. S. Bemba. *Une eau dormante.* 1975.

21. G. Diawara. *L'Aube des béliers.* 1975.

22. M. Gana Kébé. *L'Afrique Une.* 1975.

23. A. Kone. *De la chaire au trône.* 1975.

24. P. Asseng. *Trop, c'est trop.* 1981.

25. M. Maindouba. *L'Etudiant de Soweto.* 1981.

26. B. Moustapha. *Le Commandant Chaka.* 1983.

Selected Bibliography

Boulton, M. *The Anatomy of Drama*. London: Routledge & Kegan Paul, 1960, 212p.

Chevrier, J. *Littérature nègre*. Paris: Armand Colin, 1984, 220p.

Elam, K. *The Semotics of theatre and drama*. London : Routledge, 1993, 248p.

Guingane, J. P. "De Ponty à Sony", *Notre Libraire*, 102, juil-oct, 1990, pp.6-11.

Ngandu-Nkashama, P. *Theatres et scènes de Spectacle (Etudes sur les dramaturgies et les arts gestuels)*. Paris: L'Harmattan, 1973, 384p.

Ngandu-Nkashama, P. "Littératures africaines et enseignement", *Notre Libraire*, 125, janv - mars, 1996: pp 46 - 61.

Ricard, Alain. *Littérature d'Afrique noire. Des langues aux livres*. Paris : Karthala (CNRS Editions) 1995, 304p.

Roubine, J. J. *Introduction aux grandes théories du théâtre*. Paris:Bordas, 1990, 205p.

Scherer, J. *Le théâtre en Afrique noire francophone*. Paris:, P.U.F, 1992, 210p.

Volterrani, E., (Ed). *Teatro africano*. Turin: Einaudi, 1987, 334p.

Index

Lightning Source UK Ltd.
Milton Keynes UK
UKOW051947040412

190187UK00001B/23/A